Anonymous

The Parian Chronicle Or The Chronicle

Of The Arundelian Marbles 1788

Anonymous

The Parian Chronicle Or The Chronicle
Of The Arundelian Marbles 1788

ISBN/EAN: 9783337730840

Printed in Europe, USA, Canada, Australia, Japan

Cover: Foto ©ninafisch / pixelio.de

More available books at **www.hansebooks.com**

THE

PARIAN CHRONICLE.

THE PARIAN CHRONICLE,

OR

THE CHRONICLE

OF THE

ARUNDELIAN MARBLES;

WITH

A DISSERTATION

CONCERNING ITS AUTHENTICITY.

———

EA, QUÆ DISPUTAVI, DISSERERE MALUI, QUAM JUDICARE.
CIC.

———

LONDON,

PRINTED FOR J. WALTER, CHARING-CROSS.
MDCCLXXXVIII.

THE

PREFACE.

IN a late publication, entitled, An Essay on Punctuation, the Author, having occasion to mention the celebrated Chronicle of the Arundelian Marbles, subjoins this note:

" The Parian Chronicle is said to have been engraved 264 years before the Christian æra; but is there no room to question its authenticity?"

This note occasioned the following letter in the Gentleman's Magazine.

" The author of an Essay on Punctuation has thrown out a hint, which has surprised me not a little, as it will certainly do many others, viz. that there is some reason to question the authenticity of the Arundel Marbles.

"I do not doubt the judgement of this writer; but I wish to be informed by him, or any other competent judge, what foundation there is for this surmise.

A LOVER OF ANTIQUITIES."

As I am thus desired to assign my REASONS for a question, which I proposed without any particular investigation, I shall freely and ingenuously submit them to the consideration of the learned reader.

I must however previously observe, that I propose my DOUBTS with the utmost deference to the sentiments of abler judges, and with the highest respect for those learned writers, who have given their sanction to the Parian Chronicle.

ADVERTISEMENT.

THE original *Greek*, and the *Latin translation*, of the *Chronicle*, are taken from the elegant and accurate edition of the *Marmora Oxoniensia*, published by Dr. *Chandler*, in 1763.

The editions of *Selden*, *Prideaux*, and *Maittaire*, are much inferior to that of Dr. *Chandler*; and the translations, which have been made from them, by Count *Scipio Maffei* in *Italian*, M. *Du-Fresnoy* in *French*, and Dr. *Playfair* in *English*, are, on that account, proportionably defective.

In the following pages, the *Greek* is not divided into distinct epochas, like the *Latin* translation, but into lines, as it stands on the marble. This arrangement is preserved, with a design to give the reader some idea of the lacunæ in each line; though it must be observed, that there is not one line now remaining in its perfect state.

The

ADVERTISEMENT.

The words and letters, which are added by the commentators, in order to supply the deficiencies in the Greek inscription, are placed between two brackets; and, in the English translation, the corresponding words and letters are printed in Italics.

CHRONICON PARIUM,

EX

MARMORIBUS ARUNDELIANIS.

Lin. 1. . . . . . ου . . . . υπαν . . . ων
. . . . νων ανεγραψα τους αν[ωθεν

2. χρονους] αρξαμ[εν]ος απο Κεκροπος του πρωτου βασιλευσαντος Αθηνων, εως αρχον]ος εμ Παρῳ [μεν

3. Ας]υανακτος, Αθηνησιν δε Διογνητου. Αφ ου Κεκροψ Αθηνων εβασιλευσε, και η χωρα Κεκροπια εκληθη, το προτερον καλου-

4. μενη Ακτικη απο Ακτιου του αυτοχθονος, ετη ΧΗΗΗΔΠΙΙΙ. Αφ ου Δευκαλιων παρα τον Παρνασσον εν Λυκωρειᾳ εβασιλευσε, [βα]σιλε[υ

. . . . de-
fcripfi fuperiora *tempora* orfus à Cecrope, qui primus regnavit Athenis, ufque ad Archontem in Paro *quidem* Aſtyanaɾtem, Athenis verò Diognetum.

Epoch. 1. A quo Cecrops Athenis regnavit, & regio Cecropia dicta eſt, quæ priùs dicebatur Actica ab Actæo indigenâ, anni MCCCXVIII.

Ep. 2. A quo Deucalion apud Parnaſſum in Lycoriâ regnavit, reg-

B

5. ο]υτος Αθηνων Κεκροπος, ετη ΧΗΗΗΔ. Αφ ου δικη Αθηνησι[ν εγε]νετο Αρει και Ποσειδωνι υπερ Αλιρροθιου του Ποσειδωνος, και ο τοπος εκληθη

6. Αρειος Παγος, ετη ΧΗΗ𐅅ΔΠΙΙΙ, βασιλευοντος Αθηνων Κρ[ανα]ου. Αφ ου κατακλυσμος επι Δευκαλιωνος εγενετο, και Δευκαλιων τους

7. ομβρους εφυγεν εγ Λυκωρειας εις Αθηνας προ[ς Κρανα]ον, και του Διο[ς του Ολυμπιου το ιερ]ον ιδ[ρυσατ]ο, [και] τα σωτηρια εθυσεν,

8. [ε]τη ΧΗΗ𐅅ΔΠ, βασιλευοντος Αθηνων Κρ[α]ν[α]ου. Α[φ ου Αμφι]κτυων Δευκαλιωνος εβασιλευσεν εν Θερμοπυλαις, και συνηγε

9. [τ]ους περι τον ορον οικουντας, και ω[νο]μασεν Αμφικτυονας, και Π[υλαια]ν, ου[περ] και νυν ετι θυουσιν Αμφικτυονες,

10. [ε]τη ΧΗΗ𐅅ΔΠΙΙΙΙ, βασιλευοντος Αθηνων Αμ-

nante Athenis Cecrope, anni MCCCX.

Ep. 3. A quo lis Athenis intercessit Marti & Neptuno super Halirrothio Neptuni *filio*, & locus dictus est Arius Pagus, anni MCCLXVIII, regnante Athenis Cranao.

Ep. 4. A quo diluvium tempore Deucalionis evenit, & Deucalion imbres fugit è Lycoriâ Athenas ad Cranaum, & Jovis *Olympii* templum extruxit, & sacra pro salute fecit, anni MCCLXV, regnante Athenis Cranao.

Ep. 5. A quo Amphictyon Deucalionis *filius* regnavit in Thermopylis, & congregavit populos in viciniâ habitantes, & appellavit Amphictyonas, & *Pylæam*, ubi & nunc etiam sacrificant Amphictyones, anni MCCLVIII, regnante Athenis Am-

EX MARMORIBUS ARUNDELIANIS.

φικτυονος. Αφ ου Ελλην ο Δευκ[αλιωνος Φθι]ωτιδος ε-
βασιλευσε, και Ελληνες

11. [ων]ομασθησαν το προτερον Γραικοι καλουμενοι,
και τον αγωνα Παναθ[η]ναι[κον συνεςησαντο, ετη]
XHHΔΠII, βασιλευοντος

12. Αθηνων Αμφικτυονος. Αφ ου Καδμος ο Αγηνο-
ρος εις Θηβας αφικετο [κατα χρησμον, και] εκτισεν
την Καδμει-

13. αν, ετη XHHΔΠ, βασιλευοντος Αθηνων Αμφικτυονος. Αφ ου [Ευρωτας και Λακεδαιμων Λακω]-
νικης εβασιλευσαν,

14. ετη XHHΔII βασιλευοντος Αθηνων Αμφικτυονος. Αφ ου ναυ[ς πεντ]η[κοντα κωπ]ων εξ Αι-
γυπτου

15. [ε]ις την Ελλαδα επλευσε, και ωνομασθη Πεντη-
κοντορος, και αι Δαναου θυγατερες . . . . [Αμυμ]-
ωνη, και Βα . .

phictyone.

Ep. 6. A quo Hellen Deucalionis *filius* in Phthiotide regnavit, & Hellenes appellati funt, qui prius Græci dicebantur, & certamen Panathenaicum inſtituerunt, anni MCCLVII, regnante Athenis Amphictyone.

Ep. 7. A quo Cadmus Agenoris *filius* Thebas advenit *secundùm oraculum, &* condidit Cadmeam, anni MCCLV, regnante Athenis Amphictyone.

Ep. 8. A quo *Eurotas & Lacedæmon in* Laconiâ regnârunt, anni MCCLII, regnante Athenis Amphictyone.

Ep. 9. A quo navis *cum quinquaginta remis* ab Ægypto in Græciam appulſa eſt, & vocata eſt Pentecontorus, & Danai filiæ . . . . Amymone, & B . . . .

16... λαρευώ, και Ελικη και Αρχεδικη αποκληρω-
θεισαι υπο των λοιπων [ιερον ιδρυσ]αντ[ο,]
17. και εθυσαν επι της ακτης εμ παρα[λι]αδι εν
Λινδῳ της Ροδίας, ετη ΧΗΗΔΔΔΔΠΙΙ, βασιλευο[ν-
τος Αθηνων Εριχθονιου. Αφ ου Εριχ]-
18. θονιος Παναθηναίοις τοις πρωτοις γενομενοις αρμα εζευξε, και τον αγωνα εδειχνυε, και Αθηναι[α με-
τω]ν[ομασε, κ]αι [αγαλμα της
19. Θ]εων μητρος εφανη εγ Κυβελοις, και Υαγνις ο
Φρυξ αυλους πρωτος ηυρεν εγ Κ[ελαι]ναι[ς τη]ς Φρυ-
γ[ι]ας, [και την Αρμονιαν την κ[α-
20. λουμενην Φρυγιςι πρωτος ηυλησε, και αλλους
νομους Μητρος, Διονυσου, Πανος, και τον επ[ιχωριων
Θεων, και
21. Ηρωων,] ετη ΧΗΗΔΔΔΔΙΙ, βασιλευοντος
Αθηνων Εριχθονιου του το αρμα ζευξαντος. Αφ ου Μινως

.... & Helice, & Archedice forte lecta a cæteris
templum condidere, & facrificarunt super littus in maritima regione in Lindo, quæ Rhodi urbs est, anni
MCCXLVII, regnante *Athenis Erichthonio.*

Ep. 10. *A quo* Erichthonius Panathenæis primis celebratis currum junxit, & id certamen monstravit, & Athenæôn *nomen mutavit*, & *simulachrum* matris Deorum apparuit in Cybelis *montibus*, & Hyagnis Phryx tibias primus invenit in Celænis urbe Phrygiæ, *& harmoniam* quæ vocatur Phrygia primus tibiis cecinit, & alios nomos magnæ Matris, Dionysi, Panis, & illum *patriorum Deorum & Heroum*, anni MCCXLII, regnante Athenis Erichthonio, qui currum junxit.

Ep. 11. A quo Minos *ejus nominis*

EX MARMORIBUS ARUNDELIANIS. 5

[ο] πρ[ωτος ε]βα[σιλευσε,

22. και Κυ]δωνιαν ωκισε, και σιδηρος ηυρεθη εν τη Ιδη, ευρontων των Ιδαιων Δακτυλων Κελμιος κ[αι Δαμναvεως, ετη ΧΗΙΔΙΔΠΙΙΙ,

23. βασι]λευοντος Αθηνων Πανδιονος. Αφ ου Δημητηρ αφικομενη εις Αθηνας καρπον εφυ[τε]υεν, και πρ[ος αλλους επεμψε πρ]ωτη δ[ια

24. Τ]ριπτολεμου του Κελεου και Νεαιρας, ετη ΧΗΔΔΔΔΠ βασιλευοντος Αθηνησιν Εριχθεως. Αφ ου Τριπτο[λεμος

25. καρπον] εσπειρεν εν τη Ραρια καλουμενη Ελευσινι, ετη Χ[Η]ΔΔΔΔ[ΙΙ], βασιλευοντος Αθηνων [Εριχθεως. Αφ ο-]

26. υ [Ορφευς την] αυτου ποιησιν εξ[ε]θηκε, Κορης τε αρπαγην, και Δημητρος ζητησιν, και τ[η]ν αυτου [καταβα-

primus regnavit, & Cydoniam condidit; & ferrum inventum eſt in Idâ, inventoribus Idæis Dactylis Celmi & *Damnaneo, anni MCLXVIII*, regnante Athenis Pandione.

Ep. 12. A quo Ceres adveniens Athenas fruges feminavit, & ad *alias gentes miſit* prima per Triptolemum *filium* Celei & Neæræ, anni MCXLV, regnante Athenis Erichtheo.

Ep. 13. A quo Triptolemus *fruges* ſevit in Rhariâ dictâ Eleuſine, anni MCXLII, regnante Athenis *Erichtheo.*

Ep. 14. *A quo Orpheus* ejus Poeſin edidit, & Proſerpinæ raptum, & Cereris inveſtigationem, & ipſius *ad Inferos deſcen-*

27. σιν, και μυ]θο[υ]ς των υποδεξαμενων του καρπου, ετη ΧΗΔΔΔΠ, βασιλευοντος Αθηνων Εριχθεως. [Αφ ου

28. Ευμολπος ο Μουσαι]ου τα μυστηρια ανεφηνεν εν Ελευσινι, και τας του [πατρος Μ]ουσαιου ποιησ[ει]ς εξεθηκ[εν, ετη ΧΙΙ... βασιλευοντος Αθηνων

29. Εριχθε]ως του Πανδιονος. Αφ ου καθαρμος πρωτον εγενετο [δια φον]ου πρωτω αον... εαυτ......

30. [ετη ΧΙΔΙ]ΔΙΙ, βασιλευοντος Αθηνων Πανδιονος του Κεκροπος. Αφ ου [ε]ν Ελευσινι ο γυμνικος [αγων ετεθη, ετη Χ...., βασιλευοντος Αθηνων Πανδιονος του Κεκροπος.] Αφ ου [αι ανθρωπο-

31. θυσι]αι, [και] τα Λυκαια εν Αρκαδια εγενετο, και λ..κκε.....Λυκαονος εδοθησαν [εν] τοις Ελλ[η]σι[ν, ετ]η [Χ]. ν... βασιλευον-

sum, & fabulas de iis, qui fruges accipiebant, anni MCXXXV, regnante Athenis Erichtheo.

Ep. 15. A quo *Eumolpus Musæi filius* mysteria exhibuit in Eleusine, & *patris sui* Musæi poemata edidit, *anni MC...*, *regnante Athenis Erichtheo filio* Pandionis.

Ep. 16. A quo lustratio primò facta fuit *per cædem*..
.... *anni MLXII*, regnante Athenis Pandione *filio* Cecropis.

Ep. 17. A quo in Eleusine gymnicum *certamen proponebatur*, *anni M*.... *regnante Athenis Pandione filio Cecropis*.

Ep. 18. A quo *humana sacrificia*, & Lycæa in Arcadiâ celebrata fuere, &............ Lycaonis dabantur *inter* Græcos, anni M......, regnan-

32. τος Αθηνων Πανδιονος του Κεκροπος. Αφ ου κα[θαρισθεις εν Ελευσιν]ι Ηρακλης [εμυηθη ξεν]ω[ν πρωτ]ος, [ετη X] . . .

33. βασιλευοντος Αθηνησιν Αιγεως. Αφ ου Αθηνησι [σπανι]ς των καρπων εγενετο, και μαντευομενος [τοις] Αθην[αιοις Απολ]λων ην[αγκασεν

34. δικα]ς υποσχε[ι]ν, α[ς] αμ Μινως αξιωσει, ετη XΔΔΔI, βασιλευοντος Αθηνων Αιγ[εως.] Αφ ου Θησ[ευς]

35. Αθηνων τας δωδεκα πολεις εις το αυτο συνῳκισεν, και πολιτειαν και την δημοκρατειαν [πρωτος καθ-

36. εςηκω]ς Αθηνων, τον των Ισθμιων αγωνα εθηκε, Σινιν αποκτεινας, ετη ⌐HHHH⌐ΔΔΔΔΠ. Απο της Αμμον[ιας] τη[ς πρωτης, ετη ⌐HHH

37. H⌐]ΔΔΔΔII, βασιλευοντος Αθηνων Θησεως.

te Athenis Pandione *filio* Cecropis.

Ep. 19. A quo *lustratus in Eleusine* Hercules initiatus fuit hospitum primus, anni *M*. . regnante Athenis Ægeo.

Ep. 20. A quo Athenis *inopia* frugum contigit, & confultus ab Athenienfibus Apollo *coegit eos* pœnas fubire, quafcunque Minos poftularet, anni MXXXI, regnante Athenis Ægeo.

Ep. 21. A quo Thefeus Athenis duodecim urbes in unam civitatem collegit, & reipublicæ formam & ftatum popularem *cùm primus conftituiſſet* Athenis, Ifthmiorum certamen propofuit, poftquam Sinin occiderat, anni DCCCCLXXXXV.

Ep. 22. *A fefto Ammon dicto primùm celebrato*, anni DCCCCLXXXII, regnante Athenis Thefeo.

Αφ ου Αργειοι[σιν] Αδρα[ϛος ε]βασιλευσ[ε]ν, και τον
αγωνα [ε]ν [Νεμεᾳ ε]θ[εσ]αν [οι

38. Επτα,] ετη 𝟙𝟙HHIIH𝟙ΔΔΔΠΙΙ, βασιλευοντος Αθηνων Θησεως. Αφ ου οι [Ελλη]νες εις
Τροιαν ε[ϛ]ρατευ[σαν,] ετη 𝟙𝟙HHHH𝟙ΙΙΙΙ, βασιλευοντος Αθη[νων

39. Μεν]εσθεως τρεις και δεκατου ετους. Αφ ου
Τροια ηλω, ετη 𝟙𝟙HHHHΔΔΔΔΠ, βασιλευοντος
Αθηνων [Μενεσθε] ως, [εικοϛου και] δευτερου ετους, μη-
νος Θ[αρ-

40. γηλιω]νος εβδομη φθινοντος. Αφ ου Ορεϛη[ϛ εν
Σκυθ]ιᾳ των αυτο[υ μανιων ιαθη, και Α]ιγισθου θυγα-
τρι [Ηριγ]ον[η υπερ Αι]γισθου και αυ[τῳ δικη

41. εγενετ]ο εν Αρειου Παγῳ, ην Ορεϛης ενικησεν
[ισων ψηφ]ων [ουσων,] ετη [𝟙𝟙]HHHHΔΔΔ[Δ]ΙΙ, .

Ep. 23. A quo Argivorum *Adraſtus* rex fuit, & certamen in Nemeâ propoſuerunt Septem Duces, anni
DCCCCLXXXVII, regnante Athenis Theſeo.

Ep. 24. A quo Græci ad Trojam expeditionem ſuſ-
ceperunt, anni DCCCCLIV, regnante Athenis Meneſtheo, anno *regni ejus* decimo tertio.

Ep. 25. A quo Troja capta fuit, anni DCCCC
XLV, regnante Athenis *Meneſtheo*, *viceſimo* ſecundo
regni ejus anno, menſis Thargelionis die ſeptimo ante
finem.

Ep. 26. A quo Oreſtes in Scythiâ ab *inſaniâ ſuâ
liberatus fuit*, & Ægiſthi filiæ Erigonæ *de* Ægiſtho
& illi *lis* interceſſit in Areopago, in quâ Oreſtes
vicit *æqualibus numero* ſuffragiis *exiſtentibus*, anni
DCCCCXLII.

EX MARMORIBUS ARUNDELIANIS. 9

βασιλευοντος Αθηνων Δημοφωντος.   Αφ ου [Σαλα-

42. μινα εν] Κυπρῳ Τευκρος ῳκισεν, ετη ΠΗΗΗΗ ΗΔΔΔΠΙΙΙ, βασιλευοντος Αθηνων Δημοφωντος. Αφ ου Νη[λ]ευς ῳκισ[εν εγ Καριᾳ Μιλητον αγειρας Ιωνας, οι

43. ῳκισ]αν Εφεσον, Ερυθρας, Κλαζομενας, [Πριηνην, και Λεβεδον, Τηω,] Κολοφωνα, [Μ]υουντα, [Φωκαιαν,] Σαμον, [Χιον, και] τα [Παν]ιωνι[α] εγενετο, ετ[η

44. ΠΗΗΗ]ΔΙΙΙ, βασιλευοντος Αθηνων Με[δοντο]ς τρεις και δεκατου [ετ]ους. Αφ ου [Ησ]ιοδος ο ποιητης [εφαν]η, ετη ΠΗΙΔΔΔ[Δ, βασιλευοντος Αθηνων Με-

45. γακλους.]   Αφ ου Ομηρος ο ποιητης εφανη, ετη ΠΗΔΔΔΔΙΙΙ, βασιλευοντος Αθηνω[ν Δ]ιογνητου.

regnante Athenis Demophonte.

Ep. 27. A quo *Salamina in* Cypro Teucer condidit, anni DCCCCXXXVIII, regnante Athenis Demophonte.

Ep. 28. A quo Neleus condidit *in Cariâ Miletum congregatis Ionibus qui condiderunt* Ephefum, Erythras, Clazomenas, *Prienen, & Lebedum, Teon,* Colophonem, Myuntem, *Phoceam,* Samum, *Chium, &* Panionia inftituta fuere, anni DCCCXIII, regnante Athenis *Medonte,* anno decimo tertio.

Ep. 29. A quo Hefiodus poeta claruit, anni DCLXX, regnante Athenis *Megacle.*

Ep. 30. A quo Homerus poeta claruit, anni DCXLIII, regnante Athenis Diogneto.

Αφ ου Φ[ει]δων ο Αργειος εδημ[ευθη, και μετρα και

46. ϛαθμα] εσκευασε και νομισμα αργυρουν εν Αι-
γινη εποιησεν, ενδεκατος ων αφ Ηρακλεους ετη ⅢΗΔΔ
ΔΙ, βασιλευοντος Αθηνων [Φε-

47. ρεκλε]ους. Αφ ου Αρχιας Ευαγητου δεκατος ων απο Τημενου εκ Κορινθου ηγαγε την αποικιαν [εις] Συρακου[σας, ετη ΗΗΗΗⅢΔΔΔΔΙΙΙΙ,

48. βασιλευον]τος Αθηνων Ασχυλου ετους εικοϛου και ενος. Αφ ου κατ ενιαυτον ηρ[ξ]εν[ο Κ]ρ[ε]ων, ετ[η] ΗΗΗΗΔΔ. Αφ ου [Λακεδαιμ.]ο[νιοις Τ]υ[ρ-

49. ταιος συνεμαχησεν,] ετη ΗΗΗΗΔΠΙΙΙ, Αρ-
χοντος Αθηνησι Λυσι[ου.] Αφ ου Τερπανδρος ο Δερδενεος ο Λεσβιος τους νομους του[ς π]α[λαι]ων [καιν]ουσθαι αυλητ[ας

50. εθε]λησε, και την εμπροσθε μουσικην μετεϛησεν,

Ep. 31. A quo Phidon Argivus *proscriptus fuit, & menfuras atque pondera* paravit, & nummum argenteum in Ægina cudit, undecimus ab Hercule, anni DCXXXI, regnante Athenis *Pherecle*.

Ep. 32. A quo Archias Euageti *filius*, decimus a Temeno, e Corintho eduxit coloniam Syracufas, anni CCC CXCIIII, regnante Athenis Æfchylo, anno vicefimo primo.

Ep. 33. A quo annuus Archon exftitit primus Creon, anni CCCCXX.

Ep. 34. A quo *cum Lacedæmoniis Tyrtæus militavit*, anni CCCCXVIII, Archonte Athenis Lyfiâ.

Ep. 35. A quo Terpander Derdenei *filius* Lefbius nomos *antiquos* novare auletas voluit, & vetuftam muficam mutavit,

EX MARMORIBUS ARUNDELIANIS. 11

ετ[η] ΗΙΗΗ⊡ΔΔΔΙ, Αρχοντος Αθηνησιν Δρωπιλου.
Αφ ου Α[λυαττη]ς Λυδ[ων εβα]σιλευσ[εν, ετη

51. ΗΗΗΔ]ΔΔΔΙ, Αρχοντος Αθηνησιν Αριςοκλεους.
Αφ ου Σαπφω εγ Μιτυληνης εις Σικελιαν επλευτε
φυγουσα, ... ολ . . . . . θ . . . . [ετη ΗΗ
ΗΔΔΠΙΙΙ,

52. Αρχον]τος Αθηνησιν μεν Κριτιου του προτερου,
εν Συρακουσαις δε των [Γεω]μορων κατεχοντων την αρ-
χην. [Αφ ου Αμφικτυονες ενικη-

53. σαν ελ]οντες Κυρραν, και ο αγων ο γυμνικος
ετεθη χρηματιτης απο των λαφυρων, ετη ΗΙΙ[Η]ΔΔΠ
ΙΙ, Αρχοντος Αθηνησι Σιμω[ν]ος. Αφ ου

54. [ο ςεφ]ανιτης αγων παλιν ετεθη, ετη ΗΗΗΔ
[Δ]ΙΙ, Αρχοντος Αθηνησι Δαμασιου του δευτερου.
Αφ ου εν α[πην]αις Κωμω[διαι εφορεθησαν υ-

anni CCCLXXXI, Archonte Athenis Dropilo.

Ep. 36. A quo *Alyattes* in Lydiâ regnavit, *anni* CCC
XLI, Archonte Athenis Ariftocle.

Ep. 37. A quo Sappho e Mitylene in Siciliam traje-
cit fugiens . . . . *anni CCCXXVIII*, Archonte
Athenis quidem Critiâ priore, Syracufis autem rerum
potitis Geomoris.

Ep. 38. A quo *Amphictyones vicerunt* captâ Cyrrhâ, &
certamen gymnicum editum fuit pecuniarium ex fpoliis,
anni CCCXXVII, Archonte Athenis Simone.

Ep. 39. A quo coronarium certamen iterum editum
fuit, anni CCCXXII, Archonte Athenis Damafiâ fecundo.

Ep. 40. A quo in plauftris comœdiæ vectæ fuerunt

55. πο] των Ικαριεων, ευροντος Σουσαριωνος, και αθλον ετεθη πρωτον ισχαδων αρσιχο[ς] και οινου [αμ-φορευς, ετη ΗΗ ... Αρχοντος Αθηνησι ......

56. ...] Αφ ου Πεισιςρατος Αθηνων ετυραννευσεν, ετη ΗΗΔΔΔΔΠΙΙ, Αρχοντος [Αθηνησ]ι Κ[ωμι]-ου. Αφ ου Κροισος [εξ] Ασιας [εις] Δελφο[υ]ς α-[πεπεμψεν,

57. ετη ΗΗ⊡]ΔΔΔΔΙΙ, Αρχοντος Αθηνησι[ν Ευ-θυ]δημου. Αφ ου Κυρος ο Περσων βασιλευς Σαρδεις ελαβε, και Κροιτον υπο [Πυθι]ης σφαλ[λομενον εζω-γρησεν, ετη ΗΗ⊡ΔΔΔΠ, Αρχοντος Αθηνησιν Ερξι-κλειδου.

58. Ην δε]·και Ιππωναξ κατα τουτον ο Ιαμβοποιος. Αφ ου Θεσπις ο ποιητης [εφανη, πρωτος ος και] εδιδαξε [Τραγωδιαν, ης αθλον ε]τεθη ο [τ]ραγος, ετη ΗΗ⊡[Δ ΔΙΙΙ,] Αρχοντος Αθ[ηνησιν

ab Icarienfibus, inventore Sufarione; & præmium pofitum fuit primum ficuum cophinus & vini *dolium, anni* CC ... *Archonte Athenis* .....

Ep. 41. A quo Pififtratus Athenis tyrannidem occupavit, anni CCLXXXXVII, Archonte Athenis *Comiâ.*

Ep. 42. A quo Crœfus *ex* Afiâ *ad* Delphos *mifit, anni* CCXCII, Archonte Athenis Euthydemo.

Ep. 43. A quo Cyrus Perfarum rex Sardes expugnavit, & Crœfum a Pythiâ deceptum *vivum cepit, anni* CC LXXXV *Archonte Athenis Erxiclide. Vixit autem et* Hipponax hujus tempore Iambicus poeta.

Ep. 44. A quo Thefpis poeta *floruit, qui porro primus* docuit *Tragœdiam, cujus præmium* fuit hircus, anni CCI, XXIII, Archonte *Athenis*

EX MARMORIBUS ARUNDELIANIS. 13

59. Αλκ]αιου του προτερου. Αφ ου Δαρειος Περσων εβασιλευσε, Μαγου τελευτησαντος, ετη [ΗΗ]ΔΙ[Π]Ι, Αρχοντος Αθη[νησι] . . . . . Αφ ου Αρμοδιος και [Αρισογε]ιτων απεκτε[ιναν

60. Ιππα]ρχον Πεισιςρατου Α[θηνων τυραν]ον, και Αθηναιοι σ[υνανες]ησαν τους Πεισιςρατιδας εκ[βαλλειν του Πελασγικ]ου τειχους, ετη ΗΗΔΔΔΔΙΙ ΙΙΙ, Αρχοντος Αθηνησι

61. [Κλισθενους.] Αφ ου χοροι πρωτον ηγωνισαντο ανδρων, ον διδαξας Υπο[δι]κος Χαλκιδε[υς] ενικ[ησεν,] ετη ΗΗΔΔΔ[ΔΙΙΙΙ,] Αρχοντος Αθηνησι[ν Ι[σαγορου. Αφ ου νε[ως Αθηνας της] Ιππια[ς ιδρυτ-

62. θη] Αθηνησιν, ετη ΗΗΔΔΔΙ, Αρχοντος Αθηνησι Πυθοκριτου. Αφ ου εμ Μαραθωνι μαχη εγενετο

Alcæo priore.

Ep. 45. A quo Darius in Perſia regnavit, Mago defuncto, anni *CCLVI*, Archonte Athenis . . . .

Ep. 46. A quo Harmodius & Ariſtogiton interfecerunt Hipparchum Piſiſtrati *filium Athenarum tyrannum*, & Athenienſes *confurrexerunt ut* Piſiſtratidas *ejicerent ex Pelaſgico* muro, anni CCXLVIII, Archonte Athenis *Cliſthene.*

Ep. 47. A quo chori primùm certârunt virorum, cujuſmodi primum cum docuiſſet Hypodicus Chalcidenſis, vicit, anni CCXXXIV, Archonte Athenis Iſagora.

Ep. 48. A quo *templum Minervæ* Hippiæ *ſtructum fuit* Athenis, anni CCXXXI, Archonte Athenis Pythocrito.

Ep. 49. A quo in Marathone pugna commiſſa eſt

Αθηναιοις προς τους Περσας, [και Αρταφερνεα το]ν Δαρειου αδελ-

63. [φιδεο]ν, τον ϛρατηγον ενικων Αθηναιοι, ετη ΗΗΔΔΠΙΙ, Αρχοντος Αθην[ησι του] δευτερου [Φαινιππου, και] εν μαχη συνηγωνισατο Αισχυλος ο ποιητης

64. [ετ]ω[ν] ων ΔΔΔΠ. Αφ ου Σιμωνιδης ο Σιμωνιδου παππος του ποιητου, ποιητης ων και [αυτος Αθη]νησι, και Δαρειος τελευτα, Ξερξης δε ο υιος βασιλευει, [ετη

65. ΗΗΔ]ΔΠ[Ι], Αρχοντος Αθηνησιν Αριϛειδου. Αφ ου Αισχυλος ο ποιητης τραγωδια πρωτον ενικησε, και Ευριπιδης ο ποιητης εγενετο, και Στησιχορος ποιητης ε[ις]

66. την Ελλαδα αφικετ]ο, ετη ΗΗΔΔΙΙ, Αρχοντος Αθηνησι Φιλοκρατους. Αφ ου Ξερξης την σχεδιαν

ab Atheniensibus contra Persas, & *Artaphernem* Darii nepotem, ducem, superârunt Athenienses, anni CCXX VII, Archonte Athenis secundo *Phænippo, &* in prælio unà certavit Æschylus poeta *cum esset annos natus* XXXV.

Ep. 50. A quo Simonides Simonidis avus poetæ, poeta fuit qui & *ipse* Athenis ; & Darius obiit, Xerxes verò filius *ejus* regnavit, *anni* CCXXVI, Archonte Athenis Aristide.

Ep. 51. A quo Æschylus poeta tragœdiâ primùm vicit, & Euripides poeta natus fuit, & Stesichorus poeta *in* Græciam *venit*, anni CCXXII, Archonte Athenis Philocrate.

Ep. 52. A quo Xerxes navigiorum pontem

EX MARMORIBUS ARUNDELIANIS. 15

εζευξεν εν Ελλησποντῳ, και τον Αθω διωρυξε, και η εν Θερμο-

67. [πυ]λαις μαχη εγενετο, και ναυμαχια τοις Ελλησι περι Σαλαμινα προς τους Περσας, ην ενικων οι Ελληνες, ετη ΗΗΔΠΙΙ, Αρχοντος Αθηνησι Καλλιαδου. Αφ ου η εν

68. [Π]λαταιαις μαχη εγενετο Αθηναιοις προς Μαρδονιον τον Ξερξου ςρατηγον, ην ενικων Αθηναιοι, και Μαρδονιος ετελευτησεν εν τῃ μαχῃ, και το πυρ ερυη[σε

69. εν Σικ]ελια περι την Αιτναν, ετη Η[Η]ΔΠΙ, Αρχοντος Αθηνησι Ξαντιππου. Αφ ου [Γε]λων ο Δεινομενους [Συρακουσων] ετυραννευσεν, ετη ΗΗΔΠ, Αρχοντος Αθηνησι Τιμοσθεν-

70. [ους. Α]φ ου Σιμωνιδης ο Λεωπρεπους ο Κειος, ο το μνημονικον ευρων, ενικησεν Αθηνησιν διδασκων, και

junxit in Hellesponte, & Athonem perfodit, & in Thermopylis pugna commissa fuit, & pugna navalis a Græcis ad Salaminem contra Persas, in qua vicerunt Græci, anni CCXVII, Archonte Athenis Calliade.

Ep. 53. A quo ad Platæas pugna commissa fuit ab Athenienfibus contra Mardonium Xerxis ducem, in qua vicerunt Athenienses, & Mardonius occubuit in pugna, & ignis *defluxit in Sicilia* circa Ætnam, anni CCXVI, Archonte Athenis Xantippo.

Ep. 54. A quo Gelon Dinomenis filius Syracusis tyrannidem occupavit, anni CCXV, Archonte Athenis Timosthene.

Ep. 55. A quo Simonides Leoprepis filius Ceius, qui memorandi artem invenit, vicit Athenis docens, &

αι εικονες εςαθησαν Αρμοδιου και Αριςογειτονος, ετ*η*
ΗΗ[ΔΙΙΙΙ,]

71. Αρχοντος Αθηνησι[ν Λ]δειμαντου. Αφ ου Ιερων Συρακουσων ετυραννευσεν, ετη ΗΗΠΙ[Ι]ΙΙ, Αρχοντος Αθηνησι Χ[αρ]ητος. Ην δε και Επιχαρμος ο ποιητης κατα του-

72. τον. Αφ ου Σοφοκλης ο Σοφιλλου ο εκ Κολωνου ενικησε τραγωδια, ετων ων ΔΔΠΙΙΙ, ετη ΗΗΠΙ, Αρχοντος Αθηνησιν Αψηφιονος. Αφ ου εν Αιγος ποταμοις ο λιθος επεσε,

73. και Σιμωνιδης ο ποιητης ετελευτησεν, βιους ετη ⊠ΔΔΔΔ, ετη ΗΗΠ, Αρχοντος Αθηνησιν Θεαγενιδου. Αφ ου Αλεξανδρος ετελευτησεν, ο δε υιος Πε[ρ]δικ-

74. κας Μακεδονων εβασιλευει, ετη Η⊠ΔΔΔΔΠ[ΙΙΙ,] Αρχοντος Αθηνησιν Ευθιππου. Αφ ου Αισχυλος

ftatuæ pofitæ fuerunt Harmodii & Ariftogitonis, anni CCXIV, Archonte Athenis Adimanto.

Ep. 56. A quo Hiero Syracufis tyrannidem occupavit, anni CCIX, Archonte Athenis Charete. Vixit autem & Epicharmus poeta hujus tempore.

Ep. 57. A quo Sophocles Sophilli *filius,* qui e Colono fuit, vicit tragœdiâ, cùm eſſet annos natus XXVIII, anni CCVI, Archonte Athenis Apfephione.

Ep. 58. A quo in Ægos flumen lapis cecidit, & Simonides poeta obiit, cùm vixiſſet annos XC, anni CCV, Archonte Athenis Theagenidâ.

Ep. 59. A quo Alexander obiit, filius autem illius Perdiccas apud Macedonas regnavit, anni CXCVIII, Archonte Athenis Euthippo.

Ep. 60. A quo Æfchylus

EX MARMORIBUS ARUNDELIANIS.

ο πο[ι]ητης βιωσας ετη ⊡ΔΠΙΙΙΙ ετελευτησεν εν [Γε-

75. λ]α της [Σι]κελιας, ετη Η⊡ΔΔΔΔΙΙΙ, Αρχοντος Αθηνησ[ι] Καλλ[ι]ου του προτερου. Αφ ου
Ευριπιδης ετων ων ΔΔΔΔΙΙΙ τραγῳδιᾳ πρωτον ενικησεν, ετη Η⊡Δ[ΔΠΙΙΙΙ,]

76. Αρχοντος Αθηνησι Διφι[λου. Η]σαν δε κατα
Ευριπιδην Σωκρατης, και [Ανα]ξαγορας. Αφ ου Αρ-
χελαος Μακεδονων εβασιλευσε Περδικκου τελευτησαντος,
ετη Η[⊡ΠΙ,

77. Αρχ]οντος Αθηνησι Ασυφιλου. Αφ ου Διονυσιος Συρακουσων ετυραννευσεν, ετη ΗΔΔΔΔΙΙΙΙ, Αρχοντος Αθηνησιν Ευκτημονος. Αφ ου Ευριπιδης βι[ω-
σας ετη ⊡ΔΔΠΙΙ

78. ετε]λευτησεν, ετη ΗΔΔΔΔ[ΙΙΙ,] Αρχοντος
Αθηνησιν Αντιγενους. Α[φ] ου Σο[φ]οκλης ο ποιητης

poeta, cùm vixiſſet annos LXIX, obiit in *Gela* Siciliæ,
anni CXCIII, Archonte Athenis Callia primo.

Ep. 61. A quo Euripides, cùm eſſet annorum XLIII,
tragœdiâ primùm vicit, anni CLXXIX, Archonte Athenis Diphilo. Vixerunt verò tempore Euripidis Socrates
& Anaxagoras.

Ep. 62. A quo Archelaus in Macedoniâ regnavit,
Perdiccâ defuncto, anni CLVI, Archonte Athenis Aſty-
philo.

Ep. 63. A quo Dionyſius Syracuſis tyrannidem occupavit, anni CXLIV, Archonte Athenis Euctemone.

Ep. 64. A quo Euripides, cùm *vixiſſet annos LXX
VII*, obiit, anni CXLIII, Archonte Athenis Antigene.

Ep. 65. A quo Sophocles poeta,

βιωσας ετη [ΔΔ]ΔΔΔΔΙ ετελευτησεν, και Κυρος ανεβ[ησε επι τον αδελφον, ετη ΙΙΔΔΔΔΙΙ,

79. Αρχ]οντος Αθηνησι Καλλιου του Πρ.τ..ου. Αφ ου Τελεςης Σελ[ινουντιος ε]νικησεν Αθηνησιν, ετη ΗΔΔΔΠ[ΙΙΙ,] Αρχοντος Αθηνησι Μικωνος. Αφ ου [επανηλθον οι

80. μετ]α Κυρου αναβαντες, και Σωκρατης φιλοσοφ[ο]ς ετελευτησε [βιους] ετη ΙΔΙΔΔ, ετη ΗΔΔΔΠ [Ι,] Αρχοντος Αθηνησι Λαχητος. Αφ ου Λ[ευδαμας πρωτον εδιδαξεν]

81. Αθηνησιν, ετη ΗΔΔΔΠ, Αρχοντος Αθηνησιν Αρισοκρατους. Αφ ου Ξ[ανθος ο ποιητης Σαρδ]ιανος διθυραμβῳ ενικησεν Αθηνησιν, ετη ΙΙ.. [Αρχοντος Αθηνησι.......

82. Αφ] ου Φιλοξενος διθυραμβοποιος τελευτᾳ βιους ετη ΔΠ, ετη ΙΙΔΠΙ, Αρχοντος Αθηνησι Πυθεου.

cùm vixiſſet annos XCI, obiit, & Cyrus *invaſit fratrem ejus*, anni CXLII, Archonte Athenis Calliâ........

Ep. 66. A quo Teleſtes *Selinuntius* vicit Athenis, anni CXXXVIII, Archonte Athenis Micone.

Ep. 67. A quo *ii rediêre qui cum* Cyro iverunt, & Socrates philoſophus obiit *cùm vixiſſet* annos LXX, anni CXXXVI, Archonte Athenis Lachete.

Ep. 68. *A quo Aſtydamas primùm docuit* Athenis, anni CXXXV, Archonte Athenis Ariſtocrate.

Ep. 69. A quo *Xanthus poeta Sardianus* dithyrambo vicit Athenis anni C ... *Archonte Athenis* .....

Ep. 70. *A* quo Philoxenus dithyramborum ſcriptor obiit, cùm vixiſſet annos LV, anni CXVI, Archonte Athenis Pytheâ.

EX MARMORIBUS ARUNDELIANIS. 19

Αφ ου Αναξανδριδης ο κωμ[ῳδοποιος ενικησεν Αθηνησιν,
ετη ΗΔΙΙΙ, Αρχοντος]

83. Αθηνησι Καλλεου. Αφ ου Αςυδαμας Αθηνησιν
ενικησεν, ετη ΗΠΙΙΙΙ, Αρχοντος Αθηνησιν Αςειου.
Κατεκαη δε τοτε κα[ι εν ουρανῳ η μεγαλη λαμπας.
Αφ ου εν Λευκτροις

84. μαχη ε]γενετο Θηβαιων και Λακεδαιμονιων, ην
ενικων Θηβαιοι, ετη ΗΠΙΙ, Αρχοντος Αθηνησιν Φρασι-
κλειδου. [Κατα τουτον δε και Αλεξανδρος ο Αμυντου
Μακεδονων]

85. βασιλευει. Αφ ου Στησιχορος ο Ιμεραιος ο
δευτερος ενικησεν Αθηνησιν, και ῳκισθη Μεγαληπολ[ις εν
Αρκαδιᾳ, ετη ΗΠΙ, Αρχοντος Αθηνησι Δυσκινητου.]

86. Αφ ου Διονυσιος Σικελιωτης ετελευτησεν, ο δε υιος

Ep. 71. A quo Anaxandrides comicus *poeta vicit
Athenis, anni* CXIII, *Archonte* Athenis Calleā.

Ep. 72. A quo Aftydamas Athenis vicit, anni CIX,
Archonte Athenis Afteio. Exarſit autem tunc & *in
cœlo magna lampas.*

Ep. 73. *A quo in Leuctris pugna* commiſſa fuit inter
Thebanos & Lacedæmonios, in quā vicerunt Thebani,
anni CVII, Archonte Athenis Phraſiclide. *Hujus autem tempore Alexander Amyntæ filius in Macedoniā reg-*
navit.

Ep. 74. A quo Steſichorus Himeræus ſecundus vicit
Athenis, & condita fuit Megalopolis *in Arcadiā, anni*
CVI, *Archonte Athenis Dyſcineto.*

Ep. 75. A quo Dionyſius Siculus obiit, filius autem
ejus

Διονυσιος ετυραννευσεν, και Αλε[ξα]ν[δρου τελευτησαντος Πτολεμαιος Μακεδονων

87. βασι]λευει, ετη ΗΙΙΙΙ, Αρχοντος Αθηνησι Ναυ-
σιγενους. Αφ ου Φωκεις το εν Δελφοις [ιερον εσυλευ-
σαν, ετη ⌐ΔΔΔΔΙΙΙΙ, Αρχοντος Αθην-]

88. ησι Κηφισοδωρου. Αφ ου Τιμοθεος βιωσας ετη
⌐ΔΔΔΔ ετελευτησεν, [ο δε Φιλιππος Αμυντου των
Μα-]

89. κεδονων βασιλευει, και Αρτοξερξης ετελευτησεν·
Ωχος δε ο υιος β[ασιλευει των Περσων, και] . . . . . .
. . . . . .

90. . . . . . ενικησεν, ετη ⌐ΔΔΔΔΙΙΙ, Αρχοντος
Αθηνησιν Αγαθοκλε[ους. Αφ ου Αλεξανδρος ο Φιλιπ-

91. που εγε]νετο, ετη ⌐ΔΔΔΔΙ, Αρχοντος Αθηνησι
Καλλις[ρατου, ... Ην δε και Αριςοτε-
λης ο

Dionyſius tyrannidem occupavit, & *Alexandro defunc-
te, Ptolemæus in Macedoniâ* regnavit, anni CIV, Archonte Athenis Nauſigene.

Ep. 76. A quo Phocenſes Delphicum *templum ſpoliâ-
runt, anni* LXXXVIIII, *Archonte* Athenis Cephiſodoro.

Ep. 77. A quo Timotheus cum vixiſſet annos LXX
XX obiit, *Philippus autem Amyntæ filius in Macedonia
regnavit,* & Artaxerxes obiit, Ochus verò filius *ejus regnavit in Perſia,* & . . . . vicit, anni LXXXX
III, Archonte Athenis Agathocle.

Ep. 78. *A quo Alexander Philippi filius natus fuit,
anni* LXXXXI, Archonte Athenis Calliſtrato . . . .
. . *Vixit autem &* Ariſtoteles

92. φιλο]σοφος κατα τουτο[ν.] Αφ ου Κα . . . .
. . . . . .
93. . . . [ετ]η ΙΔΙ . . . . Αρχοντος . . . .

philofophus hujus tempore.
Ep. A quo Ca . . . . anni L . . . . Archonte . . . .

Cætera defiderantur.

ADVERTISEMENT.

IN order to give the English reader a proper notion of the lacunæ in this inscription, and to discriminate the assertions of the author from the conjectures of the commentators, the translator has followed the original, as closely as possible, without any regard to elegance of style.

THE

PARIAN CHRONICLE.

* * * * * * I have described *preceding times*, beginning from Cecrops, the first who reigned at Athens, to *Astyanax*, archon in Paros, and Diognetus at Athens *.

   Epoc. 1. Since Cecrops reigned at Athens, and the country was named Cecropia, before called Attica, from Acteus, a native †, 1318 years.   -   -   -   1582

   2. Since Deucalion reigned near Parnassus ‡, in Lycoria, Cecrops reigning at Athens, 1310 years.   -   -   -   1574

Bef. Chr.

---

* Diognetus was archon, Olymp. cxxix. 1. that is, bef. Chr. 264 years.

† Αυτοχθων, *autochthon*, an original inhabitant of the country.

‡ Παρα τον Παρνασσον, apud Parnassum. Lycorea, or Lycoria, was a town on the top of Parnassus. Those who were able to fly from the deluge, says Pausanias, retired εις τα ακρα, to the summits of Parnassus, and there built a city, which they called Lycorea. Pausan. l. x. c. 6. Strab. l. ix. p. 640. I do not find, that the country near Parnassus was ever distinguished by that name. Vid. Steph. Suidas, &c.

3. Since

3. Since the cause was *tried* at Athens between Mars and Neptune, concerning Halirrothius [the son] of Neptune, and the place was called Areopagus, 1268, Cran*a*us reigning at Athens. - - - **1532**

4. Since the deluge happened in the time of Deucalion; and Deucalion escaped the rains [and went] from Lycoria to Athens, to *Cran*a*us*, and bui*lt the temp*le of Jupit*er Olympius*, *and* offered sacrifices for his preservation, 1265 *years*, Cran*a*us reigning at Athens. - - - - **1529**

5. S*ince Amphi*&yon [the son] of Deucalion reigned in Thermopylæ, and assembled *t*he people inhabiting that district, and ca*l*led them Amphi&yones, and [the place of council] P*ylæa, where* the Amphi&yones still sacrifice, 1258 *years*, Amphi&yon reigning at Athens *. - - - - **1522**

6. Since Hellen [the son] of Deuc*alion* reigned in *Phth*iotis, and they were *n*amed Hellenes, who before were called Graikoi [Greeks] and *they instituted* the Panathen*æan* † agon [games] 1257 *years*, Amphictyon reigning at Athens. - - **1521**

---

* Suidas says, ὁ τοπος, the place, where the Amphictyones assembled, and the assembly itself, were called πυλαια. Suid. in v. Πυλα-γοραι. Strab. l. ix. p. 643.

It is observed by M. Goguet, that the marbles distinguish very plainly Amphictyon, the son of Deucalion, from Amphictyon, king of Athens. Goguet, Orig. of Laws, &c. b. i. c. 1. But if this be the case, the marbles are expressly contradicted by Apollodorus, who asserts, that Amphictyon, the son of Deucalion, reigned μετα Κραναου, with Cranaus, at Athens. Apollod. l. i. c. 7. § 2.

† See note to Epoc. 10.

10. Since

THE PARIAN CHRONICLE.

	Bef. Chr.
7. Since Cadmus [the son] of Agenor came to Thebes *, *according to the oracle,* and built Cadmea, 1255 years, Amphictyon reigning at Athens. - - -	1519
8 Since *Eurotas and Lacedæmon* reigned in *Laconia,* 1252 years, Amphictyon reigning at Athens. - - -	1516
9. Since a ship *with fifty oars* sailed from Egypt *to* Greece, and was called Pentecontorus, and the daughters of Danaus . . . . *Amym*one and Ba . . . . . and Helice and Archedice, elected by the rest, *built a temple,* and sacrificed upon the shore, *in the maritime country* †, in Lindus [a city] of Rhodes, 1247 years, *Erichthonius reigning at Athens.* - - - -	1511
10. *Since Erich*thonius, the first Panathenæa ‡ being celebrated, yoked [horses to] a cha-	

* Diodorus and Eusebius make Danaus go into Greece, before Cadmus went in search of Europa. Diodorus having related the story of Danaus, says, μικρον δ' υστερον τουτων των χρονων, Καδμος, κ. τ. λ. " a short time afterwards, &c." Diod. Sic. l. v. p. 329. Our chronologer places Cadmus 8 years before Danaus.

† Επι της ακτης, εμ παρα[λι]αδι, super littus, in maritimâ regione. It is very probable, that παραλιαδι is not the word, which was originally engraved on the marbles. Παραλιας is an uncommon term; and, joined with ακτη, in this place, occasions a tautology.

‡ Panathenæa, an Athenian festival in honour of the goddess Athena, or Minerva. Apollodorus and Harpocration tell us, that it was instituted by Erichthon; for which the latter produces the authority of Hellanicus and Androtion. He adds, on the testimony of Ister the historian, that, before the time of Erichthon, this festival was called Athenæa, and not Panathenæa. But Pausanias asserts, that it did not receive the name of Panathenæa, till Theseus formed the twelve cities of Attica into one community, and ordained a common feast and sacrifice for all the united Athenians.

Apollod.

a chariot, and shewed the contest *, and changed the name of Athenæa; and the image, of the mother of the gods appeared in [the mountains of] Cybele †; and Hyagnis the Phrygian first invented flutes at Celænæ [a city] of Phrygia, and first played on the flute the harmony called Phrygian, and other nomes ‡ of the mother [of the gods] of Dionyſus, of Pan, and that of the deities of the country, and the heroes, 1242 years, Erichthonius, who yoked [horses to] the chariot, reigning at Athens. - - - 1506

11. Since Minos the first reigned and built Cydonia; and iron was found in Ida, by the Idæi Dactyli Celmis and Damnaneus [1168] years, Pandion reigning at Athens. - - 1432

12. Since Ceres coming to Athens planted corn ‖, and first sent it to other [countries], by

---

Apollod. l. iii. c. 13. § 6. Plut. in v. Thesei, p. 11. Harpocration in v. Παναθηναια. Pauſan. l. viii. c. 2. Schol. Ariſtoph. Nub. v. 385.

* Primùm junxit quadrigas Erichthonius. Plin. l. vii. c. 55.

† Diod. Sic. l. iii. p. 193. Απο των Κυβιλων ἡ Κυβελη, à Cybelis Cybele nominata. Strab. xii. p. 852.

‡ Νομος ſignifies a tune, or a piece of muſic; and ſometimes an ode or ſong. Νομῳ τινι ᾀδοντες, " ſinging a particular tune." Xenoph. Anab. l. v. Non antè cantare deſtitit, quàm incohatum abſolveret νομον, " he did not leave off, till he had finiſhed the piece of muſic he had before him." Suet. in v. Ner. § 20. Διεξιλθειν νομον τον Ορθιον, " to ſing the Orthian ſong." Herod. l. i. c. 24. Ariſtotle propoſes this problem, " Why is the ſame word, νομος, uſed for laws and ſongs? Is it," ſays he, " becauſe men, before they had diſcovered the art of writing, ſung their laws, that they might not forget them?" Ariſt. Prob. ſect. xix. 28. Vid. Plut. de Muſicâ.

‖ Καρπον ςπειρασα, planted fruit. Some writers ſuppoſe, that barley

THE PARIAN CHRONICLE. 27

	Bef. Chr.
by *Triptolemus* [the fon] of Celeus and Neæra, 1145 years, Erichtheus reigning at Athens. - - - -	1409
13. Since Triptolemus fowed *corn* in Rharia, called Eleufin*, 1[1]42 years, *Erichtheus* reigning at Athens. - -	1406
14. Since *Orpheus* publi/hed his poem [on] the rape of Proferpine †, the fearch of Ceres, his *defcent* [to the fhades], and the fables concerning thofe, who received the corn †, 1135 years, Erichtheus reigning at Athens. - - - -	1399
15. Since *Eumolpus* [the fon] of *Mufæus* celebrated the myfteries in Eleufin, and publi/hed the poems of *his father Mufæus*, 11 .. years, Erichtheus [the fon] of Pandion, reigning at Athens. - - -	13..

* Icy was the firft grain fown in Attica. Pharnutus afferts, that Eleufis was the place, where the ufe of *barley* was firft difcovered. Phurn. de Nat. Deor. c. 28. Paufanias likewife obferves, that corn was firft fown in the Kharian plain ; and that the cakes offered in facrifice to Ceres, were made of the *barley*, which grew there. Paufan. l. i. c. 38. But Apollodorus, Diodorus, and others, when they fpeak of the firft effays of agriculture, under the direction of Ceres, ufe the words σιτος, πυρος, and καρπος, indifcriminately, as well as ουλαι. Apollod. l. i. c. 5. § 2. Diod. Sic. l. v. p. 336.

* Eleufin.——Talis elt in Græcis ratio : nam *actin* et *actis* dicunt, *delphin* et *delphis*, *Eleufin* et *Eleufis* ; fed veriùs in *n* definunt, quòd in obliquis habent, et *actinos*, *delphinos*, *Eleufinos*. Serv. Virg. Georg. l. i. 161.

† A fragment, which is cited by Paufanias, and afcribed to Homer, mentions the names of thofe, who received the corn, and were firft initiated into the myfteries of Ceres. Thefe were, according to that poet, Celeus, Triptolemus, Eumolpus, and Diocles. Paufan. l. ii. c. 14. Clemens Alexandrinus fays, their names were Baubo, Dyfaules, Triptolemus, Eumolpus, and Eubuleus. Clem. Alex. Cohort. § 2. p. 17.

F. 2

16. Since

16. Since a luftration was firft performed by *flaying* .... 10[6]2 *years*, Pandion [the fon] of Cecrops [the fecond] reigning at Athens. - - - | Bef. Chr. 1326

17. Since the gymnic *agon* * *was inftituted* in Eleufin, 1 ... *years*, Pandion [the fon] *of Cecrops reigning at Athens*. - - | ....

18. Since *human facrifices and* the Lycæa were celebrated in Arcadia † and ...... of Lycaon were given *among* the Greeks, 1 ... *years*, Pandion [the fon] of Cecrops reigning at Athens. - - - | ....

19. Since Hercules, having been pu*rified* ‡ *in Eleufin, was initiated the firft* of *ftrangers* ||, 1 ... *years*, Ægeus reigning at Athens. - - - - | ....

20. Since a *fcarcity* of corn happened at Athens, and *Apollo* being confulted by *the* Athen*ians* ob*liged them* to undergo *the penalties*, which Minos § fhould require, 1031 years, Ægeus reigning at Athens. | 1295

21. Since

---

* Agon, conteft, exercifes or games.

† Τα Λυκαια, an Arcadian feftival inftituted by Lycaon, in honour of Jupiter, celebrated with games, and a human facrifice. Εθυσι τε βρεφος, immolavit infantem. Paufan. l. viii. c. 2.

‡ Hercules underwent a purgation for killing the centaur. Apollod. l. ii. c. 5. § 12.

|| Ην δε ουκ εξον ξενοις τοτε μυεισθαι. At vero externis ad ea facra tunc admitti non licebat. Apollod. ibid.

§ The author of the Chronicle fuppofes, that there were two kings of Crete of the name of Minos. See Epoc. 11. Abbé Banier maintains the fame opinion, and fpecifies feveral diftinguifhing circumftances in the hiftory of thefe two princes. According to this hypothefis, the former was the celebrated legiflator, a pacific monarch, the fon of Jupiter, or rather of Afterius, and the father of Lycaftus.

THE PARIAN CHRONICLE.

	Bef. Chr.
21. Since Thefeus incorporated the twelve cities of Attica * into one [community] and *having firft eftablifhed* a civil conftitution and a popular government † at Athens; he inftituted the Ifthmian games, after he had flain Sinis ‡, 995 years.	1259
22. From the *firft* [celebration of the feftival called] Ammon, 992 *years*, Thefeus reigning at Athens.	1256
23. Since Adraftus reigned over the Argives, and *the feven* [commanders] *inftituted* the games *in Nemea*, 987 years, Thefeus reigning at Athens.	1251
24. Since the Greeks *undertook their* expedition to Troy, 954 years, Meneftheus reigning at Athens, in the thirteenth year [of his reign].	1218
25. Since Troy was taken, 945 years, Meneftheus reigning at Athens, in the [twenty-]fecond ‖ year [of his reign] on the	

Lycaftus. The latter was of an ambitious and enterprizing character; the grandfon of the former, and the father of Molus, Deucalion, Androgeus, Glaucus, Phædra, and Ariadne. Banier, Mythol. vol. iii. p. 514. Diod. Sic. l. iv. p. 263.

* The twelve cities of Attica were Cecropia, Tetrapolis, Epacria, Decelea, Eleufis, Aphydna, Thoricus, Brauron, Cytherus, Sphettus, Cephiffia, and Phalerus. Thefeus, it is faid, collected them, εις μιαν πολιν, into one city, which was Athens. Strab. l. ix. p. 609. Paufan. l. viii. c. 2. Ille vicatim difperfos cives fuos, in unam urbem contraxit. Val. Max. l. v. c. 3.

† Πολιτειαν και την δημοκρατιαν, i. e. πολιτειαν δημοκρατικην. Maittaire, Marm. Arund. p. 650.

‡ Plut. in v. Thefei, p. 4. Apollod. l. iii. c. 15. § 2.

‖ The fiege of Troy commenced in the thirteenth year of Meneftheus; confequently the deftruction of that city could not be in
the

30   THE PARIAN CHRONICLE.

	Bef. Chr.
the twenty-fourth day of the month Thargelion. - - - -	1209
26. Since Orestes *in Scyth*ia was *freed from* his *madness*, and *à cause* between him and *Erigone*, the daughter of Ægisthus, con*cerning* Ægisthus, was *tried* in Areopagus, which Orestes gained, *the votes being equal*, [942] years, Demophon reigning at Athens. - - - -	1206
27. Since Teucer built *Salamis in* Cyprus, 938 years, Demophon reigning at Athens. - - - -	1202
28. Since Ne*l*eus buil*t* * *Miletus in Caria*, *having collected the Ionians*, who *bu*ilt Ephesus, Erythræ, Clazomene, P*riene*, and *Lebedus*, *Teos*, Colophon, *Myus*, *Phocea*, Samos, *Chios*; *and* the *Pan*ionia † were instituted, [813] year*s*, Me*don* reigning at Athens, in the thirteenth *year* [of his reign]. - -	1077
29. Since *Hes*iod the poet *flouris*hed 680 years, *Megacles reigning at Athens*. -	944

the second, as it is stated in the inscription. Quadratarii incuriâ omissum est proculdubiò heic εικοςον και, ita ut annus Menesthei vigesimus secundus ab autore signatus fuerit.   Seld. p. 85.

* Homer tells us, that Miletus was inhabited at the time of the Trojan war.
Οἱ Μιλητον εχον ———
Qui Miletum tenebant. Il. ii. 868.
But Strabo, on the authority of Ephorus, informs us, that Neleus built a new city, at a distance from the old one, which he likewise called Miletus.   Strab. l. xiv. p. 941.

† A festival, celebrated by a concourse of people from all the cities of Ionia.

30. Since

THE PARIAN CHRONICLE. 31

	Bef. Chr.
30. Since Homer the poet flourifhed 643 years, *D*iognetus reigning at Athen*s*. -	907
31. Since Ph*ei*don the Argive was profcribed, and made *measures and weights*, and coined filver money in Ægina, being the eleventh from Hercules, 631 years, P*herec*les reigning at Athens. - -	895
32. Since Archias [the fon] of Euagetus, being the tenth from Temenus, conducted a colony from Corinth *to* Syracu*se*, [494] *years*, Æfchylus *reign*ing at Athens, in the twenty-firft year [of his reign]. - -	758
33. Since *C*reon was arc*h*on for the year *, 420 years †. - - -	684

34. Since

---

* In this epocha the infcription is imperfect. Palmerius, Marfham, Prideaux, Maittaire, and Chandler, fill up the lacunæ in this manner: Αφ' ὁυ κατ' ενιαυτον η*ρ*[ξ]εν [ὁ Κ]*ρ*[ε]ων. But the author of the Chronicle never ufes the prepofitive article ὁ before proper names. Perhaps the original expreffion might have been, η*ρ*ξεν ὁ α*ρ*χων, "the archon governed."

Κατ' ενιαυτον generally fignifies quotannis, fingulis annis, annually, or year by year; and, in this acceptation, it is improperly applied to an archon, who was in office only one year.

This phrafe however, if the paffage be not an interpolation, is ufed by Thucydides in the fenfe, in which it is employed by the author of the Chronicle. Themiftocles, fays that hiftorian, perfuaded the Athenians to finifh the Piræus; "for it was begun before this, during that year, in which he himfelf was chief magiftrate at Athens:" ὑπηρκτο δ' αυτου πρωτε*ρ*ον επι της εκεινου αρχης, ἡ κατ' ενιαυτον Αθηναιοις η*ρ*ξε. Ejus enim *pars* ædificari prius est cœpta, quo tempore ipfe, annuum magiftratum gerens, Athenis præfuit. Thucyd. l. i. § 93.

Dodwell endeavours to prove, that Themiftocles was archon, and began the fortifications of the Piræus in the year 481, the year before the coming of Xerxes. But it cannot be proved by any
good

† J. Per. 4031. bef. Chr. 683. Corfin.

34. Since *Tyrtæus joined the army* * *of the Lacedæmonians* [againſt the Meſſenians] 418 years, Lyſias † being archon at Athens. - **682**

35. Since Terpander [the ſon] of Derdeneus the Leſbian, *directed* the flute-players to *reform* the nomes of the *ancients*, and changed the old muſic, 381 *years*, Dropilus ‡ being archon at Athens. - - **645**

36. Since *Alyattes reigned over* the Lydians, [34]1 *years*, Ariſtocles being archon at Athens. - - - **605**

37. Since Sappho ſailed from Mitylene to Sicily, flying . . . . [328] *years*, Critias ‖ the firſt *being archon* at Athens; the *Geomori* poſſeſſing the government in Syracuſe. - **592**

38. Since *the Amphictyones obtained a victory, having taken* Cyrrha §, and a gymnic agon

good authority, that Themiſtocles, the celebrated commander, was ever the archon eponymus. Admitting, that he was an inferior magiſtrate, in ſome preceding year, we do not find, that the Piræus was fortified, till the year 477, when Adimantus was archon. Diodorus, C. Nepos, Plutarch, Pauſanias, and ſeveral other writers, relate, that this work was undertaken AFTER the concluſion of the Perſian war. Diod. l. xi. p. 32. C. Nep. in v. Themiſt. c. 6. Plut. in v. Themiſt. p. 121. Pauſan. l. i. c. 2.

I am therefore inclined to think, that the foregoing paſſage in Thucydides is, as I have already intimated, an interpolation.

* συνεμαχησεν, cum Lacedæmoniis militavit.—Tyrtæus, a lame, crack-brained poet, was ſent by the Athenians to command the Spartan army.

† Lyſias archon. J. P. 4033. bef. Chr. 681. Corſin.

‡ Dropilus archon. J. P. 4070. bef. Chr. 644. Id.

‖ Critias archon. J. P. 4118. bef. Chr. 596.—In marmore 3 jā ſcribendum eſſe putaverim. Id.

§ Cirrha, a town in Phocis, near the bay of Corinth. The inhabitants had waſted the territory of Delphi, and beſieged the city,

THE PARIAN CHRONICLE. 33

	Bef. Chr.
agon was celebrated, rewards being allotted out of the spoils, [3]27 years, Simon * being archon at Athens. - - -	591
39. Since [the Pythian] games were again celebrated, in which the conqueror received *a crown*, 3[22] years, Damasias the second † being archon at Athens. - -	586
40. Since com*edies were carried* in carts *by* the Icarians ‡, Susarion being the inventor, and the first prize proposed was a basket of figs, and *a small vessel* of wine, 2.. *years*, ... being archon at Athens. - -	57.
41. Since Pisistratus became tyrant ‖ at Athens,	

from a desire of seizing the riches, contained in the temple of Apollo. Plut. in v. Solonis, p. 83.

* Simon five Simonides archon. J. P. 4124. bef. Chr. 590. Corsin.
† Damasias II. archon. J. P. 4129. bef. Chr. 585. Id.
‡ Icaria or Icarius, a little borough, or, as Bentley calls it, " a country parish," in Attica. Athen. l. ii. p. 40. Dissert. on Phal. § 8. p. 147.
‖ The word τυραννος, tyrant, among the Greeks, signified a person, who had by any means acquired a sovereign authority in a republican state, though he afterwards exercised his authority with justice and virtue. This was the case of Pisistratus, Gelo, and his brother Hiero. Some were even raised to the dignity of tyrant, by a voluntary decree of the people. Plutarch mentions particularly Tynnondas thus elected by the Eubœans, and Pittacus by the Mitylenæans; and he adds, that the Athenians would have thus elected Solon. Plut. De his qui serò, &c. p. 551. Id. in v. Solonis, p. 85.

The word τυραννις, or τυραννος, does not occur in the poems of Homer or Hesiod, and probably was not used in their time. It is employed in a favourable sense by Euripides, in the Supplices; by Aristophanes, who calls Jupiter, θεων τυραννος, Nub. act. i. sc. 6; by Sophocles, in Oedipus Tyrannus; by Plato, in his Αντεραςαι, § 8; by Æschines, in the following passage: τοις εστι πολιτειαι ... τυραν-

Athens, 297 years, *Comias* * being archon at *Ath*ens.   -   - | Bef. Chr. 561

42. Since Crœsus sent [ambassadors] *out of* Asia *to* Delphi, [2]92 *years,* *Euth*ydemus being archon at Athens.   -   - | 556

43 Since Cyrus king of Persia took Sardes, and *apprehended* Crœsus, dec*eived* by the *Pyth*ia, [285] *years,* Erxiclides † *being archon at Ath*ens. At this time *lived* Hipponax, the Iambic poet.   -   - | 548

44. Since Thespis the poet *flourished, the first who* exhibited ‡ *tragedy,* for which a goat

---

νις, και ολιγαρχια, και δημοκρατεια. Orat. in Ctesiph. init. and frequently by the Roman writers. See Virg. Æn. vi. 266. Hor. l. iii. od. 17.

* Comias archon, J. P. 4154. bef. Chr. 560. Corsin.

† Erxiclides archon, J. P. 4166. bef. Chr. 548. Id.

‡ Εδιδαξε, docuit. Δραμα διδασκειν, signifies to publish, exhibit, or act a play. This phrase was applied to the poets, who wrote for the stage. Αστυδαμας δ' ὁ τραγῳδιογραφος τοτε πρωτον εδιδιξεν. Sub hoc tempus Astydamas, tragœdiarum scriptor, primùm docere cœpit. Diod. Sic. l. xiv. p. 270. Θεσπις εδιδαξεν, Thespis docuit. Suidas. Σοφοκλης εδιδαξε δραματα, Sophocles docuit fabulas. Id. The authors themselves were called διδασκαλοι, teachers : ιδιως διδασκαλους λεγουσι τινας ποιητας των διθυραμβων, η των κωμῳδιων, η των τραγῳδιων, peculiariter vocant διδασκαλους ipsos dithyramborum, aut comœdiarum, aut tragœdiarum poetas. Harpocration. Suidas. The Latin writers adopted this mode of expression. Livius, qui primus fabulam docuit. Cic. de Clar. Orat. § 72. Cum Thyestem fabulam docuisset, mortem obiit Ennius. Ibid. § 78. Cum Orestem fabulam doceret Euripides. Cic. Tusc. l. iv. § 63. Epist. ad Attic. l. vi. 1. De Senect. c. 14. Hor. de Art. Poet. ver. 288. A. Gell. l. xvii. 21. Casaubon gives the following reason for this phrase : " Studiorum ea fuit quondam ratio, ut maxima eruditionis pars in dramaticorum poetarum, ac præsertim comicorum, lectione et intelligentiâ poneretur. Inde puriorem Hellenismum, inde notitiam rerum, quæ in republicâ erant gesta, inde vitam & mores primorum

goat was *appointed as the prize*, 2[73] years, Alcæus the firſt being archon at Ath*ens* *. -   Bef. Chr. 537

45. Since Darius † reigned over the Perſians, Magus being dead, [2]5[6] years, ... being archon at Ath*ens*.   -   -   520

46. Since Harmodius and *Ariſtogiton* ſlew *Hipp*archus [the ſon] of Piſiſtratus, *the tyrant of* Ath*ens*, and the Athenians co*nſpir*ed to ex*pel* the Piſiſtratidæ from [their retreat within] the *Pelaſg*ic wall, 248 years, *Cliſthenes* ‡ being archon at Athens. -   -   512

47. Since choruſes of men firſt contended, [and] Hypo*di*cus the Chalcidi*an*, having taught ‖ one [of them] gained the vi*ct*ory, 24[4] years, *Iſ*agoras being archon at Ath*ens*.   -   -   -   -   508

48. Since *the temple of Minerva* Hippia §

---

morum civitatis Athenienſium hauriebant." Caſaub. in Athen. l. vi. c. 7.

* Alcæus I. archon. J. P. 4178. bef. Chr. 536. Corſin.

† Darius began his reign, J. P. 4193. bef. Chr. 521. Id. Petav. Do*ct*. Temp. l. x. c. 19. Newt. Chron.

‡ Cliſthenes archon. J. P. 4205. bef. Chr. 509. Corſin.

‖ Διδαξας. Plut. in v. Themiſt. p. 114. vid. Epoc. 44. note ‡.— Χοροδιδασκαλοι, qui choros docuerunt, nempe muſices periti. Taylor, Com. ad Marm. Sandv. p. 72. Demoſth. c. Midiam. p. 47. edit. 1743. Plut. in v. Ariſt. init.

§ Minerva equeſtris. Pauſan. l. i. c. 30. Harpocration. Suidas. The application of this mutilated paſſage to Minerva Hippia is ingenious; yet it is very probable, that it relates to Hippias, the brother of Piſiſtratus, who was expelled from Athens; and as ſome writers aſſert, was ſlain at the battle of Marathon. Cic. Epiſt. ad Attic. l. ix. 10. Juſt. l. ii. c. 9. Tertul. adv. Gentes, c. 46. Or, as others tell us, died afterwards in Lemnos. Suid. in v. Ἱππιας.—Vid. Herod. l. vi. § 107, 108. Thucyd. l. vi. §. 59.

was built at Athens, 231 years, Pythocritus * being archon at Athens. - - -
Bef. Chr.
·495

49. Since the battle at Marathon † was fought by the Athenians againſt the Perſians, and the Athenians defeated *Artaphernes*, the nephew ‡ of Darius, the commander [of the Perſian forces], 227 years, *Phænippus* ‖ the ſecond being archon at Athens; and Æſchylus the poet was engaged in the action, being [then] 35 years [of age]. - - - -
491

50. Since Simonides, the grandfather of Simonides the poet, he alſo being a poet, [dies] at *Ath*ens; and Darius dies, and Xerxes his ſon reigns, [226] years, Ariſtides § being archon at Athens. -
·490

51. Since Æſchylus the poet firſt gained the victory in tragedy, and Euripides the poet was born, and Steſichorus the poet went into Greece, 222 years, Philocrates ¶ being archon at Athens. - - -
486

52. Since Xerxes formed a bridge of boats on the Helleſpont, and cut [a navigable canal] through Athos, and the battle was fought in Thermopylæ, and the ſea-fight by the Greeks at Salamis, againſt the Perſians,

* Pythocritus archon. J. P. 4220. bef. Chr. 494. Corſin.
† Corſini places the battle at Marathon in the year bef. Chr. 490. Quum Salaminia pugna die 20 Boëdromionis, anno 1. Olymp. LXXV. contigerit, Marathonia clades 6 ejuſdem Boëdromionis menſis diei anni 3 Olymp. LXXII. certiſſimè aſcribi debet. Corſini Faſt. Attic. vol. iii. p. 150.
‡ Αδελφιδεον. Herod. l. vi. §. 94.
‖ Phænippus archon. J. P. 4224. bef. Chr. 490. Corſin.
§ Ariſtides archon. J. P. 4225. bef. Chr. 489. Id.
¶ Philocrates archon. J. P. 4229. bef. Chr. 485. Id.

in

THE PARIAN CHRONICLE. 37

	Bef. Chr.
in which the Greeks were victorious, 217 years, Calliades * being archon at Athens. -	481
53. Since the battle at Plataeæ was fought by the Athenians against Mardonius, Xerxes's general; in which the Athenians conquered, and Mardonius fell in the battle; and [torrents of liquid] fire flow*ed in Si*cily round Ætna; [2] 16 years, Xanthippus † being archon at Athens. - -	480
54. Since Gelon [the son] of Dinomenes became tyrant *of Syracuse*, 215 years, Timosthenes ‡ being archon at Athens. -	479
55. Since Simonides [the son] of Leoprepes, the Cean, who invented the art of memory ‖, teaching [a chorus] at Athens, gained the victory § ; and the statues of Harmodius and Aristogiton were erected, 2[14] years, *A*dimantus ¶ being archon at Athens. - - - -	478
56. Since Hiero became tyrant of Syra-	

* Calliades archon. J. P. 4234. bef. Chr. 480. Corsin.
† Xanthippus archon. J. P. 4235. bef. Chr. 479. Id.
‡ Timosthenes archon. J. P. 4236. bef. Chr. 478. Id.
‖ Simonidem primum ferunt artem memoriæ protulisse. Cic. de Orat. l. ii. § 84. Artem memoriæ primus ostendisse dicitur Simonides. Quint. l. xi. c. 2. Plin. l. vii. c. 24.

§ Ενικησεν Αθηνησιν δικασκων. Bentley thinks, these words relate to the teaching of *a chorus*, and translates the passage in this manner : " Simonides, the son of Leoprepes the Cean, that found the art of memory, got the prize at Athens, as teacher of a chorus, when Adimantus was archon." Dissert. on Phal. p. 29, 30.

Plutarch mentions a victory, which Simonides obtained by teaching a chorus : Επγε Σιμωνιδης μεν εν γηρα χορεις ταια. Siquidem senex Simonides choris victoriam reportavit. Plut. Ans. eni, &c. p. 785. Val. Max. l. viii. c. 7. § 13.

¶ Adimantus archon. J. P. 4237. bef. Chr. 477. Corsin.

cuse,

cuse, 20[9] years, Chares * being archon at Athens: Epicharmus the poet lived at this time. - - - - | 473

57. Since Sophocles [the son] of Sophillus, who was of Colonus †, gained the victory in tragedy, being 28 years of age, 206 years, Apsephion ‡ being archon at Athens. | 470

58. Since the stone fell in Ægos-potamos, and Simonides the poet died, having lived 90 years, 205 years, Theagenidas ‖ being archon at Athens. - - | 469

59. Since Alexander died, and his son Perdiccas reigns over the Macedonians, 19[8] years, Euthippus § being archon at Athens. - - - | 462

60. Since Æschylus the poet, having lived 69 years, died at *Gela*, in *Sicily*, 193 years, Callias the first ¶ being archon at Athens. - | 457

61. Since Euripides, being 43 years of age, first gained the victory in tragedy, 1[79] years, Diphi*lus* ** being archon at Athens. Socrates and *Ana*xagoras *l*ived in the time of Euripides. - - - | 443

62. Since Archelaus reigned over the Macedonians, Perdiccas being dead, 1[56] years, Astyphilus being *arch*on at Athens. - | 420

---

* Chares archon. J. P. 4242. bef. Chr. 472. Corsin.
† Colonus, about ten stadia from Athens. Thucyd. l. viii. § 67. Cic. de Fin. l. v. c. 1.
‡ Apsephion archon. J. P. 4245. bef. Chr. 469. Corsin.
‖ Theagenides archon. J. P. 4246. bef. Chr. 468. Id.
§ Euthippus archon. J. P. 4253. bef. Chr. 461. Id.
¶ Callias I. archon. J. P. 4258. bef. Chr. 456. Id.
** Diphilus archon. J. P. 4272. bef. Chr. 442. Id.

63. Since

THE PARIAN CHRONICLE. 39

	Bef. Chr.
63. Since Dionyſius became tyrant of Syracuſe, 144 years, Euctemon being archon at Athens. - - - -	408
64. Since Euripides, having lived ſeventy-ſeven years, died, 14[3] years, Antigenes being archon at Athens. - -	407
65. Since Sophocles the poet, having lived ninety-one years, died; and Cyrus went up [into Perſia] againſt his brother*, 142 years, Callias the firſt † being archon at Athens. -	406
66. Since Teleſtes ‡ the Selinuntian gained the prize at Athens, 13[8] years, Micon being archon at Athens. - -	402
67. Since thoſe returned, who went up with Cyrus [into Perſia] and Socrates the philoſopher died, having lived 70 years, 13[6] years, Laches being archon at Athens. -	400
68. Since Aſtydamas firſt taught at Athens, 135 years, Ariſtocrates being archon at Athens. - - -	399
69. Since Xanthus, a poet of Sardes, gained the victory at Athens in dithyrambics, 1.. years, ... being archon at Athens. -	...

70 Since Philoxenus, a writer of dithy-

---

* Κυρος ανβ[ησε επι τον αδελφον]. Theſe four letters, ανβ... apparently refer to the celebrated Anabaſis of the younger Cyrus.

Ανεβησε or αναβαντες, epoc. 67. is a form of expreſſion very common among the Greek writers, when they ſpeak of going up to a metropolis. εις την Ρωμην αναβαινουσι. Joſ. Antiq. l. xx. 7. Ανεβησαν ες Σουσα. Herod. l. vii. § 136. Vid. Matth. xx. 17, 18. Mark, x. 32, 33. Luke, x. 30. John, v. 1. vii. 8. Κυρου Αναβασις. Xenoph. Αλεξανδρου Αναβασις. Arrian.

† Του πρ.τ. ου ſhould rather be του δευτερου, the ſecond. Corſin. Faſt. Attic. vol. iii. p. 260.

‡ Diod. Sic. l. xiv. p. 272.

rambics,

iambics, dies, having lived 55 years, 116 years, Pytheas being archon at Athens. — | 380

71. Since Anaxandrides the comic poet gained the victory at Athens, [113] years, Calleas being archon at Athens. - - | 377

72. Since Aftydamas gained the victory at Athens, 109 years, Afteius being archon at Athens. Then alfo *a great light* * blazed *in the fky*. - - - | 373

73. *Since the battle was fought at Leuctra* between the Thebans and the Lacedæmonians, in which the Thebans conquered, 107 years, Phraficlides being archon at Athens. *At this time Alexander* [the fon] *of Amyntas* reigns *over the Macedonians*. - | 371

74 Since Stefichorus, the Himerian, the fecond [of that name] gained the victory at Athens, and Megalopolis *in Arcadia* was built, [106] *years, Dyfcinetus being archon at Athens*. - - - - | 370

75. Since Dionyfius the Sicilian died, and his fon Dionyfius became tyrant, and Alexander being dead, Ptolemy reigns over the

---

* Ἡ μεγαλη λαμπας.—This phenomenon is mentioned by Diodorus Siculus; but is faid to have happened the year afterwards, Olymp. CII. 1. bef. Chr. 372. Ὤφθη μεν γαρ κατα τον ουρανον επι πολλας νυκτας λαμπας μεγαλη καρομενη, απο του σχηματος ονομασθεισα πυρινη δοκις. Ingens enim fax in cœlo multis noctibus ardens apparuit, quæ propter figuram igneam trabs appellata fuit. Diod. Sic. l. xv. p. 365. Ariftotle tells us, that in the archonship of Ariftæus, μεγας αςηρ εφανη, magna ftella apparuit. Meteor. l. i. c. 6. Corfini thinks, that Ariftæus fhould be Afteius; and that the author of the Chronicle, Diodorus, and Ariftotle allude to the fame phenomenon. The δοκις πυρινη, ignea trabs, or fiery beam, was undoubtedly the tail of a comet.

Macedonians,

THE PARIAN CHRONICLE.

	Bef. Chr.
Macedonians, 104 years, Naufigenes being archon at Athens. - - -	368
76. Since the Phocæans *plundered the temple* of Delphi, [94] *years*, Cephifodorus *being archon at Athens*. - -	358
77. Since Timotheus, having lived 90 years, died, *and Philip* [the fon] *of Amyntas reigns over the Macedonians*, and Artaxerxes died; and Ochus his fon *reigns over the Perfians, and* .... gained the victory, 93 years, Agathocles being archon at Athens. - - - -	357
78. *Since Alexander* [the fon] *of Philip was born**, 91 years, Calliftratus being archon at Athens: *Ariftotle the philofopher* lived at that *time*. - - -	355
79. Since *Calippus, having flain Dion, became tyrant of Syracufe*, [90] *years*, Diotimus *being* archon *at Athens*. - -	354

* * * * * * * * * *

---

* Plutarch, Juftin, and other writers, inform us, that Alexander was born at the time of the celebration of the Olympic games. The birth of Alexander therefore fhould have been placed in the preceding year, namely, the firft year of the cvi Olympiad. Plut. in. v. Alex. p. 666. Juft. l. xii. c. 16. Eufebius is guilty of the fame error. Chron. p. 136.

A

DISSERTATION

ON THE

PARIAN CHRONICLE.

CHAP. I.

THE Parian Chronicle, engraved on a marble tablet of confiderable extent, is fuppofed to have been written 264 years before the Chriftian æra *. In its perfect ftate, it contained a chronological detail of the principal events of Greece, during a period of 1318

* Bef. Chr. 263 years, according to Selden, Prideaux, &c.—An. J. P. 4450, bef. Chr. 264, according to Corfini and Taylor. Fafti Attici, tom. iv. p. 88. Marm. Sandv. p. 5.—In the fourth year of the CXXVIII Olympiad, bef. Chr. 265 or 264, according to Sir Ifaac Newton. Chron. p. 47.

All the dates in this Differtation refer to the commencement of the Chriftian æra, according to the COMMON computation. But it muft be obferved, that, in many cafes, it is difficult, if not impoffible, to adjuft the Olympic year to the year before Chrift; becaufe the former began περι τας τροπας θεριυας, about the fummer folftice, and comprehended part of two Julian years.

years,

years, beginning with Cecrops, before Chrift 1582 years, and ending with the archonfhip of Diognetus, bef. Chr. 264. But the chronicle of the laft ninety years is loft ; fo that the part now remaining ends at the archonfhip of Diotimus, 354 years before the birth of Chrift ; and in this fragment the infcription is at prefent fo much corroded and effaced, that the fenfe can only be difcovered by very learned and induftrious antiquaries, or, more properly fpeaking, fupplied by their CONJECTURES.

The date of the Chronicle coincides with the twenty-firft year of the reign of Ptolemy Philadelphus in Egypt, the fplendid age of the Poëtarum Pleias [*]; of Lycophron, Theocritus, Callimachus, Aratus, &c. the reign in which chronologers ufually place the Seventy Interpreters [†], Pfeudo-Arifteas, Manetho, and others.

The Chronicle, which is the fubject of this enquiry,

---

[*] Authors are not agreed about the names of thefe poets. The fcholiaft to Hephæftion makes this poetical conftellation confift of the following tragic writers : Homerus the fon of Myro, Sofitheus, Lycophron, Alexander Ætolus, Æantides, Sofiphanes, and Philifcus or Philicus. Hephæft. Schol. p. 93. edit. 1553. Their names are mentioned again, with fome variation, ibid. p. 32. Tzetzes includes in the lift of thefe poets Lycophron, Theocritus, Aratus, Nicander, Æantides or Apollonius Rhodius, Philicus, and Homerus tragicus. Tzetzes de Gen. Lycoph. edit. 1601.

Saxius and others place the Poëtarum Pleias in the year bef. Chr. 277 ; yet it is certain, that all the poets above mentioned did not flourifh at the fame time. Gerald. Dial. iii. p. 330. Voff. de Poet. Græc. c. 8. p. 64. Id. de Hift. Græc. l. ii. c. 12. p. 74. Fabric. Bibl. Græc. l. ii. c. 19. vol. i. p. 688.

[†] Bef. Chr. 277. Prid. Connect. vol. iii. p. 38. The hiftory of the tranflation of the Bible by the feventy-two elders, as related by Arifteas, is A CONTEMPTIBLE FICTION. Prideaux fays: "No Arifteas, or heathen Greek, but fome Helleniftical Jew, under his name, was the author of that book." Ibid. p. 50. Hodius de Bibl. Text. Orig. l. i.

and

and many other relics of antiquity, were purchased in Asia Minor, in Greece, or in the islands of the Archipelago, by Mr. William Petty, who in the year 1624 * was sent by the Earl of Arundel †, for the purpose of making such collections for him in the East. They were brought into England about the beginning of the year 1627, and placed in the gardens belonging to Arundel-house in London, the site of which is now occupied by Arundel, Norfolk, Surrey, and Howard Streets, in the Strand.

Soon after their arrival they excited a general curiosity, and were viewed by many inquisitive and learned men; among others, by Sir Robert Cotton, who went immediately to Selden, and entreated him to exert his

* "I heare your grace hath written by one Mr. Petty, that is arriued at Smirna, ymployed by my lord of Arundell to buy books and antiquities." Letter from Sir T. Roe to archbishop Abbot, Dec. 9-19, 1624. Roe's Negot. Let. 229. p. 320.

† THOMAS, the son of Philip Howard, earl of Arundel, was born in 1592. In 1603, he was restored to all the titles of honour, which his father lost by his attainder; and also to the dignity of earl of Surrey, &c. In 1613, he went into Italy; but returned the next year. In 1621, he was constituted earl marshal of England. In 1627, he obtained the Parian marbles, which were sent by Mr. Petty. In Feb. 1641-2, he embarked for Italy. In 1644, he was created earl of Norfolk. He died at Padua, Oct. 4, 1646. This excellent nobleman was a great favourer of arts and learning. His designs, paintings, statues, &c. were numerous and valuable, and collected, at a great expence, from various parts of Europe and Asia.

He was succeeded in his estate and honours by his son HENRY Howard, who died 1652, and left nine sons, THOMAS, HENRY, Philip, Charles, Talbot, Bernard, Esme; and three daughters. Thomas was restored to the title of duke of Norfolk in 1664. Afterwards traveling into Italy, he died at Padua, unmarried, Dec. 1, 1677, whereby his honours and estate descended to his brother HENRY; of whom a farther account will be given in a subsequent note.

abilities

abilities in explaining the Greek inscriptions. Selden readily complied with his request; but desired the assistance of their common friends, Patrick Young, or, as he styled himself in Latin, Patricius Junius, and Richard James *.

The next morning, these gentlemen met in Arundel-gardens, and commenced their operations, by cleaning and examining the marble, containing the league, which the cities of Smyrna and Magnesia entered into, in favour of Seleucus Callinicus, king of Syria. Afterwards, they proceeded to the Parian Chronicle, and other inscriptions.

The following year Selden published a small volume in quarto, including twenty-nine Greek, and ten Latin inscriptions, copied from the marbles, with a translation and a commentary, under this title:

> Marmora Arundelliana; sive saxa Græcè incisa, ex venerandis priscæ Orientis gloriæ ruderibus, auspiciis et impensis herois illustrissimi, Thomæ, comitis Arundelliæ et Surriæ, comitis marescalli Angliæ, pridem vindicata, & in ædibus ejus hortisque cognominibus, ad Thamesis ripam, disposita.

* Patrick Young was librarian to James the First, and Charles the First. He was a man of distinguished learning; and, among other things, published,
> Clementis ad Corinthios Epistola prior, Gr. et Lat. cum interpretatione & notis, 4to. Oxon. 1633; and, in the same volume, Fragmentum Epistolæ secundæ, Græcè.
> Catena Græcorum Patrum in Jobum, Gr. & Lat. fol. Lond. 1637.

He died in 1652, in the sixty-ninth year of his age.

Richard James was born at Newport, in the Isle of Wight, and was fellow of Corpus Christi College, in Oxford. In 1636, he published an English translation of Minucius Felix, which he dedicated "to Lady Cotton, wife of Sir Robert Cotton, of Conington." He was likewise the author of several sermons, &c. He died, Dec. 7, 1638.

Accedunt

Accedunt inſcriptiones aliquot veteris Latii, ex locupletiſſimo ejuſdem vetuſtatis theſauro ſelectæ: Auctariolum item aliundè ſumtum.
Publicavit et commentariolos adjecit
Joannes Seldenus, J. C.
" Ipſo rore mihi ſeges eſt, quo gramen onagris."
Prudent. [*in Sym.* v. 812.]
Londini, typis & impenſis Guilielmi Stanesbeii, MDC XXVIII. Some copies have, Apud Johannem Billium typographum, MDCXXIX.

In the turbulent reign of Charles the Firſt, and the ſubſequent uſurpation, Arundel-houſe was often deſerted by the illuſtrious owners; and, in their abſence, ſome of the marbles, which were depoſited in the gardens, were defaced or broken; and others either ſtolen, or uſed for the ordinary purpoſes of architecture *.

This appears to have been the fate of the collection in general. With reſpect to the chronological marble, we find, that during the civil wars, it was moſt unfortunately broken and defaced. The upper part, containing almoſt half of the inſcription, is ſaid to have been worked up in repairing a chimney in Arundel-houſe. But a copy of it has been luckily preſerved by Selden. The fragment now remaining begins with theſe words: ——εσκευασε, και νομισμα. l. 46. epoc. 31.

In the year 1667, the Hon. Henry Howard †, grandſon

* Hæc tamen vix ultra dimidiam partem eorum conficiunt, quæ inſigniſſimus Arundelliæ comes collegerat; cætera, cùm tempore nuperrimi belli civilis incendii, in hortis Arundellianis Londini, pulſis inde dominis, diu neglecta jacuerint, aut furtim ſurrepta, aut ſervorum negligentiâ corrupta, aut à lapicidis ad reficiendas ædes adhibita, in magnum rei literariæ damnum, amittuntur. Prid. Marm. Oxon. præf. p. ix.

† HENRY HOWARD was the ſecond ſon of Henry earl of Arundel above mentioned. He was born in 1628. In 166., he ſet out

son of the first collector, on the application of John Evelyn, Esq. presented these curious remains of antiquity to the university of Oxford.

At that time Selden's work was become scarce *. It was therefore thought necessary, that another edition of the inscriptions should be published. Accordingly, bishop Fell † engaged Mr. Prideaux in this important work. Prideaux, though he had not then been six years at the university ‡, acquitted himself with great reputation. His edition was printed at Oxford in 1676, under the following title:

Marmora Oxoniensia, ex Arundellianis, Seldenianis, aliisque conflata, recensuit, et perpetuo commentario explicavit, Humphridus Prideaux, Ædis Christi alumnus, appositis ad eorum nonnulla Seldeni & Lydiati annotationibus. Accessit Sertorii Ursati Patavini de Notis Romanorum Commentarius. Oxonii, è Theatro Sheldoniano. MDCLXXVI. folio.

In 1721, Dr. Prideaux being then advanced in years ‖, and unable to superintend the republication of his own work, Mr. Robert Pearse, of Edmund Hall, in Oxford,

for Constantinople, and returned in 1665. In 1667, he presented the marbles to the university of Oxford. In 1668, he was created LL.D. In 1669, he was advanced to the dignity of baron, by the title of lord Howard of Castle Rising. In 1672, he was created earl of Norwich, and earl marshal. Upon the death of his elder brother Thomas, in 1677, he became duke of Norfolk. His Grace died at his house in Arundel-street, Jan. 11, 1683-4. Collins's Peerage.

* Selden died, Nov. 30, 1654, aged 70.
† Optimus igitur Fellus noster Humphredo Prideaux, A. B. et Ædis Christi alumno, demandandum voluit. Chand. Marm. Oxon. præf. p. iii.
‡ Qui nondum tum sextum annum in his musarum scholis compleveram. Prid. Marm. Oxon. præf. p. x.
‖ Dean Prideaux died in 1724, aged 76.

proposed

propofed to reprint it, and obtained the author's permiffion to make what corrections in it he might think neceffary. But Mr. Pearfe never carried his fcheme into execution.

In 1726, Dr. David Wilkins, who the fame year * had publifhed the works of Mr. Selden, promifed to give a new edition of the Arundelian infcriptions. In the mean time, fome other engagements engroffed his attention, and he likewife relinquifhed his defign.

In 1732, Mr. Maittaire obliged the public with a more comprehenfive view of the Marbles, than either of his predeceffors, in a work, entitled,

Marmorum Arundellianorum, Seldenianorum, aliorúmque Academiæ Oxonienfi donatorum, cum variis commentariis et indice, fecunda editio. Londini, typis Gulielmi Bowyer. MDCCXXXII. folio.

In this publication the editor has given, Firft, the Greek and Latin infcriptions in capitals, and four infcriptions in Hebrew; then the Greek text in fmall letters, with a Latin tranflation by Selden, Prideaux, and Price, p. 1. to 99.

Secondly, the differtations and comments of learned men feparately, and at full length : namely,

1. Selden commentary, from p. 99 to 197.
2. Price's notes on the third marble [Marmor Cretenfe] p. 197—200.
3. Palmerius's notes and fupplements to the firft marble [the Parian Chronicle] p. 200—222.
4. Lydiat's annotations on the fame. p. 222—295.
5. Marfham's commentaries on the firft 58 epochas of the fame marble. p. 295—309.
6. Prideaux's commentary on the marbles. p. 309—509.

* This edition of Selden's works, in three volumes folio, was begun in 1722, and finifhed in 1726.

7. Some

7. Some notes on the marbles by Reinesius. p. 509—524.
8. Spon's notes on some of the marbles. p. 524—527.
9. Chishull's notes on the third marble. p. 527—532.
10. Extracts from Smith's Epistle concerning the Seven Churches of Asia. p. 532—533.
11. Extracts from Bentley's Dissertation on the Epistles of Phalaris. p. 533—540.
12. Maffei's Italian version of the first and second marbles, with notes. p. 540—549. [The second marble contains the Smyrnean and Magnesian league.]
13. Dodwell's chronological tables of the first marble. p. 549—553.
14. Conjectures and remarks on the marbles and the preceding comments, by the editor. p. 553—605.
Lastly, A copious index, interspersed with many critical notes and observations.

Mr. Prideaux, in his edition, had ranged the inscriptions in the order, in which the marbles were placed, while they stood in the court-yard belonging to Sheldon's Theatre *. But as they were afterwards removed to a more convenient situation †, Maittaire reduced them, as nearly as he could, to the order observed by Gruter and others, who have arranged such ancient monuments, according to the nature and importance of their respective subjects.

In 1763, after the university had acquired a great variety of other ancient marbles, by the benefactions of Sir

---
* Delata sunt Oxonium, in platea Theatri Sheldoniani deposita, vel muro qui eam ambit infixa, & initiali literâ Howardiani nominis notata. Chand. Marm. Oxon. præf. p. iii.

† They are now carefully preserved in a room, adjoining to the public schools at Oxford, called the Museum Arundelianum.

George

George Wheler, the Countess of Pomfret in the year 1755, Mr. Dawkins, Dr. Rawlinson, and others, Dr. Chandler undertook to give the public a new and improved copy of these valuable remains of antiquity; and accordingly published a very magnificent volume, entitled, MARMORA OXONIENSIA.

This work is divided into three parts. The first consists of 59 copper-plates, representing 167 statues, busts, urns, vases, altars, &c. without inscriptions.

The second contains 100 Egyptian, Palmyrene, Greek, and other inscriptions, and eleven plates.

The third consists of 145 inscriptions in Latin, Arabic, and other languages, and six plates.

To the whole is subjoined a verbal index.

This learned and ingenious editor has corrected the mistakes of his predecessors; and in some of the inscriptions, particularly that of the Parian Chronicle, has supplied the lacunæ by many happy CONJECTURES.

CHAP. II.

IT seemed necessary to premise a general account of the marbles, that the reader may the more easily comprehend the following observations.

The DOUBTS, which have sometimes occurred to me, with respect to the authenticity of the Parian Chronicle, arise from the following considerations:

I. The characters have no certain or unequivocal marks of antiquity.

II. It is not probable, that the Chronicle was engraved for PRIVATE USE.

III. It does not appear to have been engraved by PUBLIC AUTHORITY.

IV. The Greek and Roman writers, for a long time after the date of this work, complain, that they had no chronological account of the affairs of ancient Greece.

V. This Chronicle is not once mentioned by any writer of antiquity.

VI. Some of the facts seem to have been taken from authors of a later date.

VII. Parachronisms appear in some of the epochas, which we can scarcely suppose a Greek chronologer, in the CXXIX Olympiad, would be liable to commit.

VIII. The history of the discovery of the marbles is obscure and unsatisfactory.

Lastly, The literary world has been frequently imposed upon, by spurious books and inscriptions; and therefore we should be extremely cautious, with regard

THE PARIAN CHRONICLE. 53

gard to what we receive under the venerable names of antiquity.

I. The characters in this infcription have no certain or unequivocal marks of antiquity.

It is written, like other ancient infcriptions, in capitals, without any diftances between the words, and without any points or accents.

Selden informs us, that all the letters, except Π and Z, are EXACTLY reprefented by the common Greek types; that the *Pi* has the perpendicular line, on the right hand, only half as long as the parallel line on the left, thus, Γ; and the *Zeta*, the form of a proftrate H, in this manner, ⌶ *.

It is generally fuppofed, that this was the more ancient way of writing the *Zeta* †; and that afterwards the

* Non licuit per operarum formas, omnes archetyporum figuras ubique repræfentare; quod tamen plerumque in univerfis, fed in prioribus binis EXACTE, fecimus, EXCEPTIS TANTUMMODO Π et Z. Το Π tum in chronologico hôc Marmore, tum in Smyrnæorum Decretis et Fœdere, perpetuò, crus, quod ad dextram vergit, habet dimidiatum ad hunc modum Γ. In recentioribus infcriptionibus quas dedimus, utrumque crus æquè femper extenditur; et Ζητα etiam non aliter quàm ufitatis typographorum formis exaratur. In vetuftioribus autem hifce binis Ζητα hâc femper figurâ ⌶ occurrit, quæ ητα ὕπτιον, five eta fupinum, dicitur Alypio. Seld. Marm. Arund. p. 76.

† Vetus ejus figura ⌶ paulatim in z deflexa eft. Chifhul. Antiq. Afiatic. p. 20.

ΓΠ. Hâc utrâque formâ PASSIM fcribitur, ut videre eft in alphabeto Cyziceni marmoris. [Montf. Palæog. Græc. p. 144.] Prior forma Γ, decurtatâ poftremâ lineâ, vetuftior eft; unde factum P Latinum, mutando quadrata rotundis. Ibid. p. 142.—ΠΓ prima forma prifca eft: fecunda item in marmoribus vetuftiffimis PASSIM habetur. Ibid. p. 337.

Z. Sic incifum habetur in nummis & marmoribus; fed hâc formâ etiam NON INFREQUENTER obferves ⌶, quo pacto fcribitur in Cyziceno marmore. Ibid. p. 142.

middle

middle bar was drawn diagonally from the extremity of the upper line on the right hand, to the end of the lower line on the left, as it now ſtands in our modern alphabets.

Yet theſe two characters, Γ and Η, ſo frequently occur, and are ſo well known, that any modern fabricator of a Greek inſcription, which he intends to impoſe upon the world, as a relic of antiquity, would moſt probably uſe them, in preference to the more common and ordinary forms.

It is however obſervable, that the letters in the Parian Chronicle have no appearance of antiquity, except this very equivocal one.

They do not in the leaſt reſemble the Sigean *, the Nemean †, or the Delian ‡ inſcriptions, which are ſuppoſed

---

* See a copy of the Sigean inſcription in Chiſhull's Antiquitates Aſiaticæ, p. 4.—This celebrated inſcription is on part of an antient pilaſter, eight feet ſeven inches long, ſomething more than eighteen inches wide, and a little above ten inches thick. It was intended to record the donations, which one Phanodicus of Proconneſus had made to a temple at Sigeum. The ſtone, at preſent, is uſed as a ſeat at the door of a Greek church, in a little village called Giaurkioi, in a place, where the city Sigeum formerly ſtood, three miles from the Sigean promontory. The inſcription is written in the manner, which the Greeks called bouſtrophedon; that is, the lines turn on the marble, as *oxen turn* in plowing, *from the left* to the right, and from the right to the left, alternately. The retrograde order of the letters is a relic of the oriental way of writing. This inſcription is ſuppoſed to have been engraved about 560 years before the vulgar æra. Chandler's Trav. in Aſia Minor, ch. xii.

† The Nemean inſcription may be ſeen in the Theſaurus Inſcriptionum, collected by Muratori, and illuſtrated by M. Bimard, who ſuppoſes it to be next in antiquity to the Sigean.

‡ The Delian inſcription was brought from the Eaſt by M. Tournefort, who copied it from the baſe of a ſtatue, ſuppoſed to be that of Apollo, thrown down in the iſle of Delos. It conſiſts of about

posed to be of a more ancient date. They differ, in many respects, from the letters on the Marmor Sandvicense *, which, according to the learned editor of that inscription, was engraved in the year before Christ 374. They bear no sort of resemblance to the characters on the Farnesian pillars †, to those of the Alexandrian manuscript, or others of a later date. They seem to resemble, perhaps more than any other, the letters of the alphabet, taken by Montfaucon from the Marmor Cyzicenum, at Venice ‡. They are plain and simple in

about eight words, in uncouth letters, which, Montfaucon thinks, were the ancient Ionian characters. Tournef. Voyages, let. 7. Chish. Antiq. Asiat. p. 16. Montf. Palæog. Græc. l. ii. c. 1. p. 122.

* The Marmor Sandvicense was found at Athens, and brought to England by lord Sandwich, in 1739. The inscription contains an account of the public money, collected for the festival of Apollo at Delphi, for four years, by the Amphictyones. The letters are placed at equal distances ; and each letter of every subsequent line stands exactly under each letter of the preceding line ; consequently, all the lines contain the same number of letters. In this position, the letters, with the interstices, appear like small perpendicular columns, extending from the bottom to the top of the marble. Marmor Sandvicense, cum commentario & notis J. Taylori, LL.D. 4to. 1743.

† Two columns found on the Appian road, about three miles from Rome, and removed from thence to the Farnesian palace. They are supposed to have been erected by Herodes Atticus, at his villa Triopia. Herodes was a scholar, and an admirer of antiquities. He was consul at Rome in the year 143.

"Part of the inscription is on one pillar, and part on the other." It is intended to exhibit a specimen of the old Ionic letters ; but seems to be a mere " simia vetustatis," and is perhaps a forgery. Montf. Palæog. Græc. p. 135. 140. Scal. Animadv. in Euseb. p. 110. Salmas. Duarum Inscript. Explic. p. 29. See Letters from a Young Painter, let. 22. 51.

‡ Montf. Palæog. Græc. l. ii. c. 4. p. 144.—Montfaucon thinks, that this inscription must have been engraved before the time of Alexander the Great.

their

their form, and such as an ordinary stone-cutter of the present age would probably make, if he were employed to engrave a Greek inscription, according to the alphabet now in use. The small letters, intermixed among the larger, have an air of affectation and artifice, rather than genuine antiquity *.

For my own part, I am persuaded, that the antiquity of an inscription can never be proved by the mere form of the letters; because the most ancient characters may be as easily counterfeited, as those, which now compose our present alphabets.

That the learned reader may form a competent idea of the characters in the Parian Chronicle, a small specimen, accurately copied from a plate in the Marmora Oxoniensia, published by Dr. Chandler, is annexed to this Dissertation.

It may be said, that there are several archaïsms in this Chronicle, which are evident marks of antiquity: as,

Εγ instead of εκ.

εγ Λυκωρειας, è Lycoriâ. l. 7.
εγ Μιτυληνης, è Mitylene. l. 51.

Εγ instead of εν.

εγ Κυβελοις, in Cybelis. l. 19.
εγ Κελαιναις, in Celænis. ibid.

Εμ instead of εν.

εμ Παρῳ, in Paro. l. 2.
εμ παρα .. αδι, in maritimâ regione. l. 17.
εμ Μαραθωνι, in Marathone. l. 62.

Αμ instead of αν.

ὡς αμ Μινως αξιωσῃ, quascunque Minos postularet. l. 34.

* But see Montf. Palæog. Græc. l. ii. c. 4. p. 142.

But

Specimen literarum, quibus exaratum est **CHRONICON MARMOREUM**, *ex editione Chandleriana parte secunda. Tab. VIII. p. 104.*

ΕΛΛΗΣΠΟΝΤΩΙΚΑ ΤΟΝΑΘΩΔΙΩΡΥΞΕΚΑΙΗΕΝΘΕΡΜΟ

Ἑλλησποντῳ, και τον Ἀθω διωρυξε, και η εν Θερμο-

In Hellesponto, et Athonem perfodit,

et in Thermopylis. Lin. 66. epoc. 52.

THE PARIAN CHRONICLE. 57

But from these and other similar expressions in the inscription, we can draw no conclusion in favour of its authenticity.

Some grammarians and commentators on the Marbles have indeed observed, that, in ancient inscriptions, γ is used instead of ν, at the end of a word, when the next begins with γ, κ, or χ: as, την γραφην, των κατοικων, μεγ καταλοχισμους, τογ χρονον; and instead of ν, when the following word begins with δ, λ, or μ: as εγ δε, εγ Λυκωςιας, εγ Μιτυληνης; and that μ likewise, at the end of words *, is used instead of ν, before β, μ, π, φ; ὁ: as, γηραιομ βιοτας, εμ Μαγνησια, εμ Πλαδοις, την πολιν, τομ πολεμον, τημ φιλιαν, τημ ὁμολογιαν †, &c.

But what reason could there be for introducing these archaïsms, as they are called, into the Parian Chronicle? We do not usually find them in Greek writers of the same age, or even in those of the most early date. The reign of Ptolemy Philadelphus was not an age of rude antiquity, with respect to the Greek language. It was 600 years after the time of Homer and Hesiod, and 130 after that of Xenophon and Plato, when the

---

* As a labial before another labial, β, μ, π, φ, ψ, in composition, μ is COMMONLY used for ν: as, εμβαινω, εμμενω, εμπιπτω, εμφημι, συμψηφις; but not as a final.

Pleraque nos illâ quasi mugiente literâ claudimus M, quâ nullum Græcè verbum cadit. Quint. l. xii. c. 10.

Vocibus in Graiis nunquam ultima conspicitur M.
          Auson. Idyl. 12.

It may be observed, by the way, that this is not an irregular verse, as some have erroneously imagined, who have called the final letter em, instead of mu.

In M, says J. Cæs. Scaliger, nullam vocem Græcam terminavit: barbaris nobisque modus nullus. De Caus. Ling. Lat. l. i. c. 10. Vid. Scalig. Animadv. in Euseb. p. 114.

† Maittaire, Marm. Arund. p. 615. 636. Id. Ling. Græc. Dialect. p. 163. 381.

I   Greek

Greek language was spoken and written in its utmost purity and elegance.

We can scarcely suppose, that even a stone-cutter, in that refined age, would have been permitted to disgrace a superb and learned monument with such barbarisms.

However this may be, the preceding archaïsms are not uniformly observed in the Chronicle. We find the author writing, a little inconsistently,

του Παρνασσον, Parnassum. l. 4.
την Καδμειαν, Cadmeam. l. 12.
τον καρπον, fructum. l. 27.
μεν Κριτιου, quidem Critiæ. l. 52.
εν μαχη, in prælio. l. 63.
εν Πλαταιαις, ad Plataeas. l. 67.

I am almost tempted to suspect, that εμ Παρω, εμ Μαραθωνι, and other pretended archaïsms, are owing to a mere affectation of antiquity, or to a corrupted dialect and pronunciation in later ages. For, if we may depend on the authority of Dr. Bentley, " the modern Greeks, though they write the ν in these cases, pronounce that letter as μ *."

These archaïsms, I know, appear on other marbles; but, for that very reason, they would naturally be adopted by the fabricator of a supposititious inscription. And the authenticity of those inscriptions, in which they appear, must be established, before they can be produced, in opposition to the present argument.

* Dissert. on Phal. § 14. p. 334.

CHAP. III.

II. IT is scarcely probable, that such an expensive and cumbersome work, as the chronological marble, would have been executed by a private citizen, a philosopher, or an historian, at Paros, either for his own amusement, or for the benefit of his fellow-citizens.

This will appear by the following considerations. First, a long inscription, containing a general system of chronology, could not be engraved on marble, without such an expense, as few learned Greeks were able to afford. Or, if the author, by an uncommon felicity, was able to erect such a literary monument, the scheme would have been useless and imprudent; as all the contents of the inscription might have been published more commodiously and effectually, by the common mode of writing, in use at that time. For,

Secondly, a manuscript is more readily circulated from hand to hand, and copies of it more easily multiplied and dispersed. This inscription, it is true, might have been copied; but no writer of antiquity seems to have either seen or heard of such a copy.

Thirdly, a manuscript is easily corrected and improved, as the author, from time to time, may see occasion. But an inscription on marble is unalterable. On this account, a league, a statute, a decree, an epitaph, &c. which do not usually require any alteration, may be very properly inscribed on marble. Whereas a system of chronology, attended with innumerable difficulties, and frequently founded on mere conjectures, must necessarily demand repeated corrections. A writer therefore, of common prudence and discretion, would not subject himself to the impossibility of making occasional emendations in his own performance.

Fourthly, in a work of considerable extent, like the Parian Chronicle, containing a multiplicity of names, facts, and dates, a stone-cutter will inevitably make a number of mistakes *, which can never be rectified on the marble. For instance, there is an error in the twenty-fifth epocha, either of the author, or of the stone-cutter, which it was not easy, or perhaps not possible, to correct, after the subsequent letters were engraved †.

Fifthly, the letters of an inscription on stone are liable to be defaced by a variety of accidents; and the smallest mutilation, in a numeral character, will totally destroy a chronological computation.

Lastly, ancient writers seem to have agreed, that a manuscript is more likely to be transmitted to posterity, than an inscription, either on marble or brass.

Ovid was certainly of this opinion, when he thus congratulated himself on the immortality of his writings, and bade defiance to the ravages of war and conflagrations, to the fury of winds and storms, and the devastations of time:

> Jamque opus exegi, quod nec Jovis ira, nec ignes,
> Nec poterit ferrum, nec edax abolere vetustas ‡.

Horace, on the publication of his odes, exclaims,

---

* Plurima passim occurrunt errata quadratariorum. Id enim genus opificies, extra mechanicam artem lapidariam, non forsan admodum periti, uti nunc saepe, ita et olim, errare soliti sunt. Marm. Arund. edit. Maitt. p. 573.

† See epoc. 25, where the omission of ιππου και occasions a gross impropriety.

‡ Ovid. Met. l. xv. 871.

Exegi

Exegi monumentum ære perennius *,

"I have raised a monument more lasting than brass;" and consequently more durable than marble.

Thucydides, likewise, when he wrote the history of the Peloponnesian war, entitled it, κτημα ες αει, "an everlasting possession †."

But the author of the Parian Chronicle, supposing it to be genuine, must be supposed to have deviated from the common mode of writing, without any sort of propriety, or any reasonable motive; he must be supposed to have put himself to a considerable, and, at the same time, a useless expense; and to have committed his elaborate performance to a stone, which he could neither alter, nor conveniently remove, nor secure from violence, or the depredation of those, who might value the marble more than the inscription.

For these reasons it does not seem probable, that the Parian Chronicle was the production of a private citizen, either for his own use, or for the benefit of the public.

It may be said, that the practice of writing upon pillars, stones, or marble, whatever was thought worthy of being transmitted to posterity, was very common among the nations of antiquity; that we read of the pillars of Seth ‡, of Hermes or Mercury ||, and Acicarus the Babylonian §; and that Sanchoniatho,

---

* Hor. l. iii. od. 30.
† Thucyd. l. i. § 22.
‡ The Jews had an old tradition, that the descendants of Seth erected two pillars, on which they inscribed their inventions; and one of them, if we may believe Josephus, remained in his time, κατα γην την Σιριαδα, in terrâ Siriade, in the land of Siriad, or Sirias. Jos. Antiq. Jud. l. i. c. 2. § 3.
|| Jamblic. de Myst. Ægyp. sect. i. c. 2.
§ Clem. Alex. Strom. l. i. § 15. p. 356. edit. Oxon. 1715.—

choniatho *, Pythagoras, Plato †, Manetho ‡, and other ancient authors, collected many things in their writings from such ancient monuments.

In answer to this objection, we may remark, that nothing can be more fabulous and uncertain, than the accounts, which are transmitted to us, concerning the pillars, said to have been erected in the early ages. The pillars of Seth, for example, may be reckoned among the fictions or the mistakes ‖ of Josephus. The place

---

Who Acicarus was, is uncertain. A late writer supposes him to have been Achiacharus, mentioned in the book of Tobit, c. i. 22. Dissert. in Daniel. secund. LXX. p. 381. Diogenes Laertius ascribes a book, entitled, Acicharus, to Theophrastus; but we know nothing of its contents. l. v. § 50.

* Euseb. Præp. Evang. l. i. c. 9. p. 32.

† Jamb. loc. cit.

‡ Εν τῃ Σηριαδικῃ γη. Manetho pretended, that he extracted his Egyptian dynasties from the pillars of Hermes. Euseb. Chron. Græc. p. 6. Maneth. apud Syncell. p. 40. Goari Annot. in loc.

‖ Herodotus tells us, that he himself had seen some of the pillars of Sesostris, εν τῃ Παλαιστινῃ Συρῃ, in the Syrian Palestine, l. ii. § 106.

The pillar, which, Josephus says, was remaining in his time, was probably one of these; and having the name of Sesostris, or Sethos, inscribed upon it, he imagined it had been erected by the descendents of Seth. Or perhaps the pillar, which he ascribed to those antediluvian philosophers, was one of the pillars of Mercury or Thoth, mentioned by Manetho. Vid. Fabric. Cod. Pseud. tom. i. p. 150. Dodwell on Sanchon. § 13.

That an antediluvian pillar should be standing in the time of Josephus, is incredible. But it is not the only legendary tale, which we find in the writings of that author. The eloquent son of Matthias, though in other respects a valuable historian, relates many ridiculous fictions: such as that of the pillar of salt being then existing. Antiq. l. i. c. 11. § 4. of Eleazar and the demon. Ibid. l. viii. c. 2. § 5. of the Sabbatic river. De Bell. Jud. l. vii. c. 5. § 1. of the plant called Baaras. Ibid. c. 6. § 3, &c.

Speaking

THE PARIAN CHRONICLE.

place where, he pretends, they existed, κατα την Συριαδα, or Συριαδα, was an unknown region, which has never been discovered.

It was no unusual thing to impose upon the world on the credit of such pillars. "Euhemerus," says the learned Mr. Dodwell, "was looked upon by antiquity, as a famous instance of it *. It was certainly the easiest way for broaching falshoods. These were monuments, which could be produced on a sudden, concerning the most remote antiquities, without the attestation of ancient writings; because they were supposed to be origi-

Speaking of the pillar of salt, he says, ιστορηκα δ' αυτος, επι γαρ και νυν διαμενει. Nam siquidem VIDI, nam et hodie usque manet. edit. Havero. 1726. In this passage, and in the story of the demon, he uses the word ιστορηκα, or ιστορησα, which is usually translated VIDI, "I have seen." But for the sake of his credit, I would rather suppose it ought to be translated, memoravi, de illa relationem accepi, or nunciatum est mihi de illa.

The author of a poem, entitled, SODOMA, annexed to the works of Tertullian, is not content with saying, the pillar of salt existed in his time, but he makes a WONDERFUL IMPROVEMENT in the story.

> Durat adhuc etenim nudâ statione sub æthram,
> Nec pluviis dilapsa situ, nec diruta ventis.
> Quinetiam, si quis mutilaverit advena formam,
> Protinus ex sese fungestu vulnera complet.
> Dicitur et vivens, alio jam corpore, sexûs
> Munificos solito dispungere sanguine menses.
>
> Tertull. Op. p. 644.

* Euhemerus the Messenian composed a history of Jupiter and other gods, from materials, which he pretended to have collected in the course of his travels; particularly from an inscription on a golden pillar in the temple of Jupiter Triphylius, in an island called Panchæa, somewhere in the Arabian ocean. Euseb. Præp. Evang. l. ii. c. 2. p. 60. Lactan. l. i. c. 11. S. D. b. l. Siculus, l. v. p. 318, 319, where this island is described. Strabo and Plutarch represent Panchæa as a fabulous region, which no body had ever seen. Strab. l. vii. p. 459. edit. 1707. Plut. de Isid. et Osir. p. 360.

nals of the times they pretended to give an account of; were fuppofed to be remote from vulgar knowledge or underftanding, being either kept in the adyta, or locked up in fome obfolete, unknown character, which none but the learned and the priefts could underftand; were contrived in hieroglyphics, or fuch ambiguous notes, as were capable of what interpretation thofe defigning perfons, who produced them, were pleafed to put upon them; were generally founded on oral tradition, than which there is not a more unfaithful conveyer of monuments to pofterity; and wholly depended on the credit of the priefts, who, at the fame time, were generally interefted in the things thus preferved, by their contributing to the fupport of their falfe religion, or to the honour of their nation for antiquity or rare inventions; and, laftly, were to be found and examined only in one place, not, like books, every where; nor even there, without the leave and direction of fuch interefted priefts. Upon this account, the ftories, with which it was fafhionable in thofe times to adorn their dialogues, were grounded on the credit of fuch pretended infcriptions: as, the table of Cebes; the Samothracian [Hyperborean] infcriptions, referred to by Axiochus *; and thofe concerning the Atlantides in Timæus †."

Almoft all the fabricators of fuppofititious writings have pretended to derive their information from fuch obfcure and fufpicious fources. Thus, the publifher of the fragments, afcribed to Sanchoniatho, would make us believe, that he compiled his Phœnician hiftory from the books of Taaut ‡, the Αποκρυφα Αμμουνεων γραμματα,

* Plato [five Æfchines] in Axiocho, p. 371. edit. Serrani, 1578.

† Plato in Timæo.—See Dodwell on Sanch. § 11.

‡ Taaut, " called by the Ægyptians Thoyth; by the Alexandrians Thoth; by the Greeks Hermes." Eufeb. Præp. Evang. l. i. c. 9.

the

THE PARIAN CHRONICLE. 65

the myftical records of the Ammoneans, concealed in the facred receffes of their temples *. Thus, Philoftratus afferts, that he took his account of Apollonius Tyaneus from the memoirs of Damis the Affyrian †. Thus, Gelafius Cyzicenus tells us, that he found in his father's houfe an ancient volume, containing a hiftory of the council of Nice ‡. And thus, Geoffrey of Monmouth would perfuade us, that he tranflated his Britifh hiftory from an old manufcript, found in Armorica by Walter Calenius, archdeacon of Oxford, in the reign of Henry the Firft ‖.

But allowing the ancient infcriptions abovementioned all the credit that can be defired; admitting it likewife as a fact, that mankind, in rude or early ages, wrote on ftones §, bricks, tiles ¶, marble, lead,

---

* Eufeb. Præp. Evang. loc. cit.—The letters or writings of the Ammoneans, according to Bochart, were infcriptions or records, ufed in חמנים hammanim, in temples or fhrines; for חמה, hamma, fignifies the fun, and חמן, hammon, the temple of the fun. Phaleg. par. ii. l. ii. c. 17.——Sir John Marfham thinks, the Ammonei were the Thebans, or inhabitants of No-Ammon. Canon Chron. fec. x. p. 244.

† Philoft. in v. Apollon. l. i. c. 3. Suidas.

‡ Cave, Hift. Liter. fub an. 476. Fabric. Bibl. Græc. l. v. c. 24. vol. viii. p. 371.

‖ Galfredi Monumet. l. xii. c. 20. Leland de Script. Brit. c. 157. p. 187. Baleus, p. 180. Pitfeus fub an. 1120, 1152.

§ Eufeb. Chron. Græc. p. 6. Lucan. l. iii. 222.——Gothes majorum acta patrii fermonis carminibus vulgata, linguæ fuæ literis, faxis ac rupibus infculpenda curaffe. Saxo-Gram. Hift. Dan. præf.

¶ Epigenes apud Babylonios DCCXXX annorum obfervationes fiderum, coctilibus laterculis infcriptas, docet. Plin. l. vii. p. 56.

In this paffage Pliny certainly wrote DCCXXX, or 720,000 years; for how could he produce the obfervations of 720 years as a

K   preed,

lead *, copper, wood †, bark, &c. this could be no reason, why the author of the Parian Chronicle should engrave his performance on any of those materials.

The most ancient nations made use of them, because they were not acquainted with any thing more proper or convenient; and as there were but few in those rude ages, who practised the art of writing, it was ne-

proof, that the use of letters among the Babylonians was *æternus*, eternal, or of the highest antiquity? Cicero mentions the observations of the Babylonians, for the space of 470,000 years; Diodorus for 473,000, and Africanus for 480,000. In a subsequent sentence Pliny says, " the lowest computation of them by Berosus and Critodemus was 480 years;" which should undoubtedly be 480,000. If these years are only *days*, as some writers maintain, 720,000 will make about 1972 Julian years. Vid. Cic. de Divinat. l. i. § 36. Diod. Sic. l. ii. p. 118. Afric. apud Syncell. p. 17.

The Babylonians wrote on tiles, because probably there were no stones at Babylon. The prophet Ezekiel, when he was a captive in that country, was ordered to make a representation of Jerusalem upon a tile, which was to be a symbolical or prophetical sign of its destruction by the king of Babylon. ch. iv. 1. Jackson, Chron. Antiq. vol. i. p. 218.

* Pausanias relates, that the Bœotians, who lived near the fountain Hippocrene, shewed him a copy of Hesiod's poem, entitled ΕΡΓΑ, inscribed on lead. Pausan. l. ix. c. 31.

Hanc [papyrum] Alexandri Magni victoriâ repertam, auctor est M. Varro, conditâ in Ægypto Alexandriâ; antea non fuisse chartarum usum; palmarum foliis primò scriptitatum; deinde quarundam arborum libris; postea PUBLICA MONUMENTA plumbeis voluminibus; mox et privata linteis confici cœpta aut cereis. Pugillarium enim usum fuisse etiam ante Trojana tempora invenimus apud Homerum, Il. vi. 169. Varronis Fragm. p. 230. Plin. l. xiii. c. 11. Front. Stratag. l. iii. c. 13. § 7. Job xix. 24.

† ——————Leges incidere ligno.
Hor. Art. Poet. v. 399.

Solenis leges Athenis axibus ligneis incisæ sunt. A. Gell. l. ii. c. 12.

cessary

THE PARIAN CHRONICLE. 67

ceſſary to uſe the moſt ſolid and durable ſubſtances, for the preſervation of their public acts and monuments. But long before the date of the Parian Chronicle, more commodious materials were invented.

In the oldeſt writings now extant, the Jewiſh ſcriptures, we frequently read of books and volumes. Moſes mentions the book of the Covenant, the book of the Law, and the book of the Wars of the Lord*. The author of the hiſtory of Joſhua refers to the book of Jaſher †. Job wiſhes, that his adverſary had written a book ‡. David appeals to the VOLUME of the book ‖. Solomon ſays, of making many books there is no end §. And, laſtly, ſeveral of the prophets ſpeak of ROLLS, and ROLLS of books ¶.

We have likewiſe an account of books and volumes, in the early ages of pagan antiquity.

Herodotus tells us, that *diphtheræ*, or the ſkins of ſheep and goats, were uſed for writing by the ancient Ionians **. Diodorus Siculus likewiſe informs us, that the ancient Perſians wrote their records on ſkins ††.

---

* Exod. xxiv. 7. Deut. xxxi. 26. Numb. xxi. 14.—Moſes died bef. Chr. 1451 years. Uſher.

† Joſhua, x. 13.

‡ Job, xxxi. 35.

‖ Pſal. xl. 7. במגלת ספר, in volumine libri. גלל fig. *volvit, convolvit*, &c.

§ Eccleſ. xii. 12.

¶ Iſa. viii. 1. Jer. xxxvi. 2. Ezek. ii. 9.

** Και τας βιβλους διφθερας καλεουσι απο του παλαιου ει Ιωνες, ὁτι ποτε, εν σπανι βιβλων, εχρεωντο, διφθερησι αιγεησι τε και οιεησι. Priſcâque conſuetudine libros Iones appellant *diphtheras*, quòd aliquandò, penuriâ biblorum, pellibus caprinis ovillíſque utebantur. Herod. l. v. § 58.

†† Εν διφθεραις οι Περσαι τας παλαιας πραξεις, κατα τινα νομον, ειχον συντεταγμενας. In membranis res antiquas Perſæ, quâdam lege, ordine deſcriptas habebant. Diod. Sic. l. ii. p. 113. Αρχαιοτερα διφθερας, *diphtherâ antiquiora*. Suidas.

K 2 Varro

Varro relates, that the use of the Egyptian papyrus for writing on, was introduced, when Alexander the Great built Alexandria in Egypt *; that is, about the year bef. Chr. 332. Guilandinus endeavours to prove from Alcæus, Anacreon, Æschylus, the ancient comic poets, Plato, Aristotle, and others, that the papyrus was used for that purpose long before the time of Alexander †. Many of his testimonies indeed, as the learned Scaliger has shewn ‡, are fallacious; yet it is evident from the words of Herodotus, cited in the margin, that the biblos or papyrus was used for writing in his time. It is not however necessary to prove, by the testimony of ancient authors, that books were written on parchment, on paper made of the Egyptian papyrus, or any such materials, before the date of the Parian Chronicle. This is sufficiently evinced by the very existence of the writings of Moses, David, Solomon, and the Jewish prophets; the works of Homer, Hesiod, Anacreon, Pindar, Æschylus, Sophocles, Euripides, Herodotus, Hippocrates, Aristophanes, Thucydides, Xenophon, Plato, Demosthenes, Aristotle, &c. and is still more incontestably proved by the libraries, which were collected in preceding ages, or about that time; such as those of Polycrates in Samos, Pisistratus ‖ and Euclides at Athens, Nicocrates in Cyprus, Euripides the poet, Aristotle the philosopher §, Clearchus at Heraclea Pontica ¶, and the most extensive and magnificent library of Ptolemy Phi-

---

* Plin. loc. cit.
† Guilandinus de Papyro, p. 16. et seq.
‡ Scalig. Animadv. in Guiland. p. 9.
‖ A. Gell. l. vi. c. 17. Tertull. Apol. c. 18. Montf. Palæog. Græc. pref. p. xvi.
§ Athen. l. i. c. 2. See below, chap. xi.
¶ Memnon de Reb. Heracliæ Ponticæ, apud Photium, cod. 224. c. 2.

ladelphus

ladelphus * in Egypt, founded in or before the year 284, which in his time is said to have contained 100,000 volumes †; and to have been enlarged by his succeſſors, to the amount of almoſt 700,000 ‡.

Not long afterwards a library was founded at Pergamus by Attalus and Eumenes, which, according to Plutarch, contained 200,000 volumes ‖.

Theſe

---

* Ptolemy, the ſon of Lagus, ſurnamed Soter, the father of Ptolemy Philadelphus, was a learned prince, as appears by his hiſtory of Alexander, which is honourably mentioned by the ancients. Vid. Arriani Præf. Plut. in v. Alex. Q. Curt. l. ix, c. 5.

Suidas ſeems to intimate, that this prince collected a library; for he obſerves, "that Zenodotus the Epheſian lived in the time of the firſt Ptolemy, and was keeper των εν Αλεξανδρεια βιβλιοθηκων, of the libraries in Alexandria." Suid. in v. Ζηνοδοτος.

† Euſeb. Chron. p. 66. Syncell. p. 271. Cedren. l. xxii. Some writers tell us, that Philadelphus collected 200,000 volumes. Joſ. Antiq. l. xii. c. 2. § 1. Alex. ab Alex. l. ii. c. 30.

‡ A. Gell. l. vi. c. 17. Am. Marcell. l. xxii. c. 16.—Four hundred thouſand volumes are ſaid to have been unfortunately burnt, when Julius Cæſar was attacked in Alexandria by Achillas, the commander of the Egyptian army. Oroſ. l. vi. c. 15. Seneca ſays, 40,000, or, according to ſome editions, 400,000. Sen. de Tranq. c. 9. A. Gellius aſſerts, that the whole library, conſiſting of near 700,000 volumes, was deſtroyed: "ea omnia incenſa ſunt." It is remarkable, that this unfortunate event is not mentioned, either by Julius Cæſar or Hirtius, in the hiſtory of the Alexandrian war.

‖ Plut. in v. Anton. p. 943. Strab. l. xiii. p. 926. Plin. l. xiii. c. 10. l. xxxv. c. 2. Reges Attalici magnis philologiæ dulcedinibus inducti, cum egregiam bibliothecam Pergami ad communem delectationem inſtituiſſent; tunc item Ptolemæus infinito zelo, cupiditatiſque incitatus ſtudio, non minoribus induſtriis, ad eundem modum contenderat Alexandriæ comparare. Vitruv. præf. l. vii. Vitruvius does not mean, that there was a library at Pergamus, before there was one at Alexandria. Some writers, who have charged him with a miſtake in this paſſage, have not attended

70 A DISSERTATION ON

These are clear and decisive proofs, that the common mode of writing, in the reign of Ptolemy Philadelphus, WAS NOT ON STONES.

to the proper force of the word *contenderat*, in the præterpluperfect tense. Galen. in Hippoc. de Nat. Hom. Com. ii. p. 17.

The Ptolemean kings were, Ptolemy Soter or Lagi [filius], bef. Chr. 305. Ptol. Philadelphus, 285. Ptolemy Soter admitted his son Philadelphus into a share of the kingdom in 285, and died in 284. Ptol. Euergetes, 247. Ptol. Philopator, 222. Ptol. Epiphanes, 205. Ptol. Philometor, 181. Ptol. Euergetes the second, surnamed Physcon, 146. Ptol. Soter or Lathyrus, 117. Ptol. Alexander, 81. Ptol. Auletes, 65. Cleopatra, 51.

The kings of Pergamus were, Philetærus, 283. Eumenes, 263. Attalus, 241. Eumenes the second, 197. Attalus the second, 159. Attalus the third, 138. This prince died after a reign of five years, and made the Roman people his heirs. Eumenes the second founded, or at least improved, the celebrated library at Pergamus. Strab. l. xiii. p. 926. The Egyptian princes having prohibited the exportation of the papyrus, Eumenes ordered, that books should be made of parchment, which, from Pergamus, was called *pergamena*. Plin. l. xiii. c. 11. Isid. Orig. l. vi. c. 3. Hieron. Epist. ad Cromatium.

It is however very certain, that the kings of Pergamus were not the real inventors of parchment: they only found out a better way of making it, and brought it into more general use. Trotzius, de primâ scribendi Orig. p. 91. Funccius de Script. vet. p. 90.

THE PARIAN CHRONICLE.

CHAP. IV.

III. THIS Chronicle does not appear to have been engraved by PUBLIC AUTHORITY, by the direction of the magiftrates, or the people of Paros.

Firft, becaufe infcriptions of that kind ufually begin in this manner :

Η ΒΟΥΛΗ ΚΑΙ Ο ΔΗΜΟΣ, " the fenate and the people ;" or, in this form :

ΕΔΟΞΕΝ ΤΗΙ ΒΟΥΛΗΙ ΚΑΙ ΤΩΙ ΔΗΜΩΙ, " it pleafed the fenate and the people."

EXAMPLES.

Infcriptions in Spon's Mifcellanea Eruditæ Antiquitatis, and other collections.

Athenis, in ædibus Jani Miftrigo. Sect. x. Infcript. 6. p. 319.

Η ΒΟΥΛΗ Η ΕΞ ΑΡΕΙΟΥ ΠΑΓΟΥ
ΚΑΙ Η ΒΟΥΛΗ ΤΩΝ Χ *
ΚΑΙ Ο ΔΗΜΟΣ ΙΟΥΛΙΑΝ ΒΕΡΕΝΕΙΚΗΝ,
κ. τ. λ.

Senatus Areopagi, & fenatus fexcentorum, & populus, Juliam Berenicem, &c. hác ftatuâ honorant.

---

* Character ille, vel figla Χ, non mille, fed *fexcentos* folùm, fignificat : hoc eft, eandem prorfus vim ac valorem obtinet, perinde ac fi minufculo charactere χ pingeretur. Etenim Berenices & Agrippæ regis ætate, Athenienfis fenatus ex fexcentis folùm civibus conflabat. Corfini Notæ Græcorum, p. 72. Id. Fafti Attici, tom. i. Differt. vi. p. 262.

Megaris,

Megaris. Infcript. 11. p. 321.

Η ΒΟΥΛΗ ΚΑΙ Ο ΔΗΜΟ.
ΤΙΒ. ΚΛΑΥΔΙΟΝ ΑΤΤΙΚΟΝ.

Senatus & populus *Megarenfis*, Tiberium Claudium Atticum, &c.

Megaris. Infcript. 14. p. 327.

Ο ΔΑΜΟΣ
ΑΥΤΟΚΡΑΤΟΡΑ ΚΑΙΣΑΡΑ ΘΕΟΥ ΥΙΟΝ
ΑΡΕΤΑΣ ΕΝΕΚΕΝ
ΚΑΙ ΕΥΕΡΓΕΣΙΑΣ.

Populus imperatorem Cæfarem, Divi filium, virtutis & beneficiorum causâ, honorat.

Δαμος et αρητας, Doricâ dialecto, quæ η in α mutat, pro δημος et αρετης.

Ibidem, ad ædem Panagias. Infcript. 16. p. 327.

Η ΒΟΥΛΗ ΚΑΙ Ο ΔΗΜΟC
Μ. ΛΙΜΙΛΙΟΝ CΑΤΟΡΝΕΙΝΟΝ.

Senatus et populus *Megarenfium* M. Æmilium Saturninum, &c. *venerantur*.

Conftantinopoli, allata ex Paro infulà. Infcript. 39. p. 334.

Η ΒΟΥΛΗ ΚΑΙ Ο ΔΗΜΟC
ΤΟΝ ΤΗC ΑΡΙCΤΗC ΜΝΗΜΗC ΠΑΙΔΑ.

Senatus & populus *Pariorum* optimæ memoriæ filium, &c. honorârunt ftatuâ æneâ.

Venetiis,

THE PARIAN CHRONICLE. 73

Venetiis, ad Cyzicum & insulam Paron pertinens inscriptio, ex Archipelago advecta *. Inscript. 45. p. 336.

ΕΔΟΞΕΝ ΤΗΙ ΒΟΥΛΗΙ ΚΑΙ ΤΩΙ ΔΗΜΩΙ
ΓΟΡΓΟΝΙΚΟΣ ΔΙΟΚΛΕΟΥΣ ΕΙΠΕΝ
ΕΠΕΙ Η ΠΟΛΙΣ Η ΠΑΡΙΩΝ.

Placuit senatui & populo. Gorgonicus Dioc. f. dixit: quandoquidem urbs Pariorum, &c.

In Co insulâ. Inscript. 51. p. 337.

Α ΒΟΥΛΑ ΚΑΙ Ο ΔΑΜΟΣ
ΤΗΣ ΛΑΜΠΡΟΤΑΤΗΣ
ΚΩΙΩΝ ΠΟΛΕΩΣ ΤΕΙΜΑΣΕΝ.

Senatus populúsque illustrissimæ Coorum civitatis honoravit Publium Sallustium, &c.

Α βουλα και ο δαμος, Doricâ dialecto, pro η βουλη και ο δημος.

Smyrnæorum Decretum †.

ΕΔΟΞΕΝ ΤΩΙ ΔΗΜΩΙ ΣΤΡΑΤΗΓΩΝ ΓΝΩΜΗ.

Placuit populo ducum sententia, &c.

Senatûs populíque Delii psephisma [decretum] quo Clinodemo, Leboti f. Siphnio, honores decernuntur ‡.

ΕΔΟΞΕΝ ΤΗΙ ΒΟΥΛΗΙ ΚΑΙ ΤΩΙ ΔΗΜΩΙ.
ΤΙΜΟΚΛΗΣ ΤΕΛΕΣΙΠΠΟΥ ΕΙΠΕ.

Placuit senatui & populo. Timocles Telesippi f. relationem fecit, &c.

* Vid. Montf. Diar. Ital. c. 3.
† Chand. Marm. Oxon. Inscript. 26. p. 41.
‡ Reinesii Inscript. Antiq. p. 499. Seld. in Mar. Arund. num. xii. Maitt. p. 566.

L This

This is the usual introductory form of inscriptions, composed by public authority. But the Parian chronologer begins HIS inscription in a very different manner, as follows :

ΑΝΕΓΡΑΨΑ τους ανωθεν χρονους, ΑΡΞΑΜΕΝΟΣ απο Κεκροπος, " I have described preceding times, beginning from Cecrops."

These are the words of a private man, speaking of his own performance in the first person singular, and do not in the least correspond with those forms of expression, which we generally find in inscriptions, composed by the order of the senate or the people of any country.

This argument cannot be much affected by observing, that the beginning of the inscription is obliterated; for it entirely depends on the words now remaining.

Secondly, the facts and dates, which are mentioned in this Chronicle, do not appear to have been extracted from any public records, or calculated to answer the purpose of authentic documents. For, in either view, it is most probable, the compiler would have preserved a regular series of kings and archons. But this is not the case. Many eminent princes and magistrates are passed over without notice. The facts, chiefly specified, are not matters of general or national importance; and, in several instances, the transactions of whole centuries are entirely omitted.

Thirdly, the Parian inscription is such a one, as we can hardly suppose the magistrates, or the people of Paros, would have ordered to be engraved.

Stately sepulchres, pillars, triumphal arches, and the like, were erected to perpetuate the glory of eminent men; and inscriptions upon them usually displayed their

various

various achievements *. Thus, we read of the pillars of Ofiris, Bacchus, Sefoftris †, Hercules ‡, and others.

The remembrance of events, in which nations were interefted, the fucceffion of princes, and perhaps the genealogies of eminent men ‖, were preferved in the fame manner.

Leagues §, decrees, laws, &c. were likewife engraved on marble or brafs, and fixed to a pillar, the walls of a temple, or other public buildings.

The Decalogue was written upon tables of hewn ftone; and Jofhua is faid to have written a copy of the law upon the fame materials ¶. In the time of Demofthenes there ftill exifted a law of Thefeus, written upon

---

* ——Incifa notis marmora PUBLICIS.
Hor. l. iv. od. 8.

† Herod. l. ii. § 106. Diod. Sic. l. i. p. 53. Strab. l. xvi. p. 1114. l. xvii. 1138.

‡ Diod. Sic. l. iv. p. 226.

‖ Ακουσιλαος εγραψε γενεαλογιας εκ δελτων χαλκων, ὡς λογος ευρειν τον πατερα αυτου, ορυξαντα τινα τοπον της οικιας αυτου. "Acufilaus wrote genealogies from tables of brafs, which, it was reported, his father found, as he was digging in fome part of his houfe." Suidas.

Nothing can be more apocryphal and fufpicious, than the origin of thefe genealogical tables. It has been always ufual with the fabricators of fuppofititious infcriptions to pretend they found them, as Acufilaus did, under ground, in fome cavern, or fecret recefs.

§ Thucydides fpeaks of Grecian pillars, on which treaties of peace and alliance were infcribed, at Olympia, at Pytho or Delphi, at the Ifthmus, at Athens, at Lacedæmon, and other places, lib. v. c. 18. Dionyfius Halicarnaffeus mentions feveral treaties, which were engraved on pillars: as, that of Romulus with the Veientes, l. ii. c. 6. p. 118. that of Tullus Hoftilius with the Sabines, l. iii. c. 8. p. 174. and that of Tarquinius Superbus with the Latins, l. iv. c. 6. p. 249.—Liv. l. ii. c. 33.

¶ Exod. xxxiv. 1. Jofh. viii. 32. Deut. xxvii. 8.

a pillar of stone *. Certain decrees, in the reign of Servius Tullus, were inscribed on a brazen column †. And the laws of the Twelve Tables were engraved on brass ‡.

Virgil alludes to this custom in the following verse:

——Fixit leges pretio, atque refixit ‖.

And Ovid, in describing the golden age,

————Nec verba minacia fixo
Ære legebantur §.

Suetonius informs us, that Vespasian, when he rebuilt the capitol, after it had been burnt by the soldiers of Vitellius, undertook to restore 3000 brazen plates, which were destroyed by the flames; and that by searching for copies of them in all places, he furnished the government with a fresh collection of curious and ancient records, containing the decrees of the senate, and the acts of the people, relative to treaties, alliances, and privileges, from times almost as early as the foundation of the city ¶.

These inscriptions, and others of the same kind, may be considered as public monuments, or public records; and were inscribed on marble or brass, with peculiar propriety, as they were professedly designed for the inspec-

---

* Εν ϛηλη λιθινη. Demosth. contra Neæram [εἰ γνωσις. Harpoc.] p. 873. edit. 1604.

† Dion. Halic. l. iv. c. 3. p. 230.

‡ Leges decemvirales, quibus tabulis duodecim est nomen, in æs incisas, in publico proposuerunt. Liv. l. iii. 57. Dion. Halic. l. x. c. 13. p. 681. Flor. l. i. c. 24.—A. Gellius informs us, that the laws of the XII Tables were written 300 years after the building of Rome. A. Gell. l. xx. c. 1.

‖ Virg. Æn. vi. 622.

§ Ovid. Met. l. i. 91.

¶ Suet. in v. Vesp. § 8. Tacit. Hist. l. iii. c. 7.

THE PARIAN CHRONICLE.

tion of the people; and essentially concerned their conduct, their property, their liberty, or their lives. But for whom could the Chronicle of Paros be intended?—It contains no encomiums on any of the patriots, the heroes, or the demi-gods, of the country; no decrees of the magistrates, no public records, no laws of state. On the contrary, it is a work of mere speculation and learning, in which the inhabitants of that island, especially the common people, had not the least interest or concern.

These words at the beginning, αρχοντος εμ Παρῳ, would naturally lead us to suppose, that the inscription related to Paros; and there were certainly many circumstances in the history of that island, worthy of notice.—I shall mention some of them.

Thucydides informs us, that the Cyclades were first inhabited by the Phœnicians and the Carians * ; that Minos fitted out a fleet, took possession of those islands, planted colonies in most of them, and, having expelled the Carians, gave the government to his sons †.

Apollodorus relates, that Hercules, when he was going to fetch the belt of Hippolyta, stopped at Paros; and that Eurymedon, Chryses, Nephalion, and Philolaus, the sons of Minos, then resided in that island ‡. The same author observes, that the mother of these four princes was a native of Paros ‖ ; and that Minos himself was there, and offering a sacrifice to the Graces, when he received the melancholy news of the death of his son Androgeus §.

* Stephanus Byzantinus says, " Paros was first inhabited by Cretans, and a few Arcadians." Steph. in v. Παρος.
† Thucyd. l. i. § 4. 8.
‡ Apollod. l. ii. c. 5. § 9. Apollodorus calls this famous belt Αρεος ζωνης, " the belt of Mars."
‖ Id. l. iii. c. 1. § 2.
§ Id. l. iii. c. 14. § 7.

Diodorus

Diodorus afferts, that after the destruction of Troy, the Carians, being grown more powerful, assumed the dominion of the sea, and having taken possession of the Cyclades, claimed some of them as their exclusive property, expelling the Cretans; and inhabited others, in conjunction with the people, who were already settled in those islands *.

Herodotus gives us the following anecdote of the Parians. The government of Miletus having been subverted by internal dissensions, the citizens requested the Parians to be arbitrators of their disputes. The Parians accepted the office; and, having surveyed the country of Miletus, appointed those to the magistracy, whose lands were best cultivated; reasonably concluding, that they who took proper care of their own estates, would not neglect the affairs of the commonwealth †. This prudent advice restored the city to its former tranquility.

C. Nepos afferts, that Miltiades subjected the Cyclades to the government of the Athenians ‡. Yet afterwards the Parians assisted Darius in his expedition against Greece. Miltiades, in order to punish them for this offence, or rather to revenge an affront offered to himself, the year after the victory at Marathon ||, invaded the island, and laid siege to the capital. But the inhabitants defended themselves with so much bravery, that, after he had invested the city for twenty-six days, without success, he raised the siege, and returned to Athens in disgrace §.

* Diod. Sic. l. v. sub fin.
† Herod. l. v. § 28, 29.
‡ C. Nepos, in v. Milt. § 2.
|| The battle of Marathon was fought in the year of the J. P. 4224. bef. Chr. 490. Petav. Rat. Temp. vol. ii. p. 126. Dodw. Annal. Thucyd. p. 44. Corsini Fast. Attic. tom. iii. p. 148.
§ Herod. l. vi. § 133. C. Nep. in v. Milt. § 7.

After

THE PARIAN CHRONICLE. 79

After the victory at Salamis, Themistocles exacted large contributions of the Parians, and other islanders in the Ægean sea, under pretence of punishing them for the favour they had shewn the Persians *.

In the year 431, at the commencement of the Peloponnesian war, we find all the Cyclades, except Melos and Thera, in alliance with the Athenians †.

In the year 405, Lysander the Spartan general totally defeated Conon the Athenian at Ægos-potamos. Not long afterwards he reduced all the cities, which had been subject to the Athenians, under the Spartan government; and, in 404, taking the city of Athens, put an end to the Peloponnesian war ‡.

In 394, Conon the Athenian, having the command of the Persian fleet, gained a complete victory over the Lacedæmonians near Cnidus; and among other states dependent on Lacedæmon, obliged the Cyclades to return to their former alliance ‖.

In 385, the Parians, by the advice of an oracle, sent a colony into the Adriatic, and took possession of an island called Parus §, and afterwards Pharus, which occasioned a war between the ancient inhabitants of that island and the Parians ¶.

C. Nepos observes, that in the time of Miltiades, Pa-

---

* Herod. l. viii. § 112.

† Thucyd. l. ii. § 9.—Thera was a Lacedæmonian colony. Strab. l. x. p. 741.

‡ Tributarias Atheniensium civitates voluntarias recepit. Just. l. v. c. 7. Xenoph. Hellen. l. ii. Diod. Sic. l. xiii. p. 226. Vid. Palmerii Exerc. p. 64.

‖ Diod. Sic. l. xiv. p. 303.

§ Φαρος, ἡ προτερον Παρος. Pharus, quæ olim Parus. Strab. l. vii. p. 484. Marcian. Herac. Perieg. v. 426.

¶ Diod. Sic. l. xv. p. 336.—The part of the Chronicle yet remaining comes down to the year 354, which is 31 years after the planting of this colony.

ros was "opibus elata," elated with its riches; and Ephorus remarks, that it was then the most flourishing, and the most considerable, of the Cyclades*.

This island is said to have taken its name from Paros, the son of Parasius, an Arcadian. Stephanus tells us, that it was likewise called Pactia, Demetrias, Zacynthus, Hyria, Hyleessa, Minoa, and Cabarnis †.

Archilochus, the inventor or the first improver of the Iambic verse, was a native of Paros ‡. This ancient poet is mentioned by many of the Greek and Roman writers with great encomiums. Horace thought his numbers and poetic spirit worthy of his imitation ‖. Quintilian says, his writings were distinguished by energy of language, comprehensive brevity, striking sentiments, and poignancy of satire §. Valerius Maximus represents him as the greatest poet, or the next to the greatest ¶. Pindar informs us, that one of the

---

* Παριν δε ευδαιμονες ατην και μεγιςην ουσαν τοτε των Κυκλαδων, Parum verò felicissimam ac maximam eo tempore Cycladum. Ephorus apud Steph. Byzant. in v. Παρος.

If the word μεγιςην means "the largest" of the Cyclades, it is not true. Pliny affirms, that Paros is but half as large as Naxos, which he reckons 75 miles in circuit. Paros therefore must be only 37; and this, according to M. Tournefort, agrees with the measurement of the natives. Plin. l. iv. c. 12. Tournef. Voyage, let. 5.

† Nicanor apud Steph. Byzant. Plin. loc. cit. Solin. c. 17.

‡ Αρχιλοχος ὁ Παριος, Archilochus ille Parius. Herod. l. i. § 12. Strab. l. x. p. 745.

‖ ————Parios ego primus iambos
Ostendi Latio, numerosque animósque secutus
Archilochi.———   Hor. l. i. ep. 19. 23.

§ Summa in Archilocho vis elocutionis, tum validæ, tum breves, vibrantésque sententiæ, &c. Quint. l. x. c. 1.

¶ Maximum poëtam, aut certè summo proximum. Val. Max. l. vi. c. 3. V. Paterc. l. i. c. 5. Cic. Orat. § 1. Id. ad Attic. l. xvi. ep. 11.

hymns

THE PARIAN CHRONICLE.

hymns of Archilochus was in such estimation, that it was usually sung three times to the honour of those, who had gained the victory at the Olympic games *.

Aristides the rhetorician places him in the first rank of those illustrious poets, who have been an ornament to their country. Homer, he observes, has added a glory to Smyrna, Archilochus to Paros, Hesiod to Bœotia, Simonides to Ceos, Stesichorus to Himera, Pindar to Thebes, Sappho and Alcæus to Mitylene †. "Wife men," says Alcidamus, as quoted by Aristotle, " are respected in all countries. For this reason, Archilochus, though he was the author of some defamatory compositions, was honoured by the Parians ‡."

Some of the foregoing circumstances, and perhaps others of more importance, which are not mentioned by the Greek historians, would have naturally occurred to an ancient writer, composing an inscription for a marble monument in the island of Paros.

But what scheme does our chronologer pursue on this occasion? Does he record the events and revolutions of his own country? Does he mention any of the battles, sieges, treaties, of the Parians? any of their public institutions? any of their poets, patriots, or warriors? Does he mention Archilochus, who was honoured by his countrymen, and distinguished, as a poet, in a general assembly of the Greeks?—Not a syllable on any of

---

* Pind. Olymp. ix. 1.
† Æl. Arist. in Epit. Alexandri.
‡ Παντες τους σοφους τιμωσι· Παριοι γουν Αρχιλοχον, καιτοι βλασφημον οντα, τετιμηκασι. Omnes sapientes honorant. Parii igitur Archilochum, quamvis maledicum, honorarunt. Apud Arist. Rhet. l. ii. c. 23.

Cicero places Archilochus about the year bef. Chr. 710. Tusc. Quæst. l. i. § 1. C. Nepos, about 668. Apud A. Gell. l. xvii. c. 21.

thefe fubjects! On the contrary, he rambles from place to place, and records the tranfactions of Athens, Corinth, Macedon, Lydia, Crete, Cyprus, Sicily, Perfia, and other foreign countries, with which Paros had no connection.

In this view, the infcription feems to have been as IMPERTINENT, in the ifland of Paros, as a marble monument would be in this country, recording the antiquities of France or Spain; or one in Jamaica, containing the revolutions of England.

Upon a fuppofition, that the infcription is a forgery, it is eafy to account for this extraordinary circumftance. A few chronological occurrences, in the ancient hiftory of Paros, would not have been fo interefting to the generality of readers; or fo valuable, in the eftimation of every lover of antiquities; or, in fhort, fo PROFITABLE to the compiler, as a general fyftem of Grecian chronology.

CHAP.

CHAP. V.

IV. IT has been frequently obferved, that the earlier periods of the Grecian hiftory are involved in darknefs and confufion.

Several of the ancients inform us, that the firft writers of Greece were poets *, whofe chief object was to amufe their readers, or to excite their admiration, by marvellous details, by perfonifying all parts of nature, and by introducing a multitude of imaginary divinities.

In the earlieft accounts of that country, we meet with fcarcely any thing but poetical fictions, the genealogies, the amours, and the adventures of gods and demigods †. Thefe mythological tales are incompatible with a regular chronology.

Herodotus, who wrote 444 years before the Chriftian æra ‡, and is emphatically ftyled the father of hiftory ‖,

---

* Πρότερον μεν εν ποιημασιν εξεφερον οι φιλοσοφοι τα δογματα, και τους λογους, ωσπερ Ορφευς, και Ἡσιοδος, και Παρμενιδης, και Ξενοφανης, και Εμπεδοκλης, και Θαλης. Antiquitùs carmine fuas fententias philofophi proferebant, ut Orpheus, Hefiodus, Parmenides, Xenophanes, Empedocles, Thales. Plut de Pyth. Orac. p. 402. Strab. l. i. p. 34. Profam orationem condere Pherecydes Syrius inftituit, Cyri regis ætate. Plin. l. vii. c. 56.—Pherecydes wrote about 540 years before Chrift.

† Και οι πρωτοι δε ιστορικοι, και φυσικοι, μυθογραφοι. Et quidem primi etiam hiftorici, ac naturæ rerum defcriptores, fabulas fcripferunt. Strab. l. i. p. 37.

‡ Herodotus was born in the year bef. Chr. 484, and died fome time after the year 432. Vid. l. ix. § 73. A. Gell. l. xv. c. 23. Corfini Fafti Attici, tom. iii. p. 157. 213. &c.

‖ Pater hiftoriæ. Cic. de Leg. l. i. § 5. Princeps genus hoc ornavit. Id. de Orat. l. ii. § 36.

M 2   feems

seems to have related all the memorable occurrences he could find in the history of the Lydians, Assyrians, Egyptians, Persians, Greeks, and other nations, within the compass of 240 years; continuing his narrative to the taking of Sestus*, or the conclusion of the Persian war in 479. But he is irregular and desultory, and seems to have had no idea of any chronological order or precision. His utmost efforts, in this department of history, consists in determining the length of a reign, and in a vague and general computation of time by the ages of men. Thus, he says, " the Heraclidæ, or the descendents of Hercules, possessed the kingdom of Lydia for the space of 505 years, during twenty-two γενεας ανδρων, generations of men †." " Semiramis lived, γενεησι πεντε, five generations, before another queen, whose name was Nitocris ‡." He mentions the Argonautic expedition,

* Diod. Sic. l. xi. p. 29.

† Herod. l. i. § 7. In this passage Herodotus makes a generation consist of near 23 years. But in book ii. § 142. he tells us, that "three generations are equivalent to a hundred years." Ancient writers observed no consistency in the use of the word γενεα. Sometimes they employed it to express a certain number of years, and sometimes a succession of father and son, or the extent of a reign. Herodoti γενεα, says Vossius, constituit annos 33⅓.—Γενεα Græcis grammaticis aliquando est spatium 20, aliquando 25, 30, 33, nonnunquam etiam plurium annorum. Imo etiam 100 aliquando: uti est apud Theophrastum; vel etiam 110 annorum intervallum continet γενεα, ut docet Phlegon. Recte itáque notatum Porphyrio, quanto vetustiores, tanto longiores esse γενεας. Is. Vossii Castig. Hornii de Ætate Mundi, c. 6. Grævii Lect. Hesiod. c. 4. p. 21. Censor. c. 17.

‡ Herod. l. i. § 184.—According to Herodotus, § 188, Nitocris was "the mother of Labynetus," or Nabonedus, supposed to be the Belshazzar of the scriptures, in whose reign Babylon was taken, bef. Chr. 539. On a supposition that she was the wife of Evilmerodach; that Evilmerodach was the son of Nebuchadnezzar; and that she assumed the government of the kingdom, soon after

pedition, the Trojan war, and other ancient events; but he never attempts to afcertain the time, when thofe perfons lived, or thofe tranfactions occurred, by referring them to any known and determinate epocha.

The antiquity, which he afcribes to the kings of Egypt, is extravagant and incredible. The Egyptians, he fays, reckoned from Menes to Sethon, 341 generations, or 11,340 years *; from Bacchus to Amafis, 15,000 †; and from Hercules to Amafis, 17,000 ‡. He feems to have collected his materials, according to

---

after the death of Nebuchadnezzar, in the year 562, the five generations of Herodotus will extend no higher, than to the year 728.

Sir Ifaac Newton thinks, this remarkable queen was the wife of Nabonaffar, the author of the famous aftronomical æra, which commenced bef. Chr. 747. Chron. p. 221. Scaliger imagines, that Nitocris was the wife of Nebuchadnezzar, and that fhe governed the kingdom during the madnefs of her hufband; and that the Semiramis of Herodotus was the celebrated wife of Ninus. Upon this principle, inftead of πεντε, five, he would read πεντηκοντα, fifty generations; that is, 1666 years, which will place Semiramis about the year bef. Chr. 2228. Not. ad Fragm. apud Emend. Temp. p. 14. 42.

Though it is perhaps impoffible to find either truth or confiftency in the hiftory of Semiramis, and the origin of the Babylonian empire, yet the Mofaic account of the early fettlement of mankind in the land of Shinar, or Babylonia, favours the fuppofition of their high antiquity. See an account of the Babylonian calculations in the notes to Chap. III.

* Herod. l. ii. § 142.—If three generations were equivalent to a hundred years, 341 generations were equivalent to 11,366 years and eight months.

† Id. l. ii. § 145.

‡ Id. l. ii. § 43.—Sethon began to reign about the year bef. Chr. 719 or 722. Amafis about 568 or 569. Ufferii Annal. Jackfon's Chron. Antiq. vol. ii. p. 230, 240.

the

the ufual cuftom of travellers, from report *, or tradition; and very feldom alleges the authority of preceding writers.

Thucydides, who was thirteen years younger than Herodotus †, begins his hiftory with a fhort account of ancient Greece, and briefly relates the events, which happened between the retreat of Xerxes in 480, where Herodotus ends, and the Peloponnefian war, comprehending a period of fifty years inclufively. After thefe preliminaries, he proceeds, in the fecond book, to the great object he had in view, the hiftory of that war, which commenced in the fpring of the year, bef. Chr. 431 (when Pythodorus had been ten months archon at Athens) and lafted twenty-feven years and fix months. In this work he records the tranfactions of every fummer and winter in a regular feries ‡, and concludes with an account of the victory obtained by the Athenian fleet at Cynoffema ‖, and a curfory view of fome other events, which happened about autumn in 411, or the twenty-firft year of the Peloponnefian war. Thucydides died before he had completed his defign, and left his eighth book unfinifhed §.

* Κατα ηκουον, "as I have heard." l. ii. § 99. See alfo l. ii. § 3. 5. 10. 12. 29. 55. 79. 100. 102. 116. 120. 122. 123. 127, &c.

† A. Gell. l. xv. c. 23.—Thucydides was born in the year bef. Chr. 471, and died in 391.

‡ The fummer, as Thucydides divides the year, extends from the vernal to the autumnal, and the winter from the autumnal to the vernal, equinox.

‖ Κυνος σημα, canis fepulchrum; called by Diodorus Ἑκαβης μνημειον, Hecubæ monumentum. Diod. l. xiii. p. 167.

§ The eighth book concludes with this remark, which feems to have been added by another hand: "When the winter following this fummer fhall be ended, the twenty-firft year of the war will be alfo completed."

The

THE PARIAN CHRONICLE. 87

The hiſtory of the Peloponneſian war, from the year 411, to its concluſion in 404, and the hiſtory of the ſubſequent affairs of Greece, is continued by Xenophon *, through a period of 48 † or 49 years, ending with the battle of Mantinea, and the death of Epaminondas in 362 ‡.

Theſe two hiſtories comprehend a period of ſeventy years, in the form of ANNALS; and this form, as far as it extends, may be thought a ſufficient notation of time. But many incidental circumſtances, many antecedent events, are related without any chronological diſtinction, or reference to any memorable epocha.

This account of the imperfect ſtate of chronology, in the time of theſe hiſtorians, correſponds with the following obſervation, made by the very learned and accurate Sir John Marſham.

Sanè ἱστορικον ſcribendi genus longè vetuſtius eſt, quàm χρονολογικον. Priſcis hiſtoricis nuda fuit rerum geſtarum narratio; nec certis temporum intervallis diſtincta; nec à termino fixo deducta. In hâc claſſe cenſendi ſunt Herodotus, Thucydides, Xenophon, et qui perierunt reliqui; quorum ſcripta, antequam nata eſſet ars chronologica, prodierunt. Hi, licèt Olympiorum aliquando obiter meminerint, tetraëtericam tamen Olympiadum computationem non agnoſcunt ‖.

* Some think there is a chaſm of near two years between the period, at which the hiſtory of Thucydides ends, and the Grecian hiſtory of Xenophon begins. Uſſerii Annal. ſub an. J. Per. 4303. But Dodwell denies, that there is any ſuch hiatus; and his opinion is now generally followed. Dodwell de Cyclis Vet. diſſ. viii. § 20. p. 342.—Xenophon was born about the year 450, and died in 360, at the age of ninety. Diog. Laert. l. ii. § 56. Lucian. in Macrob.

† Diod. Sic. l. xiii. p. 169.
‡ Id. l. xv. p. 395. Corſin. Faſt. Attic. vol. iv. p. 17.
‖ Canon. Chron. ſec. xvi. p. 486.

Thucydides,

Thucydides, in order to ascertain the time of an event, which happened in the LXXXVIII Olympiad, does not specify the number of the Olympiad, but mentions it in these terms: "It was that Olympiad, in which Dorieus the Rhodian was the second time victorious*." When the Olympiads began to be used in chronology, they were distinguished by their respective numbers.

The series of Olympiads, archons, and ephori, in Xenophon's Grecian history, is the interpolation of some impertinent annotator †.

Historians had not yet fixed upon any certain epocha, from which they might deduce their chronological computations. Neither the destruction of Troy, the institution of the Olympic games, nor the foundation of any city, was employed for that purpose.

It is very observable, that, at this period, historical records were so scarce, or so defective, that even the most inquisitive and the best informed writers were unacquainted with the revolutions and the most remarkable transactions of neighbouring kingdoms, which happened within a century of their own time ‡. Thus Herodotus and Xenophon differ EXTREMELY, in the accounts they give of several important circumstances in the history of Cyrus the Great, particularly with respect to

---

* Thucyd. l. iii. § 8.

† Ineptissima illa Olympiadum, archontum, ephororum συγχυσις, quæ in Hellenica Xenophontis irrepsit, glossatoris cujuspiam inscitiam prodit. Marsh. Can. Chron. sec. xvi. p. 487. Dodwell, Præl. Academ. inaug. § 7. Id. de Cyclis Vet. diss. viii. § 23. Fabric. Bibl. Græc. l. iii. c. 4. vol. ii. p. 73.

‡ Cyrus died in the year bef. Chr. 529. Herodotus was born at Halicarnassus, in Asia Minor, in the year 484; and Xenophon about 34 years afterwards. The latter accompanied the younger Cyrus into Persia.

THE PARIAN CHRONICLE.

the birth and the death of that prince, and the establishment of the Persian empire.

Herodotus relates, that Cyrus was the son of Cambyses, a Persian of inferior rank, and Mandane, the daughter of Astyages; that, in consequence of a dream, his grandfather Astyages ordered, that he should be put to death in his infancy; that, contrary to his directions, he was preserved, and educated among shepherds; that when he was grown to maturity, he dethroned Astyages, and transferred the empire to the Persians; that, after a reign of twenty-five years, he was slain in battle, by the forces of Tomyris, queen of the Massagetes, who cut off his head, and threw it into a vessel full of human blood, with a sarcastic reflection on his cruelty and ambition *.

Xenophon, on the contrary, informs us, that Cambyses was king of Persia; that Cyrus was educated in his father's court; that when he was twelve years of age, he went with his mother Mandane to visit Astyages, who entertained him with great liberality and affection; that Astyages died in peace, and left his kingdom to his son Cyaxares; and lastly, that Cyrus, after a reign of conquests and glory, died, like a philosopher, in his own palace, surrounded by his family and his friends.

Ctesias, in his account of this prince, differs from Herodotus and Xenophon in almost every circumstance †. Diodorus says, he was taken captive by the

---

* Herod. l. i. § 107, &c.

† Ταυτα λεγει Κτησιας περι Κυρου, και ουχ ὡς 'Ηροδοτος. Hæc dicit Ctesias de Cyro, iis quæ ab Herodoto referuntur dissimilia. Ctesiæ Fragm. apud Phot. Bibl. cod. 72. Herod. Op. p. 812.—Ctesias was of Cnidus, and attended the younger Cyrus in his Persian expedition.

queen of the Scythians, and crucified *. Joannes Malala relates, that he was killed in a sea-fight with the Samians; and for the truth of this assertion, he cites a history, falsely ascribed to Pythagoras †.

Xenophon's Cyropædia, I know, is generally regarded as a moral or political romance. But it may be observed, that the author himself disclaims this idea ‡; and that a judicious writer would scarcely venture to form a romance on a recent period of history, in direct opposition to public records and well-known facts ||. On the other hand, if there were no records, and those facts were generally unknown, or sunk into oblivion, the argument I would draw from the different accounts, given of this celebrated hero by Herodotus, Xenophon, and others, remains in its full force.

About four hundred years before the Christian æra, Hippias the Elean published a catalogue of the victors at the Olympic games §. This catalogue, as Plutarch observes, was written ὀψὲ, late, that is, 376 years after the first Olympiad, in which Corœbus was victor in the

* Ἀνεσταυρωσε, cruci affixit. Diod. Sic. l. ii. p. 128.
† Malalæ Chron. p. 201. Cedren. p. 114.
‡ Xenophon, in the beginning of his Cyropædia, tells us, " that he had taken great pains to inform himself of Cyrus's birth, education, and character; and that he would not advance any thing, but what had been told him."
|| Strabo, Plutarch, Q. Curtius, Arrian, and others, agree, that Cyrus was buried at Pasargadæ in PERSIA; which is hardly consistent with the story of Herodotus. Strab. l. xv. p. 1061. Plut. in v. Alex. p. 703. Q. Curt. l. x. c. 1. Arrian. l. vi. sub fin.

See Prid. Connect. an. 530, where the author gives several reasons, why he thinks Xenophon's account of the death of Cyrus is more probable, than that of Herodotus.

§ Των Ολυμπιονικων αναγραφη, Olympionicarum Recensio. Plut. in v. Numæ, § 1. Schol. ad Theoc. Idyl. 4.

stadion;

stadion; but, what is worse, he affirms, that it was " a performance of no authority *." Yet, as the direction of the games properly belonged to the people of Elis †, Hippias may be supposed to have had the best information, which could be obtained. His publication however seems to have been but a bare list of names, merely calculated to distinguish the victors, and excite emulation in others ‡, without being applied to any chronological purpose.

About the year 338, Ephorus of Cuma in Æolia, one of the disciples of Isocrates, wrote a history of Greece and other countries, from the return of the Heraclidæ into Peloponnesus ||, to the siege of Perinthus by Philip of Macedon, in the year 340, comprehending a period of 750 years §. He is said to have distributed his materials into different books κατα γενος, " according to the nature of the subject ¶ ;" but we are not told, that he observed the order of time. His veracity is called in question by several ancient writers **.

Callisthenes and Theopompus lived at the same time. The former was Aristotle's relation, and attended Alexander in his expedition into Asia. Among other productions ††, he wrote a history of Greece, entitled, Ἑλληνικα,

---

* Απ' ουδενος ὁρμωμενον αναγκαιου προς πιςιν. Nullis certis fultum argumentis. Plut. loc. cit.
† Strab. l. viii. p. 544, 545.
‡ Pausan. in Eliac. l. vi. c. 6.
|| The return of the Heraclidæ is placed by the generality of chronologists bef. Chr. 1103, or 1104 years.
§ Diod. Sic. l. iv. § 1. Id. l. xvi. p. 463.
¶ Κατα γενος, in certum rerum genus. Diod. Sic. l. v. p. 285.
** Id. l. i. p. 37. Sen. Nat. Quæst. l. vii. c. 16. Censor. c. 17.
†† A spurious history of Alexander the Great, under the name of Callisthenes, is said to be, or to have been, extant in manuscript, in

Ἑλληνικα, Hellenica, which commenced at the year bef. Chr. 394.

The latter was a difciple of Ifocrates, and likewife wrote a hiftory of Greece, in twelve books, beginning where Thucydides ends, and concluding with the fea-fight near Cnidus, in 395, including a period of feventeen years *. Diodorus obferves, that thefe three writers, " Ephorus, Callifthenes, and Theopompus, did not attempt to relate the occurrences of ancient times, becaufe they would not admit of any chronological computation †." Cicero informs us, that Callifthenes wrote a narrative of the fiege of Troy ‡. But this work might have no more chronology in it, than the Iliad of Homer.

Timæus Siculus lived in the time of Ptolemy Soter and Philadelphus, and is faid to have been the author of a work, entitled, Ολυμπιονικαι η Χρονικα Πραξιδια, Olympionicæ feu Acta Chronica ||. Polybius tells us, that this writer compared the times of the Ephori with the kings of Sparta; and the archons at Athens, and the prieftefles of Juno at Argos, with the Olympic vic-

---

feveral libraries. Cafaub. ad Scalig. epift. 402. 413. Voff. de Hift. Græc. l. i. c. 9. Fabric. Bibl. Græc. l. iii. c. 8. vol. ii. p. 212.

The fragment, which Fabricius quotes from Berkelius, as the beginning of the Pfeudo-Callifthenes, is the production of another writer. Bibl. Græc. l. vi. c. 12. vol. xiv. p. 148. Vide Berkel. ad Steph. Byzant. in v. Βουκεφαλεια.

* Diod. Sic. l. xiv. p. 303.

† Απεςησαν των παλαιων μυθων, ἃ prifcis fabulis abftinuerunt. Diod. Sic. l. iv. § 1. 'Η δε των χρονων απαγγελια τον ακριβεςατον ελεγχον εν τοις δεχμενοις, καταφρονειν ποιει της ἱςοριας τους αναγινωσκοντας. Et temporum notatio cum exacta fupputationis argumenta non admittat, in causa est ut hiftoriam lector afpernetur. Ibid.

‡ Callifthenes Troicum bellum [à perpetuâ fuâ hiftoriâ feparatim.] Cic. Epift. ad Famil. l. v. 12.

|| Suidas.

tors*. And Diodorus Siculus observes, that he was extremely accurate in the notation of time †.

Yet, notwithstanding this high encomium, he was usually styled γραοσυλλεκτρια ‡, which implies, that, with respect to his historical compilations, he was a mere old woman. Polybius gives us this character of him: "His works are filled with dreams, prodigies, and incredible romances; in short, with the grossest superstition, and the wonderful stories of old women ‖." Clemens Alexandrinus likewise represents him as a fabulous writer §.

Eratosthenes was one of the disciples of Callimachus. He was born in the year bef. Chr. 276, and died in 196, or 194, at the age of eighty ¶, or eighty-two **. He was made keeper of the royal library at

---

* Ὁ γαρ τας συγκρισεις ποιουμενος ανεκαθεν των Εφορων προς τους βασιλεις τους εν Λακεδαιμονι, και τους αρχοντας τους εν Αθηναις, και τας ιερειας τας εν Αργει παραβαλλων προς τους Ολυμπιονικας, ουτος ετι. Hic enim ille est, qui ephoros, à primâ institutione, cum regibus Spartanorum comparat; et archontes Atheniensium et sacerdotes Junonis apud Argivos, cum Olympicis victoribus confert. Valesii Excerpta ex Polyb. l. xii. p. 50.

† Τιμαιος μεν ουν μεγιστην προνοιαν πεποιημενος της των χρονων ακριβειας. Timæus maximam diligentiam adhibuit in exquisitâ temporum notatione. Diod. Sic. l. v. § 1.

‡ Suidas in v. Τιμαιος.

‖ Εν δε ταις ιδιαις αποφασεσιν, ενυπνιων, και τερατων, και μυθων απιθανων, και συλληβδην, δεισιδαιμονιας αγενους, και τερατειας γυναικωδους, ετι πληρης. In suis verò narrationibus ipse somniis et prodigiis refertus est, et fabulis ab omni fide remotis; ac postremò degeneri ac muliebri superstitione. Valesii Excerpt. ex Polyb. l. xii. p. 56. Suid. in v. Δεισιδαιμονια.

§ Θεοπομπῳ μεν και Τιμαιῳ μυθους και βλασφημιας συντεττουσιν. Theopompo et Timæo, qui fabulas et maledicta componunt. Clem. Alex. Strom. l. i. § 1. p. 316.

¶ Suidas. Corsini Fasti Attici, tom. iv. p. 94.

** Lucian. in Macrobiis. Prid. Connect. vol. iii. p. 182.

Alexandria

Alexandria by Ptolemy Euergetes, on the death of Zenodotus; and continued in that office to the ninth or the eleventh year of Epiphanes. He wrote a great number of books in different sciences. By the order of Ptolemy [Euergetes] he made a catalogue of the kings, who reigned at Thebes in Egypt, which he collected from the records of that city, and the tradition of the priests. The list extends from Menes to Amurthæus or Amuthantæus, and contains a series of 38 kings, who reigned in succession, during a period of 1076 years. It was preserved by Apollodorus, and is extant in the Chronographia of Syncellus *; but its authority is questionable.

The Ολυμπιονικαι of Eratosthenes are cited by Diogenes Laertius, and Athenæus †; and his Χρονολογια or Χρονογραφιαι, by Syncellus, Harpocration, and Dionysius Halicarnasseus ‡. In the opinion of Dionysius, " Eratosthenes used accurate canons" in his Chronography ||.

It may not therefore be improper to subjoin some general principles of his chronology, as they are transmitted to us by Clemens Alexandrinus §.

	Years.
From the taking of Troy to the return of the Heraclidæ - - - -	80
From that time to the settlement of Ionia -	60

---

* Syncell. p. 91—147.——According to the computation of Syncellus, who gives us this catalogue of Eratosthenes, Menes began his reign 2600 years, and Amuthantæus died 1524 years, before the Christian æra.

† Diog. Laert. in v. Emped. l. viii. § 51. Athen. l. iv. c. 13. p. 154.

‡ Syncell. p. 194. Harpoc. in v. ενιος. Dionyf. Halic. l. i. p. 60.

|| Τισιν οι κανονες ὑγιως, οἱς Γρατοσθενης κεχρηται. Sunt incorruptæ regulæ, quibus Eratosthenes usus est. Dionyf. Halic. loc. cit.

§ Clem. Alex. Strom. l. i. § 21. p. 402.

From

THE PARIAN CHRONICLE.

	Years.
From that time to the guardianship of Lycurgus	159
From that time to the first Olympiad	108
From that time to the invasion of Xerxes	297
From that time to the beginning of the Peloponnesian war	48
From that time to the end of the war	27
From that time to the battle at Leuctra *	34
From that time to the death of Philip	35
From that time to the death of Alexander	12

The accuracy of some of these numbers, as they stand in the Stromata of Clemens, is confirmed by a passage of Dionysius Halicarnasseus, from which we learn, that the four hundred and thirty-second year after the destruction of Troy was, according to the canons of Eratosthenes, the first year of the seventh Olympiad †.

As Eratosthenes had the use of the Alexandrian library, he had advantages in his chronological researches, which none of his predecessors enjoyed. But this was long after the year, in which the Parian Chronicle is supposed to have been compiled. That work was engraved in 264, when Eratosthenes was only twelve years of age; and he was not invited from Athens till the year 239 ‡, twenty-five years afterwards. The Chronicle therefore could not be copied from the writings of Eratosthenes. Besides, the computations of

---

* Ἐπὶ τριάκοντα τέσσαρα.—The Latin translation, in the editions of Sylburgius and Potter, makes it only xxx years: I suppose by mistake.

† Dionys. Halic. loc. cit.

‡ Prid. Connect. vol. iii. p. 121. and Chronol. Table at the end of the fourth volume. Saxius supposes, that Eratosthenes was not appointed keeper of the Alexandrian library, before the year 236. Onomastic. p. 109.

the Chronicle, and that of Eratoſthenes, are very different in ſome important articles, as it will appear hereafter.

Apollodorus, an Athenian, the diſciple of Ariſtarchus the grammarian, and Panætius the philoſopher, was the author of ſeveral treatiſes on the fabulous and heroic ages of Greece, particularly the following: 1. Περι Θεων, Of the Gods, a work of conſiderable extent. 2. Βιβλιοθηκα, a genealogical and mythological work. The part of it now remaining, which ſcarcely conſiſts of three books, ends abruptly with an account of ſome of the exploits of Theſeus. From paſſages cited by the ancients, the learned Dr. Gale and others infer, that the Hiſtory of the Gods, and the Bibliotheca, were different productions *. 3. Χρονικα or Χρονικη Συνταξις †, Temporum Ordo & Structura, extending from the ſiege of Troy to the time when the author wrote, which was about the year bef. Chr. 140, or ſomething later ‡. This work is ſaid to have been compoſed in tragiambic verſe ‖.

* Errant, qui [Bibliothecam] idem opus cum libris Περι Θεων faciunt. Galei Diſſert. de Script. Mythol. c. 5.—Dr. Gale likewiſe proves, that the Bibliotheca is not an EPITOME of the Hiſtory of the Gods, as ſome writers have ſuppoſed. Ibid.

† Diod. Sic. l. xiii. p. 222.

‡ Apollodorus mentions the death of Carneades, in the CLXII. 4. Olympiad, bef. Chr. 129. Diog. Laert. l. iv. § 65.

   Συνταξε τα περι [απο] της Τρωϊκης αλωσεως,
   Χρονογραφιαν ςειχουσαν αχρι του νυν βιου.

  Conſcripſit à Trojæ excidio,
  Chronographiam verſibus deſcriptam ad hoc uſque
   tempus.

   Marc. Heracl. ſive Scymni Chii Perieg. v. 22.

This author wrote in the year bef. Chr. 132. Corſini Faſti Attici, tom. iv. p. 107.

‖ A. Gellius, l. xvii. c. 4. cites three verſes from the Chronica of Apollodorus.

THE PARIAN CHRONICLE. 97

The writings of Apollodorus naturally suggest the two following obfervations:

1. Though the Bibliotheca was written 120 years after the date of the Parian Chronicle, it does not contain the fmalleft traces of a fyftematical chronology.

2. The chronicle of Apollodorus is quoted by many eminent writers of antiquity*; while that of Paros, which comprehends a more extenfive period, is entirely unnoticed.

About the fame time † Polybius wrote his Univerfal Hiftory ‡, originally confifting of forty books, of which five only are now remaining, with extracts and fragments of fome others. The firft and fecond books form a fort of introduction to the reft. In the third the author enters upon his principal fubject, which was a hiftory of the moft confiderable tranfactions of the Romans, and other nations, from the year 220, or the commencement of the fecond Carthaginian war, to the fall of the Macedonian empire, in 168 ‖.

Polybius is the moft ancient writer now extant, that has adopted the method of afcertaining the dates of civil and military tranfactions by the Olympiads. But his hiftory, excepting the fhort fketches contained in the

---

* Diodorus Siculus, Strabo, Plutarch, Phlegon, A. Gellius, Lucian, Clemens Alexandrinus, Diogenes Laertius *paſſim*, Eufebius, Stephanus Byzantinus, &c.

† Polybius was born bef. Chr. 205 years, and died 123.

‡ Ἱϛορικη Καθολικη. Polyb. l. ii. c. 37.

‖ Strabo informs us, that Polybius was prefent at the burning of Corinth by L. Mummius, in the year 146; that he had given an account of that event in his hiftory; and particularly lamented the deftruction, which was made by the Roman foldiers, of many beautiful pictures, and other works of ingenuity, when they plundered the city. Strab. l. viii. p. 584.

The fifth book of Polybius ends with the CXL Olympiad, bef. Chr. 217.

two preliminary books, included the events of only 53 years, many of which happened within the compass of his own life, and does not display any great extent of chronological science.

About this time chronology began to assume a new form, and to be established on more solid, regular, and scientific principles. The Greek historians, in general, made use of the Olympiads in the computation of time. Dionysius Halicarnasseus, Diodorus Siculus, Plutarch, Diogenes Laertius, and others, will shew us, how this epocha was regularly continued in subsequent ages. But as no records had been kept, before the establishment of the Olympiads, in the time of Corœbus; and no great accuracy observed in the Olympic catalogues, till they began to be applied to historical purposes, the transactions of preceding ages still remained in a state of obscurity and confusion; and all that the ablest chronologers could afterwards accomplish, was a precarious system, founded on the loose calculations, or the arbitrary assertions, of more ancient authors.

I am very sensible, that several writers, besides those I have mentioned, published Olympic catalogues; particularly Aristotle, Demetrius Phalereus, Philochorus, Aristarchus, Stesiclides, Hippostratus, Phlegon, &c. [*]
But

---

[*] Aristotle. Ολυμπιονικαι, Olympionicæ. Diog. Laert. in v. Arist. l. v. § 26.

Demetrius Phalereus. Των Αρχοντων Αναγραφη, Archontum Recensio. Diog. Laert. in v. Thal. l. i. § 22. See below, chap. x.

Philochorus. This writer was an Athenian, and lived about 200 years bef. Chr. Vid. Suid.

Aristarchus. ὁ των Ολυμπιασιν εξηγητης, Olympiadum enarrator. Pausan. l. v. c. 20.

Stesiclides. Των Αρχοντων και Ολυμπιονικων Αναγραφη. Diog. Laert. in v. Xenoph. l. ii. § 56.

Hippostratus. v. Jonf. de Script. Hist. Phil. l. iv. § 41.

Phlegon.

THE PARIAN CHRONICLE. 99

But from what has been obferved in the writings of the Greeks, from Herodotus to Polybius, we can find no traces of a regular fcientific chronology.

Let us confider the fentiments of the ancients on this fubject.

Phlegon. Ολυμπιονικων και χρονικων συναγωγη, Olympionicarum & Chronicorum Sylloge. Phot. cod. 97.

CHAP. VI.

JULIUS Africanus, in this Χρονογραφια, which extends from the creation to the year after Christ 221, asserts, "that the Greeks had no accurate history before the Olympiads; and that all their accounts of preceding ages are confused and inconsistent *."

Justin Martyr likewise observes, "that the Greeks had no accurate history before the Olympiads †." Justin wrote about the year 140.

Plutarch, an author of great learning and judgement, ventures no farther into Grecian antiquity, than the time of Theseus. When he attempts to give his readers the history of that hero, he says, "As geographers throw into the extremities of their maps those countries, which are unknown to them, remarking at the same time, that all beyond is nothing but hills of sand, and haunts of wild beasts, frozen seas, marshes, and mountains, inaccessible to human courage and industry; so in comparing the lives of illustrious men, when I have passed through the periods of time, which may be described with probability, and where history may find a

---

* Μεχρι μεν Ολυμπιαδων, ουδεν ακριβες ιςορηται τοις Ελλησι, παντων συγκεχυμενων, και κατα μηδεν αυτοις των πρωτου συμφωνουντων. Ante quidem Olympiades nihil certi à Græcis in historiâ traditur, omnibus confusis, nec ullâ ex parte sibi anteà consentientibus. Afric. apud Euseb. Præp. Evang. l. x. c. 10. Syncell. p. 154.—Africanus died about the year of Christ 232. Cave.

† Οτι ουδεν Ελληςι προ των Ολυμπιαδων ακριβες ιςορηται. Nihil à Græcis ante Olympiades, accuratè scriptum esse. Just. Mart. ad Græc. Cohort. p. 13. edit. 1686.—Justin was born about the year 89, and died in 164. Fabricius.

sure

THE PARIAN CHRONICLE.

sure footing in facts, I may say of the remoter ages, that all beyond is full of prodigy and fiction, the region of poets and fabulists, wrapt in clouds, and unworthy of belief *."

Plutarch's ne plus ultra is not much more than half a century before the siege of Troy; for Theseus is said to have carried away Hellen from Sparta, about 24 years before that event †.

This excellent writer takes notice of the inconsistencies of the Greek historians in many points of chronology, concerning some of the most illustrious characters, and the most important transactions of later times, in which we might have expected a general agreement. Thus, he says, " there is nothing but uncertainty and contradiction in the accounts, which historians have given us of Lycurgus, the celebrated Spartan lawgiver. Some say, he was contemporary with Iphitus, and joined with him in settling the cessation of arms, during the Olympic games ‡. Aristotle the philosopher is of this opinion, and endeavours to support it by an Olympic disc, on which the name of Lycurgus was inscribed.

---

* Plut. in v. Thesei, p. 1.—Plutarch wrote about the year aft. Chr. 120.

† Sir Isaac Newton places the birth of Theseus 74 years before the siege of Troy. Chron. an. 938.

‡ The Olympic games are supposed to have been first instituted by the Idæan Hercules, in the fabulous ages of Greece. Diod. Sic. l. v. p. 230. After many interruptions they were restored by Iphitus, prince of Elis, 884 years bef. Chr. the year in which Lycurgus gave his laws to the Lacedæmonians. But the names of the victors were not recorded, till the XXVIII Olympiad, in the year 776, when Corœbus of Elis was victor in the race. This was the first Olympiad, which the Greeks used in their chronological computations; yet these Olympiads are confounded by several authors. Aristod. apud Syncell. p. 196. Athen. l. xiv. p. 635. Pausan. l. v. c. 4.

Others,

Others, as Eratosthenes and Apollodorus *, computing the time by the succeſſion of the Spartan kings, place him much earlier than the firſt Olympiad †."

In another place he ſays, " Some authors think they can prove by chronological arguments, that the ſtory, concerning the interview between Solon and Crœſus, is a fiction. But a ſtory ſo famous, atteſted by ſuch a number of witneſſes, and, what ſtill more deſerves to be conſidered, ſo agreeable to Solon's character, and ſo worthy of his magnanimity and wiſdom, ſhould not, in my opinion, be rejected, upon a pretence of its not agreeing with ſome chronological canons ‡, as they are called, which thouſands continue to this day endeavouring to correct, without being able to bring them to any conſiſtency ||."

In this inſtance, we find the date of a moſt important tranſaction, in the moſt poliſhed ſtate of Greece, the legiſlation of Solon at Athens, a ſubject of diſpute and uncertainty.

Joſephus aſſerts, that the ancient Greek writers deſtroy one another's credit; that the genealogies of Heſiod are corrected by Acuſilaus §; that Acuſilaus is

---

* Eratoſthenes placed the legiſlation of Lycurgus 299 years after the ſiege of Troy; that is, bef. Chr. 884. And Apollodorus agreed with him in this computation. Clem. Alex. Strom. l. 1. § 21. p. 402.

† Plut. in v. Lycurgi, § 1.

‡ Plutarch ſeems to allude to the canons of Eratoſthenes.

|| Plut. in v. Solonis, p. 93.——According to Corſini, Solon was archon in 594; went into Lydia, during the tyranny of Piſiſtratus, in 560; and died the year following. Faſti Attici, tom. iii. p. 99. But ſee A. Gell. l. xvii. c. 21. Diog. Laert. l. i. § 59.

§ Clemens Alexandrinus informs us, that Eumelus and Acuſilaus turned ſome of Heſiod's poems into proſe, and then publiſhed them as their own compoſitions. Strom. l. vi. § 2. p. 752.

condemned

condemned by Hellenicus, Hellenicus accused of falshood by Ephorus, Ephorus by Timæus, Timæus by his successors, and Herodotus by all the world *.

Varro, who is applauded by Cicero, Dionysius Halicarnasseus, Seneca, and Quintilian †, for his profound learning and knowledge of antiquities, divided the time, anterior to his own age, into three parts. "The first," he says, " extends from the beginning of the world to the Ogygian deluge ‡; and may be called, αδηλον, the obscure or unknown period. The second extends from the deluge to the first Olympiad, and is called μυθικον, fabulous. The third extends from the first Olympiad to the present time, and is called ισορικον, the historic æra ‖."

Thucydides, in the beginning of his history, remarks, that " the transactions of an earlier date [than the Peloponnesian war] and those which were still more ancient, could not, through length of time, be adequately known §."

But

* Ἡροδοτον δε παντες. Jos. cont. Ap. l. i. § 3.—Josephus was born A. D. 37, and brought down his Antiquities to the year 94; but how long he lived afterwards is not known. Lib. xx. sub fin.

† Cicero de claris Orat. § 60. Dionys. Halic. l. ii. p. 92. Sen. Consol. ad Helv. c. 8. Quint. l. x. 1.

‡ Ant. Chr. 1796. Banier.

‖ Varro tria discrimina temporum esse tradit. Primum, ab hominum principio ad cataclysinum priorem, quod propter ignorantiam vocetur αδηλον. Secundum, à cataclysmo priore ad Olympiadem primam; quod, quia in eo multa fabulosa referuntur, μυθικον nominatur. Tertium, à prima Olympiade ad nos, quod dicitur ισορικον, quia res in eo gestæ, veris historiis continentur. Varronis Fragm. p. 219. Censor. de Die Nat. c. 21. Varro died bef. Chr. 26 years. Eusebius.

§ Τα προ αυτων, και τα ετι παλαιοτερα, σαφως μεν ευρειν, δια χρονου πληθος, αδυνατον ην. Quæ ante [motus Peloponnesiacos gesta] et quæ etiam

But the most important observation on this subject occurs in Diodorus Siculus, who informs us, that, when he undertook to write his Historical Library, "he travelled through many parts of Europe and Asia, in order to view those places, which he had occasion to mention, and to examine every thing, which might be of service to him in his undertaking; and that he spent thirty years in composing this work *."

Yet after all his enquiries he declares, that "he did not attempt to circumscribe those times, which preceded the Trojan war, because he could find no PARAPEGMA, on which he could place any dependence †."

In this passage the word PARAPEGMA has been variously interpreted. The Latin translators, Rhodoman and Wesselingius, render it, "certitudinis fulcrum." Sir Isaac Newton accordingly translates μηδεν παραπηγμα πιςευομενον, "no certain foundation to rely upon." Scaliger calls parapegma, tempus certum & definitum; and adds, "id autem duplex est, undè et quò. Hoc est, undè rationes temporum deducuntur, et quò referuntur." Marsham styles it, terminus fixus; Stillingfleet, "a certain fixed epocha, or a certain fixed period of

---

etiam antiquiora, liquidò investigari, propter temporis longinquitatem, non potuerunt. Thucyd. l. i. § 1.

* Τριακοντα μεν ετη περι αυτην επραγματειθημεν, μετα δε πολλης κακοπαθειας και κινδυνων επληθομεν πολλην της τε Ασιας και της Ευρωπης, ινα των αναγκαιοτατων, και πλειςων μερων αυτοπται γενθωμεν. Triginta annorum operam in id [argumentum] contulimus, magnamque Asiæ & Europæ partem, non absque periculis & ærumnis, perlustravimus; ut pleraque, et maximè instituto huic necessaria, locis inspiceremus ipsi. Diod. in Procem. Just. Mart. Cohort. ad Græc. p. 10. Diodorus flourished bef. Chr. 60 years. Blount.

† Τους μεν [χρονους] προ των Τρωϊκων ου διοριζομεθα βεβαιως, δια το μηδεν ΠΑΡΑΠΗΓΜΑ παρειληφεναι περι τουτων πιςευομενον. Quæ Troïca præcesserunt, non definimus certo spatio; quia nullum sumi potest PARAPEGMA, cui fidendum. Diod. in Procem. p. 5.

time."

time *." Suidas explains it by the word κανων, regula. But Salmasius censures the interpreters of Diodorus, and other learned men, for their ignorance and hallucination, with respect to this term, and then proceeds to define it in this manner: " Interpretes Diodori firmamentum exponunt. Scaliger ad Eusebium, quod alii εποχην, Censorinus titulum vocat, id Diodoro dici παραπηγμα, hoc est, terminum fixum et hærentem. Παραπηγμα propriè est quicquid adfigitur. Hinc παραπηγματα tabulæ dicebantur adfixæ columnis, aut pilis, in quibus leges, aut alia publica monumenta incidebantur .... Παραπηγμα ιστορικον aut μυθικον dicitur series historiarum vel fabularum, secundum ordinem temporum digesta. Et hôc sensu plane accipiendum est in illis Diodori verbis †."

This learned commentator, if I rightly comprehend his idea, supposes parapegma to signify what we call a chronological table.

To these interpretations I shall subjoin the sentiments of Vossius.

" Diodorus Siculus solùm extendit [tempus μυθικον] usque ad bellum Trojanum; atque addit, ante ea tempora nihil certi haberi, propterea quòd nullum sit παραπηγμα περι τουτων πιστευομενον. Nempe astrologi quidem habent tabulas suas, quæ παραπηγματα vocantur, ubi siderum ortus et occasus, atque tempestates, ordine annotantur; cujusmodi tabulas sequi tutò licet. At non historici similiter ante Trojana tempora, ut hic Diodorus ait, habent sua quoque παραπηγματα πιστευομενα, ubi series temporum annotetur. Extabant quidem Arctinus, Eumelus, Lesches, alii poetæ cyclici; sed negat

---

* Newton's Chron. c. 1. Scal. ad Euseb. Chron. proleg. p. vi. Ejusdem Animad. p. 71. Marsham. Canon. Chron. p. 14. 329. edit. 1672. Stillingfl. Orig. Sacræ, b. i. c. 5, 6.

† Salmas. Plin. Exercit. p. 860.

hos παραπηγμα effe, cui fedem [fidem] habere femper poffis, propter tot fabulas. Varro extendit μυθικον tempus ulterius; nimirum ufque ad primam Olympiadem *."

If we underftand the word parapegma of a chronological table, as Salmafius and Voffius explain it, fuch a table muft confift of certain fixed periods or epochas; thefe epochas muft be determined by canons or rules; and thefe canons or rules muft be the bafis, upon which a chronological fyftem is founded. Thefe different interpretations therefore feem to be, in fact, equivalent.

But in whatever fenfe we underftand this term, the affertion of Diodorus is extremely unfavourable to the credit of the Parian Chronicle. For we muft either fuppofe, that it was not EXISTING in the time of Diodorus, which at once decides the queftion; or, that Diodorus had not heard of it, which is fcarcely credible, confidering his abilities, and the pains he took to collect information from every quarter; or, laftly, that he did not think it πιςευομενον, worthy of credit; which will hardly be admitted by the advocates for the Arundelian Marbles.

The fame inference may be drawn from the foregoing remarks of Africanus, Juftin Martyr, Plutarch, Jofephus, Varro, and Thucydides; for all thefe writers agree, that the earlier periods of the Grecian hiftory were involved in darknefs and confufion.

But, if the Parian chronologer could afcertain the dates of the moft important events, which happened in Greece, five, fix, feven, eight hundred years before the Olympiads; fuch as, the firft eftablifhment of the kingdom of Attica by Cecrops, the deluge in the time

* G. I. Voffii Chron. Sacræ Ifagoge. c. 2. p. 7. edit. 1659.
De Parapegmate, vid. Vitruv. l. ix. 7. Gemini Ifagog. c. 15. Uffer. de Maced. Anno Solari, c. 6, 7. Menagii Obferv. in Diog. Laert. l. ix. § 48.

of Deucalion, the coming of Danaus into Peloponnesus, the arrival of Cadmus in Bœotia, the siege of Troy, &c. with a particularity which we scarcely find in a modern history, there could be no want of light or information, no want of parapegmata, epochas, canons, or chronological tables: consequently, the complaints of all the writers above-mentioned, and many others, which might be alleged, are groundless and absurd.

This is a flagrant imputation on the knowledge, or the integrity, of those respectable authors; but it is obviated at once on a supposition, that the Parian Chronicle is a modern compilation.

Thucydides, I know, lived 140 years before the Chronicle is said to have been written; but if Thucydides, as well as other writers, complained, that there was nothing but uncertainty in the earlier periods of the Grecian history, from whence can we suppose the author of this inscription collected such a clear, determinate, and comprehensive system of chronology?

If he had any sources of information, which were unknown to succeeding writers, how happens it, that they should all of them overlook this most considerable, most exact, most creditable author? Why did they omit this ancient account of their early ages? Why did they not copy his most memorable epochas? Why did they not produce his authority? or, at least, why did they not mention his opinion? Surely nothing, to all appearance, could be more elaborate, more important, or of higher authority, than a chronological table, which was thought worthy of being engraved on marble!—Yet, on this occasion, as we shall soon find, all the writers of antiquity are perfectly silent!

CHAP. VII.

V. THE silence of the ancients, with respect to the Parian Chronicle, is by no means a circumstance in its favour.

The learned and judicious Le Clerc, treating of the proper means of detecting supposititious books, among other rules for that purpose, lays down the following aphorism.

" Those writings, which are neither named in ancient catalogues, nor mentioned by any writer in the same age, or in ages immediately following, are, for the most part, to be accounted fictitious, or, at least, may be justly suspected *."

It is natural to suppose, that a short, insignificant inscription, like most of those which are preserved in the collections of Gruter, Reinesius, Gudius, Spon, and others, might have lain exposed to public view for many ages, without being particularly noticed by historians or antiquaries. But the Parian Chronicle is not a small inscription, of no importance in the republic of letters; it is not an inscription, which might have been concealed in a private library, or a cabinet, like a volume in manuscript. But it is a curious, learned, and comprehensive system of chronology, inscribed at a con-

---

* Scripta, quorum nulla mentio in priscis catalogis, quæ nec memorata sunt ab ullo scriptore sequentium proximè sæculorum, ut plurimùm aut ficta judicanda sunt, aut minimùm suspecta habenda. Cler. Art. Crit. p. iii. § 2. c. 3.—In this passage the author alludes to such catalogues as we find in Diogenes Laertius, or in A. Gellius. l. iii. 3.

fiderable expence on a tablet of marble, comprehending a detail of the principal epochas of Greece, during a period of 1300 years.

"In this infcription," fays Prideaux, "we have more events in the early ages of Greece, fpecified and recorded, than are to be found in almoft all the writers of antiquity *." The epochas of Cecrops, Deucalion, Hellen †, Cadmus, Danaus, Minos, Triptolemus, Hefiod, Homer, and others, about which the learned are ftill in doubt, are here exactly afcertained.

Here the queftion, which has been a thoufand times debated, whether Homer or Hefiod is the more ancient author, is precifely determined. Here likewife the year, the month, and the day of the month, in which Troy was taken, is particularly fpecified.

Thefe are fuch WONDERFUL DISCOVERIES in ancient hiftory, that if this Chronicle had exifted 264 years before the birth of Chrift, and more efpecially, if it had been compiled by PUBLIC AUTHORITY, or even KNOWN at Paros, it muft have excited a general attention, and would certainly have been copied, or cited, or praifed, or cenfured, or mentioned, by fome writers of fucceeding times.

But neither Strabo, Pliny, Paufanias, nor Athenæus, who mention the moft remarkable curiofities of different countries; neither Apollodorus, Diodorus Siculus, Tatian, Clemens Alexandrinus †, nor Eufebius,

* In uno horum, plura de antiquis Græcorum temporibus, quàm in omnibus ferè libris, habes explicata. Prid. Marm. Oxon. præf. p. v.

† From this Hellen the Greeks were called Hellenes. Apollod. l. i. c. 7. al. 6.

‡ Tatian cites fifteen, and Clemens Alexandrinus ten ancient writers, concerning a point of chronology, namely, the age of Homer, within the compafs of two pages. Tatian. § 48. Clem. Alex. Strom. l. i. § 21. p. 388.

who profeſſedly treat of the fabulous ages of Greece, take the leaſt notice of this wonderful monument of ancient learning. In ſhort, we do not find in any writer of antiquity, either poet or hiſtorian, geographer or chronologer, mythologiſt or ſcholiaſt, the moſt diſtant alluſion to the Parian Chronicle.

We have indeed loſt the works of many ancient authors; yet perhaps there never appeared a writer of any reputation, either in Greece or Rome, in all the ages of claſſical antiquity, whoſe name, and ſome account of his writings, have not been tranſmitted to the preſent age. If this obſervation be not ſtictly true, the exceptions are few and inconſiderable.

It was ſuch a common practice among the ancients, to mention the works of their predeceſſors, that in many books we find references and alluſions to three, four, five, ſix, or ſeven hundred different authors of every denomination.

Above 170 authors are mentioned by Pauſanias, 200 by A. Gellius, 320 by Servius, 340 by Diogenes Laertius, 350 in the Greek Scholia to Ariſtophanes, 430 by the two Senecas, 450 by Euſtathius, 450 by Quintilian, 530 by Plutarch, 580 by Clemens Alexandrinus, 700 by Pliny, 700 by Athenæus, and a proportionable number by many other claſſic writers; but not a ſyllable of the learned Parian, or of his elaborate ſyſtem of Grecian chronology.

At laſt, after it had exiſted above 1800 years, without being either named or cited, it is dug out of the ground, and brought to Europe in triumph; it is explained, quoted, applauded *, by critics and commentators. In a word, it is depoſited in the boſom of our

---

* Vix aliud eſt in re literariâ, anguſtius, antiquius, utilius. Maittai.e, Marm. Arund. dedic. p. i.

Alma

Alma Mater, and esteemed κτημα ες αει, "a glorious and everlasting acquisition."

Under these circumstances, it will be impossible to account for the profound silence of the ancients, and their gross inattention to a writer, who now excites the curiosity and admiration of the literary world, and professes to unravel all the chronological perplexities of the fabulous and heroic ages of Greece.

CHAP. VIII.

THERE are three objections, which may be alleged against the preceding argument.

First, as there were many chronological writers among the Greeks, the author of the Parian Chronicle might have been one of them, and cited under his proper name, without any reference to the inscription.

Secondly, this Chronicle has been ascribed to Demetrius Phalereus.

Thirdly, the works of some eminent writers of antiquity, such as Phædrus and Q. Curtius, lay in obscurity for many centuries, and were not discovered till later ages.

The supposition, on which the first of these objections is founded, is extremely improbable. The ancients almost always specified the works of their predecessors, which they had occasion to quote. Thus, Diogenes Laertius refers to Demetrius Phalereus, εν τη των Αρχοντων Αναγραφη; to Apollodorus, εν Χρονικοις; to Eratosthenes, εν τοις Ολυμπιονικαις; to Timæus, εν δεκατη Ιστοριων, &c.

In the same manner, the Parian Chronicle would certainly have been mentioned under some distinguishing title, if it had been noticed or cited by the writers of antiquity.

But let us enquire, how far the chronology of the learned Parian corresponds with that of the ancients, in two or three instances of the utmost notoriety, the epocha of the Trojan war, and the age of Homer.

THE PARIAN CHRONICLE. 113

The Epocha of the Trojan War.	Bef. Chr.
Sosibius reckoned, from the destruction of Troy to the first Olympiad, 395 years *. - Eratosthenes computed, from the taking of Troy to the return of the Heraclidæ, 80 years; from thence to the colonization of Ionia, 60 years; from thence to the tutelary government of Lycurgus, 159 years; and from thence to the commencement of the Olympiads, 108 years; in all 407 †. -	1171
	1183
Dionysius Argivus supposed, that Troy was taken in the eighteenth year of the reign of Agamemnon, and the first of Demophon ‡. - - - -	1183
P. Cato placed the building of Rome, in the first year of the seventh Olympiad, 432	

---

* Apud Censorin. c. 21.—The passage in Censorinus, on which some of the following computations depend, is confused and erroneous. The Cambridge edition in 1695, and Havercamp's in 1767, give it in this manner:

Secundum [tempus] non planè quidem scitur; sed tamen ad mille circiter et ɔc annos esse creditur: à priore scilicet cataclysmo, quem Ogygium dicunt, *ad Inachi regnum*, anni circiter cccc. hinc ad Olympiadem primam paulo plus cccc... Et quidem Sosibius scripsit esse cccxcv, &c.

The following alteration will perhaps give us a clear and consistent idea of the author's calculations.——Sed tamen ad *mille* circiter annos esse creditur à priore scilicet cataclysmo, quem Ogygium dicunt, *ad Ilii excidium*, anni circiter ɔc. Hinc ad Olympiadem primam paulo plus cccc, &c. See Jackson's Chron. Antiq. vol. iii. p. 330.

† Clem. Alex. Strom. l. i. § 21. p. 402.—Eratosthenes autem septem et cccc. Censor. loc. cit.

‡ Clem Alex. Strom. l. i. § 21. p. 381. Euseb. Chron. Græc p. 376. Præp. Evang. l. x. c. 12. p. 498.

Q   years

years after the Trojan war *. From this number deduct 25 years for the Olympiads, preceding the foundation of the city, and the remainder will be 407. - - — Bef. Chr. 1183

Dionyſius of Halicarnaſſus follows the computation of Cato. - - - 1183

Diodorus Siculus computes 779 years, from the taking of Troy to the end of the ninety-third Olympiad †; and conſequently, to the firſt Olympiad, 407 years. - - 1183

Tatian places the Trojan war 407 years before the Olympiads ‡. - - - 1183

Euſebius tells us, that from the taking of Troy to the firſt Olympiad, there were 406 years; or, according to Scaliger, 407 ‖. - - - - 1183

Apollodorus reckoned, from the Trojan war to the return of the Heraclidæ, 80 years; and from thence to the firſt Olympiad, 328 years §. - - - 1184

Solinus places the reſtoration of the Olympic games, in the four hundred and eighth year after the deſtruction of Troy ¶. 1184

The Greek chronologiſts, as Euſebius informs us, computed 408 years from the ſiege of Troy to the firſt Olympiad **. - 1184

Cenſorinus reckons, from the deſtruction

---

* Dion. Halic. l. i. p. 60.
† Diod. Sic. l. xiv. p. 235.
‡ Tatian. ad Græc. § 64.
‖ Euſeb. Chron. p. 93. Scal. Animadv. p. 53.
§ Diod. Sic. l. i. p. 5, 6.
¶ Solin. c. 1. § 28. edit. Goezü, 1777.
** Euſeb. Præp. Evang. l. x. c. 9. p. 484.

of Troy to the firſt Olympiad, a little more than 400 years *. — Aretes Dyrrhachinus makes this interval 414 years †. — Paterculus reckons 437 years from the taking of Troy to the building of Rome, 22 years after the commencement of the Olympiads ‡. — Timæus computed, from the deſtruction of Troy to the firſt Olympiad, 417 years ‖. Dicæarchus reckoned, from the reign of Nilus to the firſt Olympiad, 436 years §.— By the reign of Nilus, Sir John Marſham ſays, Dicæarchus indicates the time of the Trojan war. — — — The author of the Life of Homer, aſcribed to Herodotus, reckons, from the Trojan war to the birth of that poet, 168 years; from thence to the expedition of Xerxes into Greece in 480, 622 years ¶. — — Duris Samius, who lived in the time of Ptolemy Philadelphus, computed from the deſtruction of Troy to Alexander's expedi-

Bef. Chr.

118*

1190

1191

1193

1212

1270

---

* Cenſor. loc. cit.—This calculation depends on the correction propoſed in a former note.

† Apud Cenforin. loc. cit.—In the Cambridge edition, and that of Havercamp, &c. the number is IƆXIIII; but this ſeems to be a miſtake inſtead of CƆXIIII.

‡ V. Paterc. l. i. c. 8.—There is probably an error in the text of Paterculus.

‖ Apud Cenforin. loc. cit.

§ Apud Schol. in Apoll. Argon. l. iv. v. 276. p. 412. edit. 1641.—Per regnum Nili belli Trojani tempora Dicæarchus deſignat. Marſh. Can. Chron. ſec. x. p. 249.—Dicæarchus was one of Ariſtotle's diſciples.

¶ Vita Homeri inter Herod. Op. § 38.

tion

tion into Asia, in the year bef. Chr. 335, | Bef. Chr.
1000 years.* -   -   - | 1335

The PARIAN CHRONICLE places the destruction of Troy before the Olympic æra, 433 years. -   -   - | 1209

Several writers acquaint us with the month, and the day of the month, on which Troy was taken. Some placed this event on the twenty-third day of Scirrophorion †; Ægias or Agis, and Dercylus, on the twenty-third of Panemus ‡; Hellanicus and Dionyfius Argivus on the twelfth of Thargelion ‖; Dionyfius Halicarnaffeus, an ancient scholiast on Euripides, and others, on the twenty-third of that month §; Ephorus, Callisthenes, Damastes, and Philarchus, on the twenty-fourth ¶.

The

---

* Apud. Clem. Alex. Strom. l. i. § 21. p. 403.

† Clem. Alex. Strom. l. i. § 21. p. 381. Vid. Eufeb. Chron. Græc. p. 376.

‡ Clem. Alex. loc. cit.——According to Corfini, Panemus, among the Corinthians, coincided with Hecatombæon or July; and among the Macedonians, with Scirrophorion or June. Corfini Differt. Agonist. p. 159. Fast. Attic. Differt. iii. § 20, 21.

‖ Clem. Alex. loc. cit.

§ Ογδοη φθινοντος μηνος Θαργηλιωνος, octavâ definentis Thargelionis die; that is, the eighth from the end, or the twenty-third day of the month. Dionyf. Halic. l. i. p. 51. Schol. ad Eurip. Hecub. v. 914. apud Scal. Emend. Temp. l. v. p. 378. Clem. Alex. loc. cit.

¶ Τη εβδομη φθινοντος, septimâ definentis die, or the twenty-fourth. Plut. in v. Camilli. p. 138.

Before the first year of the LXXXVII Olympiad, that is, bef. Chr. 432, the Athenians, according to Corfini, began their year from the winter solstice, with the month Gamelion; afterwards from the summer solstice, with Hecatombæon. Their year had twelve months, confisting of 30 and 29 days alternately. This learned writer ranges them in the following order: Hecatombæon, Metagitnion, Boëdromion, Pyanepfion, Mæmacterion, Pofideon, Gamelion,

The PARIAN CHRONICLE likewise places it on the twenty-fourth of Thargelion.

With respect to the sentiments of modern chronologers, concerning the time of this event, it may be sufficient to observe, that there are two opinions, transmitted to us by the ancients, which nearly coincide, and carry with them the greatest probability. The one is adopted by Scaliger *, and his followers, Calvisius, Emmius, &c. who place it in the year bef. Chr. 1183; the other, by Petavius, Capellus, Usher, Strauchius, &c. who place it in 1184.

Some of the Greek writers, as we have already observed, have asserted, that Troy was taken on the twenty-third, and others, on the twenty-fourth of Thargelion. In order to adjust this dispute, modern chronologists have supposed, that the city was taken in the night, between the twenty-third and the twenty-fourth †. But this, I apprehend, is rather an imaginary, than a real exactness.

lion, Anthesterion, Elaphebolion, Munychion, Thargelion, Scirrophorion, which nearly corresponded with July, August, September, October, &c. Corsini Dissert. Agonist. p. 159. Fast. Attic. Dissert. ii. § 8. 22. 29. &c. Id. tom. iii. Proleg. p. xxviii.

* Emend. Temp. l. v. p. 379. Canon. Isag. l. iii. p. 289.

† Capellus colligit Ἰλίου ἅλωσιν contigisse inter Junii decimum tertium, et decimum quartum; nocte scilicet, quæ media fuit inter lunam 23 et 24, hoc est, inter ἑβδόμην φθίνοντος et ὀγδόην φθίνοντος Thargelionis. Simsonii Chron. p. 330.

Facile dissidium illud componi poterit, sive quòd nox illa, quâ urbs incensa ac direpta fuit, tum ad vigesimam tertiam, quæ præcesserat, tum ad vigesimam quartam proximè insequentem diem referri possit; sive quòd in Thargelione mense dies aliqua, juxta Metonis leges, exempta concipiatur; adeóque una eademque dies, quæ verè vigesima tertia fuerat, atque ὀγδόη φθίνοντος, à Dionysio, et Clemente quoque Alexandrino vocata fuit, vigesima quarta ab aliis appellari potuerit, si exemptilis ipsa in dierum numero computetur. Corsini Fast. Attic. Dissert. ii. p. 86.

Let us now see, how the hypothesis of the Parian Chronicle corresponds with the sentiments of the foregoing writers, in this and other articles.

Eratosthenes, Dionysius Argivus, Cato, Dionysius Halicarnasseus, Diodorus, Tatian, and Eusebius, make an interval, between the Trojan war and the Olympiads, of 407 years; other authors, an interval of 408.

The compiler of the Parian Chronicle makes the same interval consist of 433 years; in which he differs from the former 26, and from the latter 25 years.

He supposes, that Troy was taken 1209 years before the Christian æra, on the twenty-fourth day of Thargelion; and, in this particular, he agrees with Ephorus, Callisthenes, Damastes, and Philarchus. But Plutarch, who gives us the sentiments of these writers, does not mention the year, in which they placed that event.

The learned Petavius, having examined the circumstances, recorded by the ancients, relative to the year, the month, and the day, on which Troy was taken; and compared those circumstances with the lunations, by which the Grecian months were regulated, observes, that every thing coincides with the year of the Julian period 3530, bef. Chr. 1184; but that the Arundelian marbles, which place that event on the twenty-fourth day of Thargelion, in the year of the J. P. 3505, or bef. Chr. 1209, totally confound all the accounts of the ancients *.

Isocrates reckoned, that the Athenian constitution

---

* Igitur anno Per. Jul. 3530, ante Christianam æram 1184, nobilissimum illud excidium incidit. Marmora Arundelliana idem eo anno vindicant, qui sit Per. Jul. 3505, Thargelionis ιβδομη φθινοντος, hoc est, 24 die: quod antiquorum omnium rationes conturbat. Ration. Temp. par. ii. l. ii. c. 10. Ibid. p. i. l. i. c. 12.

THE PARIAN CHRONICLE. 119

had fubfifted from its firft eftablifhment by Cecrops, to the ufurpation of Pififtratus, ουκ ελαττον χιλιων ετων, not lefs than a thoufand years *. The Chronicle makes this period 1021 years.

It is obferved by Selden, that the beginning of the reign of Cecrops is placed 26 years fooner by the author of the Chronicle, than it is by Eufebius †; and that there is very feldom any greater agreement between them, before the appointment of the annual archons. It may not therefore be improper to illuftrate this obfervation by a few examples.

The difference between the Parian Chronicle and Eufebius, in the date of fome memorable occurrences.

	P. C.	Euf.	Diff.
Cecrops began to reign in Attica, bef. Chr.	1582	1556	26
Deucalion began to reign at Lycoria	1574	1541	33
Deucalion's deluge	1529	1527	2
Cadmus builds Cadmea	1519	1455	64
Danaus arrives in Greece	1511	1474	37
Erichthonius celebrates the Panathenæa	1506	1474	32
Thefeus reforms the government of Athens	1259	1233	26
The Nemean games inftituted	1251	1232	19
Mneftheus began to reign at Athens	1230	1204	26
Troy taken	1209	1183	26

* Orat. Panath. p. 409. edit. Cantab. 1686.—Ifocrates was born 436 years, and wrote his Panathenaic oration 343 years, before Chrift.

† Epocha hæc recentior eft Eufebio, annis XXVI. Nec minor firmè confenfus eft inter eum et noftrum, ante annuorum archontum initia, feu Periodi Julianæ annum 4030. Seld. Marm. Arund. p. 92.

Phædon

A DISSERTATION ON

	P. C.	Euf.	Diff.
Phædon invents weights and measures - - -	895	800	95
Creon made annual archon - -	684	684	—
Terpander - - -	645	646	1
Cyrus takes Sardes - -	542	549	7
Battle at Marathon - -	491	491	—
Sea-fight at Salamis - -	481	480	1
Gelo seizes the kingdom of Syracuse	479	487	8

Thus far we do not find any exact and uniform correspondence, between the Parian Chronicle and any writer of antiquity, with which we are acquainted.

CHAP. IX.

The Age of Homer.

	Bef. Chr.

THEOPOMPUS conceived, that Homer lived 500 years after the warriors, who were present at the siege of Troy. Others, mentioned by Tatian, were of the same opinion *. - - - 684

Euphorion imagined, that Homer lived in the time of Gyges, who, according to Clemens Alexandrinus, began to reign in the eighteenth Olympiad †. - - 708

Some writers, mentioned by Eusebius, place him 400 years after the destruction of Troy ‡. - - - - 784

Sosibius made Homer flourish 90 years before the Olympiads ‖. - - 866

Euphorbus, or Ephorus, 124 years before the building of Rome §. - - 877

Herodotus was of opinion, that Hesiod and Homer did not live above 400 years before his time ¶.—Herodotus was born bef. Chr. 484. - - - 884

Porphyry, and the generality of writers, as Suidas informs us, made Homer a hun-

---
* Clem. Alex. Strom. l. i. § 21. p. 389. Tatian. § 49.
† Tatian. Clem. Alex. loc. cit.
‡ Euseb. Chron. p. 97.
‖ Tatian. Clem. Alex. loc. cit.
§ Euseb. Chron. p. 106.
¶ Herod. l. ii. § 53.

	Bef. Chr.
dred years older than Hesiod, and supposed Hesiod to flourish only 32 years before the Olympiads *. - - -	908
Cornelius Nepos, in his Chronica, placed Homer 160 years before the building of Rome †. - - - -	912
Solinus imagines he lived 138 years before the Olympiads ‡. - - -	914
Eusebius places Homer, according to the opinion of some writers, 140 years before the first Olympiad ‖. - - -	916
Velleius Paterculus says, Homer flourished 950 years before his time. He wrote his history about 30 years after the Christian æra; Homer therefore, by his reckoning, flourished bef. Chr. 920 years §. -	920
Pliny, about the year 78, reckons, that Homer lived near 1000 years before him ¶.	920
Juvenal, about the year 98, likewise supposes, that Homer's poems had been extant a thousand years **. - - -	902
Apollodorus supposed, that Homer lived 100 years after the Ionic migration, and 240 after the Trojan war ††. - -	944

* Suidas in v. Ὅμηρος.
† Apud A. Gell. l. xvii. c. 21.
‡ Solin. c. 40. § 17.
‖ Euseb. Chron. num. 1101. p. 106.
§ Nam fermè ante annos nongentos quinquaginta floruit. Paterc. l. i. c. 5.
¶ Jam ante annos prope mille Homerus. Plin. l. vii. c. 16.
** ———— Uni cedit Homero,
    Propter mille annos.   Sat. vii. 38.
†† Clem. Alex. Tatian. loc. cit. Eusebius says, Apollodorus placed Homer 260 years after the destruction of Troy. Chron. p. 97.

Euthymenes

THE PARIAN CHRONICLE. 123

	Bef. Chr.
Euthymenes asserted, that Homer was born in Chios, about 200 years after the taking of Troy, and that Hesiod was his contemporary *. - - -	984
Archemachus was of the same opinion. -	984
Philochorus maintained, that Homer was born 180 years after the destruction of Troy †. - - - -	1003
Cassius Hemina asserted, that Homer and Hesiod lived a little more than 160 years after the Trojan war ‡. - -	1023
Aristarchus thought, that Homer lived at the time of the Ionic migration, which, according to Tatian and Clemens, was 140 years after the destruction of Troy ‖. -	1044
Eratosthenes placed τὴν ἡλικίαν, the age of Homer, 100 years after the Trojan war §. -	1083
The author of the life of Homer, ascribed to Herodotus, asserts, that Homer was born 622 years before the expedition of Xerxes into Greece, which was in 480 ¶. -	1102

* Clem. Alex. Tatian. loc. cit.
† Tatian. loc. cit. Clem. Alex. Strom. l. i. § 21. p. 388. Euseb. Chron. 97.
‡ Apud A. Gell. l. xvii. c. 21. Euseb. Chron. p. 101.
‖ Tatian. § 49. Clem. Alex. loc. cit. Euseb. Chron. p. 97. Homeri Vita, inter Opusc. Mythol. à Galeo edita.
§ Clem. Alex. Tatian. loc. cit. Euseb. Chron. p. 100. Syncell. p. 180.—Ἡλικία, in Clemens Alexandrinus, means the flourishing age, or the age of manhood.
¶ Vita Homeri, § 38.—In this passage, there is a difference of above 200 years between the computation of Homer's biographer, and that of Herodotus. This, among other circumstances, is an argument, that Herodotus was not the author of the Life of Homer. Scaliger imagines, that ἑξακόσια, 600, should be τετρακόσια, 400. Scalig. Animadv. in Euseb. num. 1548. p. 102.

Crates

Crates Mallotes suppoſed, that Homer flouriſhed juſt before, or about, the return of the Heraclidæ, 80 years after the Trojan war *. - - - - 1104

Some writers, mentioned by Euſebius, place Homer 333 years before the Olympiads †. - - - - 1109

Some, ſays Plutarch, affirm, that Homer lived at the time of the Trojan war, and was an eye-witneſs of it; others, that he lived 100 years after it ‡. - - 1184 / 1084

The author of the PARIAN CHRONICLE tells us, that Homer flouriſhed 302 years after the Trojan war, 37 years after Heſiod, 23 before the reſtoration of the Olympiads by Iphitus and Lycurgus in the year 884; and 131 before their final eſtabliſhment, when Corœbus was victor in the race, in 776. - 907

Heſiod is ſuppoſed to have been older than Homer by Ariſtophanes, [Ephorus], Accius ‖, &c.

Homer

---

* Πρὸ τῆς καθόδου. Tatian. § 49. Euſeb. Chron. num. 908. p. 97. Homeri Vita ſupra cit. Περὶ τὴν κάθοδον. Clem. Alex. Strom. l. i. § 21. p. 389.

† Homerus ſecundum quorundam opinionem his fuiſſe temporibus judicatur. Euſeb. Chron. loc. cit.

‡ Plut. in v. Homeri. p. 44.—The word uſed by Plutarch is γενέσθαι, eſſe, to live.

‖ Ariſtoph. Ran. v. 1065.—This teſtimony is of little weight, as it entirely depends on the order of the words, or the poſition of the two names, Heſiod and Homer.

Alii minorem fuiſſe Homerum; in quîs L. Accius poeta, et Ephorus hiſtoriæ ſcriptor. Ephor. apud A. Gell. l. iii. c. 11. L. Accius, ibid.—The argument, on which Accius founded his opinion, is extremely frivolous. Homer, he thinks, would have told

THE PARIAN CHRONICLE. 125

Homer and Hesiod are said to have been contemporaries by Herodotus, Ephorus, Euthymenes, Varro, Plutarch, Philostratus, Cyril,* &c.

Homer is supposed to have lived some time before Hesiod by Philochorus, Xenophanes, Cicero, Paterculus, Josephus, Pliny, A. Gellius, Solinus, Porphyry, Eustathius, and almost all other writers †.

From

---

told his readers who Peleus was; and would likewise have said, that Polyphemus had but one eye, if Hesiod had not mentioned these things before him.

* Herod. l. ii. § 53.
Ephorus apud Syncell. p. 173.—Ephorus asserted, that Hesiod was the kinsman and contemporary of Homer. In the edition of Goarus the words are, 'Ησιοδος εγνωριζετο, ον Εφορος ανεψιον και συγχρονον ομου φησιν; and translated, Hesiodus florebat, quem Ephorus nepotem et sibi coëvum celebrat. But this is absurd. The true reading is certainly συγχρονον 'Ομηρου φησιν.
Euthemenes apud Clem. Alex. loc. cit.
Varro apud A. Gell. loc. cit. Varr. Fragm. p. 78.
Plutarch. de Consol. p. 105. Sympos. l. v. quæst. 2. p. 675. Sept. Sapient. Conv. p. 153.
Philost. 'Ηρωικα, in Euphorbo.
Cyril. adv. Jul. l. i. p. 11.
† Philochorus, Xenophanes.—Alii Homerum quàm Hesiodum majorem natu fuisse scripserunt, in quîs Philochorus & Xenophanes. A. Gell. l. iii. c. 11.
Cicero.—Homerus multis, ut mihi videtur, ante [Hesiodum] seculis fuit. De Senect. § 15.
Josephus.—'Ολως δε παρα τοις Ελλησιν ουδεν ομολογουμενον ευρισκεται γραμμα, της 'Ομηρου ποιησεως πρεσβυτερον, Neque tu scriptum omnino apud Græcos ullum, cujus de fide modò constet, Homeri poëfi antiquius invenias. Cont. Ap. l. i. § 2.
Paterculus.—Hesiodus fuit circa cxx annos distinctus ab Homeri ætate. l. i. c. 7.
Pliny.—Homerus quidem primus doctrinarum et antiquitatis parens. Nat. Hist. l. xxv. c. 2.
A. Gellius.—De Homero et Hesiodo inter omnes ferè scriptores

From this enquiry, concerning the age of Homer, we may deduce the following observations.

First, that there is a variation in the conjectures of the ancients, of 500 years in this article.

Secondly, that such a diversity of sentiments, respecting the age of this illustrious poet, is a farther proof of what has been already advanced, that the Greeks had no regular history or chronology before the Olympiads.

Thirdly, that the computation on the Arundelian Marble, relative to the age of Homer, does not agree with the opinion of the principal chronologers of antiquity. It differs from the computation of Apollodorus 62 years, and from that of Eratosthenes 202, in the interval between the siege of Troy and time of Homer; and from others, in a greater or less proportion; though it must be acknowledged, that we cannot form any precise idea of this diversity; since few of these writers inform us, whether they speak of the birth, the ἡλικία, or the death of Homer.

Fourthly, that the opinion, adopted by the author of the Chronicle, which supposes Hesiod to be older than Homer, is not well supported; nor is it the most commonly received opinion. Suidas informs us, that οἱ πλεῖστοι, the generality of writers, supposed Hesiod to have been 100 years younger than Homer [*]. According to

---

tores constituit, ætatem eos egisse vel iisdem fere temporibus, vel Homerum aliquanto antiquiorem. Noct. Attic. l. xvii. c. 21.

Solinus.—Inter quem [Homerum] et Hesiodem poetam, qui in auspiciis Olympiadis primæ obiit, centum triginta octo anni medii fuerunt. c. 40. § 17.

Porphyry.—Πορφύριος, καὶ ἄλλοι πλεῖστοι, νεώτερον ἑκατὸν ἐνιαυτοῖς ἡγοῦσιν, Porphyrius, et alii plurimi, ipsum Homero juniorem centum annis statuunt. Suid. in v. Ἡσίοδος.

Eustathius.—Apud Hom. Odys. l. iv. p. 187.

[*] Suidas, loc. cit.

A. Gellius

A. Gellius, " almoſt all writers agreed, that Homer and Heſiod were either nearly contemporaries; or, that Homer was a little more ancient *." It is likewiſe atteſted by Joſephus, Sextus, Empiricus †, and others, that there was no writing remaining among the Greeks, more ancient than the poems of Homer. This then was the general voice of antiquity.

Laſtly, that in all this controverſy, ſo frequently and ſo warmly debated, both in Greece and Italy, we do not-find the leaſt reference or alluſion to the Chronicle of Paros; nor any one author of antiquity, to which this Chronicle can be fairly attributed.

But let us conſider the ſecond objection.

---

* De Homero & Heſiodo inter *omnes* ferè ſcriptores conſtitit, ætatem eos egiſſe, vel iiſdem ferè temporibus, vel Homerum aliquantò antiquiorem. A. Gell. l. xvii. c. 21.

† Joſ. loc. cit.—Ποιημα ουδεν πρεσβυτερον ηκεν εις ἡμας της Ὁμηρου ποιησεως. Sext. Empir. adv. Mathemat. p. 41.

CHAP.

CHAP. X.

THE author of four Differtations, fubjoined to the book of Daniel fecundum Septuaginta, printed at Rome in 1772, afcribes the Parian Chronicle to Demetrius Phalereus *.

This writer adopts the ftory, related by Arifteas, concerning the tranflation of the Jewifh fcriptures into Greek; and confequently maintains, that Demetrius Phalereus was principally concerned in recommending and promoting that verfion. But as it is fuppofed to have been made in the eighth year of Ptolemy Philadelphus †, 277 years before the Chriftian æra, after the

death

---

* ΔΑΝΙΗΛ κατα τους ιβδομηκοντα, εκ των Τετραπλων Ωριγενους. Daniel fecundum LXX. ex Tetraplis Originis, nunc primùm editus è fingulari Chifiano codice, annorum fupra IƆCCC. Romæ 1772. folio.

† " Within the compafs of this year archbifhop Ufher places the making of this tranflation. And here all muft place it, who with him BELIEVE the hiftory to be GENUINE, which is written of it under the name of Arifteas, and will hold what is confiftent with it herein. For, according to that author, they cannot place it later; becaufe then it would not fall within the time of Eleazar, who is therein faid to have been the high-prieft of the Jews, that fent the feventy-two elders to Alexandria to make this tranflation; for he died about the beginning of the next year. And they cannot place it fooner; becaufe then it would be before Ptolemy Philadelphus married Arfinoe, his fifter, whom Eleazar, in the epiftle, which the author makes him to have written to this prince, calls his queen and his fifter." Prid. Connect. vol. iii. p. 38. Vid. Ariftex Hift. edit. Oxon. p. 17.

The learned Dr. Hody is of opinion, that the Pentateuch only was tranflated into Greek, about the year 285, when Ptolemy Philadelphus

death of Demetrius, our author endeavours to remove this chronological objection, by proving, that Demetrius was not only alive at that time, but that he afterwards compofed a hiftory of the Jews, and the Parian Chronicle *.

I fhall briefly confider his arguments and obfervations relative to the Chronicle.

" This performance," he obferves, " is evidently the work of one perfon †."

Granted.

" The author has paid more attention to poets, and the hiftory of literature, than to warriors or military tranfactions; of which we have inftances in the fiftieth and fixty-fifth epochas, where he fpeaks of Simonides and Sophocles ‡."

Admitting the truth of this remark, it will only prove, that the writer was a poet, or a man of letters; which no perfon will controvert.

" It is well known," fays the learned editor of Daniel, " that Demetrius Phalereus was the author of a work, entitled, των Αρχοντων Αναγραφη, which was efteemed by the ancients, and is cited by Diogenes Laertius, in order to afcertain the date of fome events in the lives of

ladelphus was king of Egypt, in partnerfhip with his father; and that this verfion was not made by royal authority, but by the Jews of Alexandria, for the ufe of the fynagogue. De Bibl. Text. Orig. l. i.

* Dr. Chandler feems to have acquiefced in this opinion; for he fays: " This Demetrius was author of the ancient and famous Chronicon, infcribed on marble at Paros, and now preferved, but not entire, at Oxford. See Daniel à LXX. p. 480. Rome, 1772." Chandler's Travels in Greece, c. vii.

† Auctor certè unus fuit. Differt. iv. § 21.

‡ Poetarum potius mentionem ingerit, indèque literaram hiftoriam profequitur. Ibid.

Thales and Anaxagoras. From which it appears, that his performance was not a mere list of names; but included many historical events, such as we find in the Parian Chronicle *."

From this very slight and equivocal resemblance between the plan of the Αναγραφη, and that of the Chronicle, we can by no means infer, that they were the productions of the same writer.

For, 1. the Chronicle takes no notice of Thales or Anaxagoras, or of the circumstances, for which the Αναγραφη is quoted by Laertius. Yet we might have expected to find a perfect coincidence in these articles, if the one had been a copy of the other.

2. Demetrius, as Plutarch informs us, asserted, that Aristides was archon after the battle at Plataeae, a little before his death †, which happened in the year 467. But nothing of this kind is to be found in the Chronicle.

3. From Creon to Diotimus inclusive, there were 330 annual archons; but allowing one for each epocha, not more than forty-seven were originally mentioned in the Chronicle, within that period. The Chronicle therefore cannot, in any sense of the word, be styled, των Αρχοντων Αναγραφη, a catalogue of the archons.

There is a dispute among the ancients concerning the age of Socrates. Some say, that he lived sixty, others seventy years. The Parian Chronicle asserts, that he died at the age of seventy, when Laches was archon at Athens.

This, our author observes, is likewise asserted by Demetrius Phalereus. For, says Diogenes Laertius,

---

* In Marmore Arundelliano nihil occurrit, quod non conveniat Demetrio. Ibid. p. 481.

† Plut. in v. Arist. p. 321.

" Socrates

THE PARIAN CHRONICLE. 131

"Socrates died in the firſt year of the ninety-fifth Olympiad, when he was ſeventy years of age. Demetrius Phalereus ſays the ſame *. Others tell us, that he died at the age of ſixty."

I anſwer: fifty writers might ſay this, as well as Demetrius Phalereus; for Plato, fourſcore years before, had made Socrates tell the Athenians, in his Apology, that he was above ſeventy years of age, when he was brought to his trial †.

2. It does not appear, that Laertius took this account of the age of Socrates from the Αναγραφη of Demetrius. He moſt probably found it in another work by the ſame author, entitled, SOCRATES, which is mentioned in the liſt of his writings, and quoted by Plutarch in his Life of Ariſtides ‡.

3. This coincidence does not, by any means, prove, that the Chronicle was compoſed by Demetrius; becauſe a modern author would naturally take his account of the age of Socrates, either from Plato or Laertius.

Laertius, in his catalogue of the writings of Demetrius, takes no notice of his Αναγραφη, or however does not mention it under this title.

The author of the Diſſertation imagines, that "his account of the archons might be included in his two books Περι των Αθηνησι πολιτων, Of the Citizens of Athens,

* Και ταυτα φησι και Δημητριες ὁ Φαληρευς, eadem fermè Demetrius Phalereus. Diog. Laert. in v. Demet. l. v. § 44.

† Ετη γεγονως πλειω ἰβδομηκοντα, plures quàm ſeptuaginta annos natus. Apol. Socrat. § 1. Diod. Sic. l. xiv. p. 266.
Socrates was born in the year bef. Chr. 469, and died in 400. Corſin. Faſti Attici. tom. iii. p. 189. 281.

‡ Plutarch and Diogenes Laertius mention a book, written by Demetrius Phalereus, entitled, SOCRATES. Plut. in v. Ariſtid. § 1. Diog. Laert. l. v. § 81. Diogenes likewiſe quotes a work by Demetrius, which is probably the ſame performance, entitled, Socratis Apologia, l. ix. § 15. § 37. Vid. Athen. l. xiii. § 1.

which is mentioned by Laertius; and this," he thinks, "will be very probable, if, inftead of πολιτων, citizens, we read πολιτευσαντων, governors or magiftrates."

As this correction of the text is unfupported by any authority, it is of no weight in the argument. The omiffion of the Αναγραφη, in the Catalogue given by Laertius, would lead us to fufpect, that it was a performance of no great confequence.

If it had been either the Chronicle itfelf, or the original, from which the Chronicle was taken, it would have been accounted a work of importance to the general hiftory of Greece, and have been much oftener quoted than it is. At prefent, we have only two or three general references in Laertius to certain paffages in it, which do NOT EXIST in the Chronicle.

At the beginning of the Chronicle, we find the following remaining characters, which no commentator has attempted to explain.

. . . . . ου . . . . υπαν . . . ων . . . . .
. . . . . νων ανεγραψα τους, κ. τ. λ.

Our author fills up thefe lacunæ in this manner.

Δημητριος ὁ ΦανοςρατΟΥ Φαληρευς, εκ των συΜΠΑΝτων ὑπαρχονΤΩΝ, ανεγραψα τους, κ. τ. λ. Demetrius Phanoftrati filius Phalereus, ex omnibus quæ extant monumentis edidi, &c.

This is an ingenious fupplement; but it does not coincide with ALL the remaining letters; and any other names will fuit the place, as well as thofe of Demetrius Phalereus and Phanoftratus, provided the name of the father, in the genitive cafe, ends in ΟΥ.

Our author obferves, that Demetrius, in his computation of time, ufes an expreffion, which is conftantly employed in the Parian Chronicle: namely, αφ' ου, ex quo.

Αφ'

THE PARIAN CHRONICLE. 133

Αφ' ου δε αι φυλαι αι δεκα, ex quo autem decem tribus. Αφ' ου δε εξ Ιεροσολυμων, ex quo autem ex Hierosolymis *. Αφ' ου δε εκλεγηναι Αβρααμ, ex quo selectus est Abraamus. Αφ' ου δε εκ Χανααν αυτον ελθειν εις Αιγυπτον, ex quo venit è terrâ Chananæâ in Ægyptum †."

In anſwer to this argument we may remark, that αφ' ου is a common phraſe; and that no inference can be drawn from it. For inſtance:

Αφ' ου ο κυριος εγεννηθη, ex quo natus eſt Dominus. Αφ' ου δε επαθεν, ex quo autem paſſus eſt. Αφ' ου εςη το βδελυγμα υπο Νερωνος, ex quo ſtetit abominatio à Nerone ‡.

Clemens Alexandrinus and Euſebius have indeed quoted a writer called Demetrius, in which the foregoing paſſages occur. But he muſt have an uncommon ſhare of credulity, who can believe, that the celebrated Demetrius Phalereus wrote a hiſtory of the JEWS! The firſt paſſage above cited, if taken from Demetrius, ſeems to contain a refutation of this opinion; for the time is there computed from the captivity of the ten tribes, to the FOURTH Ptolemy ||, or Ptolemy Philopator, who did not begin his reign till the year before Chriſt 222, a long time after the death of Demetrius Phalereus §.

It

* Demetrius apud Clem. Alex. Strom. l. i. § 21. p. 403.
† Id. apud Euſeb. Præp. Evang. l. ix. c. 21. p. 425.
‡ Clem. Alex. Strom. l. i. § 21. p. 407, 408. Vid. African. apud Euſeb. Chron. p. 47.
|| Αφ' ου δε αι φυλαι αι δεκα εκ Σαμαρειας αιχμαλωτοι γεγονασιν, εως Πτολεμαιου τεταρτου, ετη πεντακοσια εβδομηκοντα τρια, μηνας εννεα. Ex quo autem decem tribus abductæ fuerunt captivæ ex Samariâ, uſque ad Ptolemæum quartum, anni DLXXIII, novem menſes. Clem. Alex. Strom. l. i. § 21. p. 403.
§ In order to remove this objection, the author tranſlates εως Πτολεμαιου τεταρτου, εως πεντακοσια εβδομηκοντα τρια, not as the words are

It has been obferved, that Jofephus * fpeaks of Demetrius Phalereus, as a writer of the Jewifh hiftory.

Huetius thinks, that Jofephus, in this cafe, has confounded Demetrius Phalereus, with Demetrius Judæus, who wrote an account of the Jewifh kings †.

Jonfius fuppofes, that in the paffage, where Demetrius is mentioned by Jofephus, the word *Phalereus* has been inferted by fome officious interpreter; or that there was a younger writer called Demetrius Phalereus ‡.

But

are ufually rendered, ufque ad Ptolemæum quartum; but, ufque ad Ptolemæi quartum annum, anni DLXXIII.

If, fays he, Demetrius had meant the *fourth* Ptolemy, he would have expreffed himfelf thus: ἕως Πτολεμαιου ΤΟΥ τεταρτου.—But this is by no means a confequence. On fimilar occafions, the numeral adjective is ufed by various authors, without the prepofitive article. Thus Joannes Malala: ιβασιλευσε τριτος Πτολεμαιος—ιβασιλευσι τεταρτος Πτολεμαιος—δωδεκατος δε Πτολεμαιος, &c. Malalæ Chronog. l. viii. p. 250.—Και γαρ τριτος Πτολεμαιος. Jof. cont. Ap. l. ii. § 5.

* Cont. Ap. l. i. § 23. See alfo Clem. Alex. Strom. l. i. § 21. p. 404.

† Huet. Demonft. Evang. prop. iv. c. 2. § 20.

‡ Demetrium quendam de Judæorum regibus fcripfiffe credo Clementi. Phalereum ejus libri auctorem effe Jofepho non credo; fed gloffematis loco habendam effe vocem *Phalereus* adferere malim; vel junior fuerit Demetrius Phalereus, et à priore diverfus. Jonfius, de Script. Hift. Phil. l. i. c. 18. § 4.

Jerom fpeaks of this Demetrius as a Jew. Clemens Alexandrinus, he fays, DE JUDÆIS Ariftobulum quendam, et Demetrium, et Eupolemum, fcriptores ADVERSUS GENTES refert, qui in fimilitudinem Jofephi Αρχαιογονιας Moyfis & Judaicæ gentis affeverant. De Script. Eccl. tom. i. p. 281.

This Demetrius, fays Prideaux, was an hiftorian, that wrote in Greek, and an inhabitant of Alexandria, where he compiled a hiftory of the Jews, and continued it down to the reign of the fourth Ptolemy, who was Ptolemy Philopator, the grandfon of Philadelphus,

THE PARIAN CHRONICLE.

But I can scarce think, that *Phalereus* is an interpolation; because Tertullian and Eusebius, who have quoted Josephus, call the Jewish historian Demetrius Phalereus *.

I rather believe, there was some counterfeit history of the Jews, in circulation, under the name of this eminent philosopher.

Fabricius is of this opinion: Demetrium intelligo Judæum quendam, qui scripserat librum de Regibus Judæorum, sub nomine fortassis Demetrii Phalerei †.

It is allowed on all hands, that Demetrius Phalereus, some time after he was driven out of Athens by the prevailing power of Demetrius Poliorcetes, retired into Egypt, and was honourably received by Ptolemy Soter. This is mentioned by Cicero, Diodorus Siculus, Ælian, Diogenes Laertius, Plutarch, Suidas, and other ancient writers ‡.

But none of these writers give us the least intimation

---

phus. His having written so agreeably to the scripture, seems to prove him to have been a Jew. Connect. vol. iii. p. 66.

Fabricius enumerates above a hundred Demetrii. Bibl. Græc. vol. x. p. 390.

* Tertull. Apoll. § 19. Euseb. Præp. Evang. l. ix. c. 42.
† Fabric. Bibl. Græc. vol. iii. p. 117.
‡ Phalereus Demetrius cum patriâ pulsus esset injuriâ, ad Ptolemæum se regem Alexandriam contulit. Cic. de Fin. l. v. c. 19.

Φυγων προς Πτολεμαιον εις Αιγυπτον, ad Ptolemæum in Ægyptum perfugit. Diod. Sic. l. xx. p. 782.

Εν Αιγυπτῳ δε, συνων τῳ Πτολεμαιῳ, νομοθεσιας ηρξε. In Ægypto apud Ptolemæum scribendis legibus præfuit. Ælian. Var. Hist. l. iii. c. 17.

Diog. Laert. l. v. § 78.

Πρωτος των Πτολεμαιου φιλων, amicorum Ptolemæi omnium primus. Plut. de Exil. p. 601.

Παρα τῳ Σατηρι Πτολεμαιῳ διατριβων, apud Ptolemæum Soterem degens. Suidas.

Strab. l. ix. p. 610.

of his continuing in favour with Ptolemy Philadelphus. On the contrary, Diogenes Laertius, on the authority of Hermippus, informs us, that Demetrius had given great offence to Philadelphus, by endeavouring to perfuade Ptolemy Soter to leave his dominions to Ceraunus *, his elder fon, by a former marriage; that Philadelphus, after the death of his father, ordered him to be taken into cuftody, and confined, till he had determined, in what manner he fhould treat him; and that, in the mean time, he was killed by the bite of an afp †. This was probably foon after he was apprehended, as his confinement was only a temporary expedient ‡.

Hermippus adds, that " Demetrius was buried near Diofpolis," a city of Egypt, in the Delta, not far from

---

* Ceraunus was Ptolemy's eldeft fon, by Eurydice the daughter of Antipater. Appian. de Bell. Syr. p. 128. al. 207. Ptolemy Philadelphus was a younger fon, by his fecond wife, Berenice.

† Και πως υπνωττων, υπ' ασπιδος την χειρα δηχθεις, τον βιον μετεθηκε. Ac forte dormitans, ab afpide manum morfus, ex vitâ migravit. Diog. Laert. l. v. § 78. edit. Meibomii. Cicero feems to intimate, that the death of Demetrius was not accidental: Afpide ad corpus admotâ, vitâ effe privatum. Orat. pro Rab. Pofth.

The excellent Corfini fuppofes, that his death was voluntary: animi ægritudine perculfus, afpidis morfu fibi mortem confcivit. Faft. Attic. tom. iv. p. 80.

Simfon, in his Chronicon, explains the words of Diogenes Laertius above-cited in a manner, fomething different from the generality of commentators; and his learned editor Wefselingius acquiefces in his interpretation: Afpidis morfum, fine dolore letiferum effe aiunt. Itaque Ælianus de Animal. l. ix. c. 11. fcripfit, τον [θανατον] εκ του δηγματος της ασπιδος, πραϋν τινα και αβληχρον, " lenem & imbecillem mortem effe, quæ afpidis morfu afferretur." Talis igitur Demetrii mors innuitur fuiffe, qui dormitanti fimilis (ὑπνωττων πως) vitâ exceffiffe dicitur. Simfonii Chron. fub an. 3721. edit. Wefseling. 1729.

‡ Petavius, Corfini, &c. place the death of Demetrius in the firft year of the CXXIV Olympiad, bef. Chr. 284. Ration. Temp. l. iii. c. 18. Corfin. loc. cit.

THE PARIAN CHRONICLE. 137

the Mendefian channel of the Nile. From which, I think, we may infer, that he had been banifhed from the court of Ptolemy Philadelphus.

The teftimony of Hermippus is of great weight in this inftance, as he was an accurate hiftorian, and lived about the time of Ptolemy Philopator *; and therefore could fcarcely be at a lofs for authentic information, relative to one of the moft illuftrious men of his age.

It muft be acknowledged, that Arifteas, Ariftobulus, Philo, Jofephus, Clemens Alexandrinus, Tertullian, Cyril of Jerufalem, Epiphanius, and others †, have afferted, that Demetrius was greatly refpected by Ptolemy Philadelphus, and principally concerned in obtaining the tranflation of the Bible, commonly called the Septuagint.

---

* Hermippus was of Smyrna. Athenæus calls him Καλλιμαχειος, from which it is fuppofed he was one of the difciples of Callimachus. Deipnof. l. ii. p. 58. l. v. p. 213. He wrote many books, and particularly the lives of eminent men, which are frequently cited by Diogenes Laertius, under the title of Βιος. D. Laert. l. i. § 33. l. ii. § 13. l. v. § 2. He flourifhed about the year bef. Chr. 220. Vid. Voff. de Hift. Græc. l. i. c. 16. Jonf. de Scrip. Hift. Phil. l. ii. c. 9. § 4. Dodwell. de Cyclis, differt. iii. § 12.

Dionyfius Halicarnaffeus, Jofephus, and other ancient writers, fpeak of him with applaufe.

Ἑρμιππος ακριβης ἐν τοις αλλοις γενομενος. Dionyf. Halic. de Ifæo, p. 104.

Ανηρ περι πασαν ιςοριαν επιμελης, vir circa omnem hiftoriam diligens indagator. Jof. cont. Apion. l. i. § 22.

† Arifteæ Hiftoria LXXII Interpretum. Oxon. 1692. Ariftob. apud Eufeb. Præp. Evang. l. xiii. c. 12.—Ariftobulus is fuppofed to have lived about 125 years before Chrift. Prid. Connect. vol. ii. p. 41. Philo de Vitâ Mofis, l. ii. Jof. Antiq. l. xii. c. 2. Clem. Alex. Strom. l. i. § 22. p. 410. Tertul. Apol. § 18. Cyril. Hierofol. Catech. iv. c. 34. Epiph. de Menf. & Pond. c. 9.

The book, which is transmitted down to us under the name of Aristeas, is apparently the foundation of all that has been said, concerning the manner of making this version by seventy-two elders, sent from Jerusalem to Alexandria for that purpose. The ecclesiastical writers adopted his narration with implicit credulity (as it seemed to do honour to the Scriptures) and embellished it with the story of the seventy-two cells *, the wonderful agreement of the interpreters, their prophetical inspiration †, and other circumstances, equally absurd and incredible ‡. But the most judicious writers reject it as a fiction, contrived by some Hellenistic Jew, in order to give a sanction to the Greek translation of the scriptures, and advance the glory of his own nation ‖.

"Demetrius Phalereus," as Plutarch relates, "advised king Ptolemy to collect and read such books, as treated of the government of states and kingdoms; for," says he, "they contain that salutary counsel, which friends never venture to give their sovereigns §."

The author of the Dissertation contends, that these words cannot be referred to Ptolemy Soter, an aged and learned prince; that it is evident they were addressed to

---

* Just. Mart. Cohort. ad Græc. p. 13. Epiph. de Menf. & Pond. c. 3.

† Philo. loc. cit.

‡ Nescio quis primus auctor, septuaginta cellulas Alexandriæ mendacio suo extruxerit, quibus divisi eadem scriptitarint. Hieron. in Pentat. præf. tom. iii. p. 14.

Quæ pridem à Ludovico Vive, Josepho Scaligero, aliisque magnis nominibus explosa ; à Pseudo-Aristæa, Judæo-Hellenistâ, ad conciliandam versioni isti auctoritatem conficta ; à veteribus credulâ nimis, ut solent, mente suscepta, avidius autem à Latinis et recentioribus defensa. Spanhemii Introd. ad Hist. p. 157.

‖ Vid. Hodii de Bibl. Text. Orig. l. i.

§ Plut. in Apophtheg. Regum, p. 189.

Philadelphus,

THE PARIAN CHRONICLE. 139

Philadelphus, who confidered Demetrius, not only as his preceptor, but as his parent.

In anfwer to this objection I muft obferve, that if Demetrius went into Egypt in the year before Chrift 308 *, as Eufebius fays he did, he might very properly give Ptolemy Soter this advice; for Ptolemy did not affume the title of king, till the year 305 †, and moft probably had not then begun to form his library.

If, as I rather think, he retired into Egypt on the death of Caffander ‡, in 298, he was there in the feventh year of Ptolemy Soter; and as he lived with that prince above 13 years, in the character of his legiflator, his counfellor, and his friend, he might give this advice without any kind of impropriety, either to the father or the fon, and yet afterwards incur the difpleafure of the latter, as Hermippus relates.

Our author, in conformity to his hypothefis, which makes Demetrius Phalereus the writer of the Parian Chronicle, maintains, that this learned Athenian was living in the cxxix Olympiad, when the Chronicle is fuppofed to have been compiled.

Let us confider the probability of this opinion in a chronological view. Demetrius was appointed governor of Athens in the year 318, and, for the fpace of ten years, difcharged that important office with fo much

---

* Fuga Demetrii in Ægyptum incidit in Olymp. cxviii. 2. i. e. bef. Chr. 307. Bruckeri Hift. Crit. Phil. vol. i. p. 857. Petavius and Corfinus place it in the fame year. Rat. Temp. l. iii. c. 18. Fafti Attici, vol. iv. p. 67.

† In this reign Ptolemy the aftronomer places the beginning of the reign of Ptolemy Soter.

‡ Μετα την Κασσανδρου τελευτην, ηναγκασθη φυγειν ας Αιγυπτον, Caffandro mortuo, fugere in Ægyptum fuerit coactus. Strab. l. ix. p. 610. In this article, Strabo corroborates the teftimony of Hermippus.

T 2   probity

probity and wisdom *, that three hundred and sixty statues were erected to his honour †. Athens was at that time in a situation, which required the most consummate policy and prudence in a governor. We may therefore presume, that his abilities were well known, and that he was 35 or 40 years of age, when he was elected ‡. If he was, it is highly improbable he should compose the Chronicle fifty-four years afterwards.

Plutarch dates the authority of Demetrius in the government of Athens, from the time of the Lamian war ‖, between the Athenians and Antipater, in the second year of the CXIV Olympiad, bef. Chr. 323 years. This makes an interval of fifty-nine years, between his appearing at Athens in a public character, and the date of the Parian inscription.

This argument may be still farther confirmed by the testimony of Athenæus. " Ctesicles," says that writer, " in the third book of his Chronica, asserts, that in the cx Olympiad, Demetrius Phalereus enumerated the inhabitants of Attica, and found that there were 21,000 Athenians, 10,000 sojourners or foreigners, and 400,000 slaves §." This was 337 years before the Christian

* Fuit enim hic vir non solùm eruditissimus, sed etiam civis è republicâ maximè, tuendæque civitatis peritissimus. Cic. de Leg. l. ii. sub fin. Αθηνησιν επιφανεϛατα επολιτευσατο, Athenis summâ cum gloriâ rempublicam rexit. Ælian. Var. Hist. l. iii. c. 17.

† Diog. Laert. l. v. § 75.

‡ Ἡρεθη, electus est. Diod. Sic. l. xviii. p. 647. Olymp. cxv. 3. bef. Chr. 318.

‖ Plut. in v. Demet. p. 893. Diod. Sic. l. xviii. p. 596.

§ Κτησικλης δε εν τριτη Χρονικων, τη δεκατη, προς ταις εκατον φησιν Ολυμπιαδι, κ, τ. λ. Athen. l. vi. p. 272. There is probably an error in the text of Athenæus; but, till we have authority to correct it, we must take it as it stands. Demetrius might be in some public station, and make this computation several years before he was appointed governor by Cassander.

THE PARIAN CHRONICLE.

æra, and 73 years before the date of the Chronicle. According to this account, it is utterly incredible, that Demetrius should be any ways concerned in that performance.

The presumptive evidence against our author's opinion, which arises from the SILENCE of all the writers of antiquity, with respect to the Parian Chronicle, is, in this instance, remarkably strong, if not decisive. Demetrius Phalereus was not a writer of an inferior class, or an obscure rhetorician; but an author of the highest distinction, whose name and character would have given so much authority to the inscription, that it must have excited the attention of succeeding historians, biographers, or chronologists. But as not one of them has either cited or mentioned it, we can never suppose, that it was the production of this illustrious philosopher and legislator.

" Cùm nusquam occurrit mentio libri," says Le Clerc, " nomine philosophi insigniti, falsa sit inscriptio, aut minimùm suspecta fiat necesse est; quia credibile non est, librum, insignis præsertim philosophi, potuisse non modò fugere diligentiam Diogenis Laertii, sed etiam ita sperni, ut nusquam citaretur ab iis, qui frequenter de eo philosopho verba fecerunt, nec raro aliorum ejus operum meminerunt *."

* Clerici Art. Crit. p. iii. sect. 2. c. 3. vol. ii. p. 337.

CHAP. XI.

THIRDLY, it may be objected, that the works of some eminent writers of antiquity, such as Phædrus, Q. Curtius, &c. lay in obscurity for many centuries, and were not discovered till later ages.

To obviate this objection, it will be necessary to consider the peculiar circumstances of these authors.

1. Phædrus is said to have been the freedman of Augustus, or Tiberius. Saxius places him in the reign of Claudius, 48 years after the Christian æra*. His fables were first published by Pet. Pithœus, in 1596.

Martial certainly means this fabulist, when he asks, if Canius Rufus, a poet of Gades,

        Æmulatur IMPROBI JOCOS Phædri †.

IMPROBUS plainly alludes to the satire, which Phædrus conceals under the actions or the dialogues of birds and beasts. Accordingly, Rigaltius, Gudius, and others, suppose, that the HYDRUS, in the second fable, represents Caligula.

The word *jocos* evidently points out the fabulist. Æsop's fables are called by Aristophanes, Hesychius, and others, γελοια, joci ‡.

The same expression is used by Avienus, when he says, the fables of Æsop, " sub *jocorum* communium

---

* Sax. Onomast. vol. i. p. 241.

† Mart. l. iii. ep. 20. Vid. l. i. 62. iii. 64.—Martial wrote about the year 94.

‡ —— Αισωπου τι γελοιον. Aristoph. Vesp. v. 564.——Αισωπειων γελοιων. Ibid. v. 1251.——Αισωπου γελοια. Hesych. Dion. Chrys. Orat. 82. p. 631.

THE PARIAN CHRONICLE. 143

fpecie, vitæ argumenta contineant;" and by Phædrus himfelf, when he fpeaks of his own productions:

> Fictis *jocari* nos meminerit fabulis.—
> Calumniámque fictis clufit *jocis* *.

We do not find, that Phædrus is mentioned by any other writer, till we come to Avienus, who is fuppofed to have lived about the year 410. This fabulift, in his dedication to Theodofius [Macrobius] exprefsly mentions the five books of Phædrus: " Phædrus etiam partem aliquam quinque in libellos refolvit."

But Seneca, it is obferved, has given fome intimation, that there were no fables in the Roman language in his time; for he thus writes to Polybius: " Non audeo te ufque eo producere, ut fabellas quoque, et Æfopeos logos †, intentatum Romanis ingeniis opus, folitâ tibi venuftate connectas ‡."

In order to account for this obfervation, fome have imagined, that Phædrus's work was in few hands, and unknown to Seneca; or that he did not think of it, when he was writing to Polybius ||. Pithœus, Lipfius, and Voffius, fuppofe, that Phædrus is not mentioned in this paffage, becaufe he was not a Roman, but a Thracian. Vavaffor conceives, that his fables were fupprefled, or not noticed, becaufe the fatirical allufions

---

* Phæd. Prol. v. 7. Id. ad Eutychum, l. iii. 37. l. iv. 6. 2.
† Æfopei logi, i. e. apologi, fabulæ.
Æfop is called by Diogenes Laertius, ὁ λογοποιος, fabularum fcriptor. Lib. i. § 72. Λογων Αισωπειων συναγωγαι, fabularum Æfopiarum collectiones, are mentioned by the fame author, among the works of Demetrius Phalereus. In the edition of Meibomius, 1692, the word λογων is improperly tranflated *orationum*, inftead of *fabularum*. Lib. v. § 80.
‡ Sen. Confol. ad Polyb. c. 27.
|| Fabric. Bibl. Lat. l. ii. c. 3. vol. i. p. 373.

they

they contain were obnoxious to the tyrants of thofe days *.

Fabricius, from the words *connectas* and *refolverit*, c. 30. infers, that Seneca could not properly mention Phædrus, as he was not then fpeaking of Æfopic fables in verfe, but of fimilar compofitions in profe †.

Upon thefe grounds learned writers have contended, that the fables of Phædrus might have been extant in the time of Seneca, notwithftanding the preceding remark.

It is acknowledged, that they are not mentioned by any writer, except Martial, before Avienus, in the fifth century.

In this cafe, we can only fuppofe, that the general filence of the ancients might have been owing to feveral caufes, or concurring circumftances; fuch as, the character of Phædrus, as a freedman, a minor poet, a copyer of Æfop, and the author of compofitions, which no hiftorian could have any occafion to cite; or probably to fome contingencies, which I fhall confider in the next article.

II. It is alleged, that the hiftory of Alexander the Great, by Q. Curtius, is neither quoted, nor mentioned by any of the ancients.

Who Q. Curtius was, and when he lived, are points, which cannot be determined with any certainty. Tacitus and the younger Pliny fpeak of one Curtius Rufus, who was proconful of Africa, in the reign of Ti-

---

* Vavaffor de Ludicrâ Dictione. p. 208. edit. 1658. Morhof. de Patav. Liviana. c. 12. p. 158.

† Fabric. Bibl. Lat. loc. cit. Id. Bibl. Græc. l. ii. c. 9. § 12. But fee the ufe of the word *refolvit*, in the paffage above cited from Avienus.

berius

berius *, about the year 37. And as Tacitus obferves, that he lived to "a very advanced age †," Voffius imagines he might be alive, and write, or finifh, his hiftory in the reign of Vefpafian: that is, in or after the year 69; for there are many paffages in it, which, he thinks, evidently allude to that period ‡.

One Q. Curtius Rufus is mentioned by Suetonius, in his catalogue of the celebrated rhetoricians; and he is fuppofed by Cafaubon, Voffius, Perizonius, Fabricius, and others, to have been the author of the hiftory in queftion.

Pliny, in an epiftle to Saturninus, applauds one of his friends, whofe name was Rufus, and fays, Legi librum omnibus numeris abfolutum, "I have read his book, which is highly finifhed ∥." But there is no circumftance in this epiftle, which can lead us to infer, with any certainty, that Pliny alludes to the Hiftory of Alexander.

It has been obferved, that Quintilian, who wrote about the year 88, and mentions the moft confiderable hiftorians §, takes no notice of Q. Curtius; and from this, and other circumftances, fome have inferred, that the Hiftory of Alexander, which is now extant under the name of Q. Curtius, is a modern compofition. But this inference is arbitrary and illogical. Quintilian does not attempt to mention all the eminent hiftorians THEN extant. He takes not the leaft notice of A. Hirtius, Cornelius Nepos, Trogus Pompeius, and many others.

* Tacit. Annal. l. xi. c. 20, 21. Plin. Epift. l. vii. c. 27.
† Longâ poft hæc feneêtâ. Tacit. loc. citat.
‡ Voff. de Hift. Lat. l. iv. c. 28. p. 146. Saxii Onomafticon, p. 258.
∥ Plin. l. ix. 38.
§ Quint. l. x. c. 1.

Montfaucon

Montfaucon asserts, that there was a manuscript copy of Q. Curtius in M. Colbert's library at Paris, above 800 years old [*]. Fabricius observes, that this historian is quoted by Petrus Blæsensis, who wrote about the year 1150; by Johannes Sarisburiensis about the year 1170; and by Vincentius Bellovacensis in the year 1244 [†].

Antonius Panormita tells us, that Alphonsus, king of Arragon, who began his reign in 1252, was cured of an obstinate indisposition by the delight he took in reading the history of Alexander, and used to rally his medical attendants by declaring, that Curtius was a much better physician than Avicenna [‡].

These testimonies, taken from writers of the twelfth and 13th centuries, are proofs, that the History of Alexander, ascribed to Q. Curtius, is not a modern composition.

Admitting then, that this history was written in the first century, and that it lay in obscurity for above a thousand years, we may account for the silence of the ancients on the following suppositions.

Let us only conceive, that the first part [||] of this work was destroyed by some accident in the author's life-time, or after his death, before a second copy of it was taken, such a disaster might prevent its publication at first, and afterwards impede its general circulation.

---

[*] Montf. Palæog. Græc. præf. p. ii.
[†] Fabric. Bibl. Lat. l. ii. c. 17. § 1.
[‡] Frequenter in medicos rex jocatus, Avicennam, velut parabolanum, parvi facere, Curtium laudibus cumulare. Ant. Panormita de Dictis & Factis Alphonsi regis Aragonum. l. i. p. 14, 15. edit. 1538.
[||] The two first books are entirely lost; and there are four other deficiencies; namely, book v. ch. 13. b. vi. ch. 1. b. x. ch. 1. and 4, which Freinshemius and others have endeavoured to supply. ——— The first edition of Q. Curtius was printed in 1474.

THE PARIAN CHRONICLE. 147

The manuscript, it is possible, might fall, as Aristotle's books did, into the hands of ανθρωποι ιδιωται, illiterate men*, or some βιβλιοταφος, some CURIOUS COLLECTOR

---

* Aristotle left his books to Theophrastus, who was his successor in the Lyceum. Theophrastus "bequeathed them to Neleus." [Diog. Laert. in v. Theoph. l. v. § 52.] who carried them to Scepsis. The heirs of Neleus were ιδιωται ανθρωποι, men of no learning, and kept them locked up. When they heard, that the king of Pergamus was collecting books for his library, they hid them in a hole under ground, where they were much damaged by the damp and worms. A long time afterwards they were sold to Apellico, a rich citizen of Athens, who was a lover of books, but no philosopher. Apellico caused them to be transcribed, and the deficiencies supplied; but this was done without either accuracy or judgement. After his death, 86 years before the Christian æra, Sylla took the city of Athens, and removed this library to Rome, where Tyrannio the grammarian had the use of Aristotle's works. Andronicus Rhodius received a copy of them from Tyrannio; and having corrected, and ranged them in order, presented them to the public. Strab. l. xiii. p. 906. Plut. in v. Syllæ, p. 468.

Athenæus reports, that all Aristotle's books, τα τουτων βιβλια παντα [legendum forté τουτου] were bought of Neleus by Ptolemy Philadelphus. Deipnos. l. i. p. 3. Yet, in another place, he says, his library was bought by Apellico, l. v. p. 214. These seeming contradictions may perhaps be reconciled by supposing, that Ptolemy bought only copies of his writings.

Neleus was the disciple of Aristotle and Theophrastus. Aristotle died bef. Chr. 322 years; Theophrastus about 286; and Ptolemy Philadelphus came to the crown about two years afterwards. If this prince had any negociation with Neleus, it must have been in the former part of his reign. However, it is very probable, that either Athenæus, or some of his editors, have made a mistake in the passage, where Philadelphus is said to have bought all Aristotle's books of Neleus.

The disasters abovementioned have occasioned innumerable omissions, disarrangements, perplexities, and difficulties, in almost all the productions of Aristotle, and opened a wide field for the combats of his followers and commentators, which, in about three centuries after Albertus Magnus, that is, between the year 1260 and 1560,

LECTOR of books, who might keep it in durance for half a century, and then bequeath it to a succeffor like himfelf. Thefe contingencies will account for the filence of Quintilian and his contemporaries.

There are various other reafons, why a manufcript may be with-held from public view, or confined to a few private hands; and thefe reafons have fo far operated, that many valuable writings have been fuffered to moulder in oblivion for feveral ages.

Diogenes Laertius informs us, that the works of Thucydides, which the author left unfinifhed, lay in obfcurity, till they were brought to light by Xenophon *.

But the cafe of the Parian Chronicle is widely different. It was neither left unfinifhed, nor was it written on paper, or parchment, and, in that condition, liable to be concealed in a bookcafe or a cheft; but it was OSTENTATIOUSLY ENGRAVED ON MARBLE.

We may therefore ftill affert, that, in this cafe, the filence of the ancients is unaccountable.

Before I conclude this chapter, I muft obferve, that a circumftance, on which the preceding objection entirely depends, is rather taken for granted than proved, which is, the authenticity of the works, afcribed to Phædrus and Q. Curtius †. If they are the productions of later ages, which indeed I do not fuppofe, the objection is at once fuperfeded.

1560, amounted to 12,000 authors. Patricii Difcuff. Peripat. l. x. p. 145.

* Diog. Laert. in v. Xenoph. l. ii. § 57.

† A collection of epiftles, in five books, was publifhed in 1500, under the name of one Q. Curtius; but they are ftupid forgeries. Fabricius has condefcended to reprint them, in his Bibliotheca Latina, vol. i. p. 644. edit. 1728.

CHAP.

THE PARIAN CHRONICLE. 149

CHAP. XII.

VI. SOME of the facts, mentioned in the Chronicle, seem to have been taken from writers of a later date.

In the following passages there is an APPEARANCE of imitation; or a stronger resemblance, than such as may be supposed to arise from accident.

PASSAGES in the PARIAN CHRONICLE.	PARALLEL PASSAGES in GREEK AUTHORS.
Epoc. 1. Αφ ου Κεκροψ Αθηνων εβασιλευσε, και η χωρα Κεκροπια εκληθη, το προτερον καλουμενη Ακτικη απο Ακταιου του αυτοχθονος. A quo Cecrops Athenis regnavit, et regio Cecropia dicta est, quæ prius dicebatur Actica ab Actæo indigenâ.	Κεκροψ της Αττικης εβασιλευσε πρωτος, και την γην, προτερον λεγομενην Ακτην, αφ' εαυτου Κεκροπιαν ωνομασεν. Cecrops in terrâ Atticâ primus regnavit, et quæ prius Acta dicebatur, de suo ipsius vocabulo Cecropiam dici voluit. Apollod. l. iii. c. 13. § 1. edit. Gal. 1675. c. 14. edit. Heyn. 1782. Απ' αυτου δε Κεκροπια η χωρα εκληθη. Syncell. p. 153. Euseb. Chron. p. 28.
Epoc. 2. Αφ ου Δευκαλιων παρα τον Παρνασσον εν Λυκωρεια εβασιλευσε. A quo Deucalion apud Parnassum in Lycoriâ regnavit.	Δευκαλιων βασιλευειν των κατα Παρνασσον ηρξατο. Deucalion iis qui ad Parnassum imperitare cœpit. Euseb. Chron. Græc. p. 28. 109.

Epoc.

Epoc. 3. Αφ ου δικη Αθηνησι[ν εγε]νετο Αρει και Ποσειδωνι υπερ Αλιρροθιου του Ποσειδωνος· και ο τοπος εκληθη Αρειος Παγος. A quo lis Athenis intercessit Marti et Neptuno super Halirrhothio, Neptuni filio, et locus dictus est Arius Pagus.

Ἁλιρρόθιος ὁ Ποσειδῶνος ὑπο Αρεος φωραθεις κτεινεται· Ποσειδων δε εν Αρειω Παγω κρινεται, δικαζοντων των δωδεκα θεων, Αρει, και [ουτος] απολυεται *. Halirrothius, Neptuni f. à Marte deprehensus occiditur. Quamobrem Neptunus Martem in Areopago cædis reum agit. Is duodecim deorum sententiâ judicatus absolvitur. Apollod. l. iii. c. 13. § 2. edit. 1675. c. 14. edit. 1782. Αρειος Παγος εκληθη. Syncell. p. 153. Euseb. Chron. p. 110.

Epoc. 4. Αφ ου κατακλυσμως επι Δευκαλιωνος εγενετο, και Δευκαλιων τους ομβρους εφυγεν εγ Λυκωρειας εις Αθηνας προ[ς Κρανα]ον . . . και τα σωτηρια εθυσεν. A quo diluvium, tempore Deucalionis evenit; et Deucalion imbres fugit è Lycoriâ, Athenas ad Cranaüm, et sacra pro salute fecit.

Εφ' ου τον επι Δευκαλιωνος λεγεται κατακλυσμον γενεσθαι . . . τω Παρνασσω προσισχει, κακει των ομβρων παυλαν λαβοντων, εκβας εθυσε Διί Φυξιω. Sub quo [Cranao] Deucalionis diluvium fuisse narratur . . . . Parnassum demum appellit, ibíque cùm imbres desiissent, egressus, Jovi Phyxio sacris opera-

---

* Scaliger, having observed, that this passage is corrupt and imperfect, says, the author means: Ποσειδωνος δε εισαγοντος, εν Αρειω Παγω κρινεται, δικαζοντων των δωδεκα θεων, Αρης, και απολυεται. Scal. in Euseb. Chron. p. 31. Gale gives the text, as it is here cited, and subjoins this remark: Græci sic loquuntur, κριεται Αρει, disceptat cum Marte. Not. in loc.

tur. Apollod. l. iii. c. 13.
§ 5. c. 14. edit. 1782. Id.
l. i. c. 7. § 2.

This account of Deucalion, in the Parian Chronicle, is not confiftent with what we find in fome of the principal writers of antiquity.

Herodotus, Apollodorus, Conon, Strabo, Ovid, Juftin, Eufebius, and others, affirm, that at the time of the deluge, Deucalion reigned in Theffaly *.

Apollodorus relates, that the mountains of Theffaly were divided or torn afunder by the flood †; and that Deucalion, after being carried along nine days and nights upon the water, landed at laft on Parnaffus, and THERE offered facrifices to Jupiter Phyxius.

There are fome improbabilities attending the ftory, as it is told in the Chronicle. 1. The deluge is fuppofed to have happened 45 years after Deucalion began his reign in Lycoria. 2. Lycoria, according to Paufanias, was a city, built on the TOP of Parnaffus, by thofe, who had efcaped the deluge; and confequently could not exift 45 years before that event. 3. It is fcarcely probable, that Deucalion would leave the top of Parnaffus, or Lycoria, where he is faid to have been long fettled, and go to another country, on this occafion, either for fafety, or for the purpofe of offering a facrifice to Jupiter for his prefervation. Laftly, if there had

---

* Herod. l. i. c. 56. Apollod. l. i. c. 7. § 2. Conon, Narrat. 27. Strab. l. ix. p. 660. Ovid. Metam. l. i. v. 317. Juft. l. ii. c. 6. Eufeb. Chron. Græc. p. 110. Hellanicus apud Schol. in Apoll. Rhod. l. iii. v. 1085.

† Τα ορη διεςη, montes dirempti funt diluvio, receffere. Thefe words are improperly rendered by Ægius Spoletinus, Gale, &c. montes aquarum diluvio immanes fuere. Vid. Herod. l. vii. c. 129. Strab. l. ix. p. 658. Sen. Nat. Quæft. vi. 25.

been

been any authority for saying, that Deucalion went to Athens, and there made his offering, and built a temple to Jupiter, it is hardly probable, that these two circumstances, so much to the honour of that city, would have been totally omitted by Apollodorus, an Athenian writer.

We are told indeed by Pausanias *, that Deucalion lived for some time at Athens, and there built a temple to Jupiter Olympius, and had a sepulchre near the temple. But Pausanias only gives us the story of his building a temple, as an uncertain tradition, λεγουσι †; and Dionysius Halicarnasseus observes, that sepulchral monuments were frequently erected to eminent men, in places, where they were not buried ‡. This objection is entirely removed, if, as Meursius asserts, the temple at Athens, ascribed to Deucalion by Pausanias and Strabo ‖, was not built by Deucalion king of Thessaly, but by Deucalion, the son of Minos, king of Crete §.

Ερος. 6. Αφ ου Ελλην ο Δευκ[αλιωνος Φθι]ωτιδος εβασιλευσε, και Ελληνες [ων]ομασθησαν το προτερον Γραικοι καλουμενοι, και τον αγωνα πανα-θ[η]ναι[κον συνεςησαντο.] A

Αυτος μεν ουν ['Ελλην] αφ' αύτου τους καλουμενους Γραικους προσηγορευσεν 'Ελληνας... Εριχθονιος των Παναθηναιων την εορτην συνεςησατο. Is quidem de se Hellenas, qui

* Paus. l. x. c. 6.
† Id. l. i. c. 18.
‡ Dionys. Halic. l. i. p. 43.
‖ Strab. l. ix. p. 651.
§ Meursius, having quoted the words of Pausanias, adds, "De hoc Deucalione, Minois filio, locus iste capiendus, non de illo altero, Prometheo nato; sub quo celeberrimum id diluvium accidisse fertur. Quin ætatem illic porro omnem egit; cùmque diem obiisset, prope extructum à se templum est sepultus. Meurs. Creta, l. iii. c. 5. p. 157.

THE PARIAN CHRONICLE. 153

quo Hellen Deucalionis f. in Phthiotide regnavit, & Hellenes appellati funt, qui prius Græci dicebantur, et certamen Panatheniacum inftituerunt *.

poftea † Græci vocati funt, nominavit. . . . Erichthonius Panathenæorum celebritatem inftituit. Apollod. l. i. c. 7. § 2. § 3. edit. 1782. l. iii. c. 13. § 6. c. 14. edit. 1782.

Epoc. 28. Αφ ου Νη-[λ]ευς ωκισ[εν εγ Καρια Μιλητον, αγειρας Ιωνας, οι ωκισ]αν Εφεσον, Ερυθρας, Κλαζομενας, [Πριηνην, και Λεβεδον, Τεω] Κολοφωνα, [Μ]υουντα, [Φωκαιαν] Σαμον [Χιον, και] τα [Παν]ιωνι[α] εγενετο. A quo Neleus condidit *in Cariâ* Miletum, congregatis Ionibus, qui condiderunt Ephefum, Erythras, Clazomenas, *Prienen, et Lebedum, Teon,* Colophonem, Myuntem, *Phoceam,* Samum, *Chium, P*anionia inftituta fuere.

Νηλευς δε εις την Ιωνιαν αφι · νετο, και πρωτον μεν ωκισε Μιλητον, Καρας εξελασας . . . αφ' ων αι δωδεκα πολεις εκληθησαν εν Ιωνια. Εισι δε αιδε· Μιλητος, Εφεσος, Ερυθραι, Κλαζομεναι, Πριηνη, Λεβεδος, Τεως, Κολοφων, Μυους, Φωκαια, Σαμος, και Χιος. Neleus autem pervenit in Ioniam, et primùm condidit Miletum, ejectis Caribus, ... à quibus duodecem Ioniæ civitates appellatæ funt. Sunt autem hæ: Miletus, Ephefus, Erythræ, Clazomenæ, Priena, Lebedus, Teus, Colophon, Myûs, Phocæa, Samus and Chius. Ælian.

---

* The Panathenæa are faid to have been firft inftituted by Erichthonius, fifteen years after the date of this epocha. See Epoc. x. and Apolled. loc. cit.

† Ægius Spoletinus and Dr. Gale infert the word *poftea*; but it is a miftake inftead of *antea* or *prius.* Οι καλουμενοι τοτε μεν Γραικοι, νυν δε Ελληνες, qui tunc appellabantur Græci, nunc autem Hellenes. Arift. Meteor. l. i. c. 14. Γραιοι and γραικοι may perhaps fignify *antiqui*, ancients, or old inhabitants.

A DISSERTATION ON

Var. Hift. l. viii. c. 5. edit. Gronov. 1731.

The names of fix, and, if the lacunæ are properly fupplied, the names of twelve cities, appear to have been engraved on the marble, exactly as we find them in Ælian's Various Hiftory. But there is not any imaginable reafon for this particular arrangement. It does not correfpond with the time of their foundation, with their fituation in Ionia, with their relative importance, or with the order, in which they are placed by other eminent hiftorians.

Thefe twelve cities are thus enumerated by Herodotus: Miletus, Myus, Priene, Ephefus, Colophon, Lebedus, Teos, Clazomenæ, Phocæa, Samos, Chios, Erythræ *.

By Strabo: Ephefus, Miletus, Myus, Lebedus, Colophon, Priene, Teus, Erythræ, Phocæa, Clazomenæ, Chius, Samus †.

By Paterculus: Ephefus, Miletus, Colophon, Priene, Lebedus, Myus, Erythræ, Clazomenæ, Phocæa, Samos, Chios, &c. ‡.

By Paufanias: Miletus, Ephefus, Myus, Priene, Colophon, Lebedus, Teus, Erythræ, Clazomenæ, Phocæa, Samus, Chius ‖.

By Suidas: Ephefus, Miletus, Myus, Priene, Colophon, Teos, Lebedus, Erythræ, Phocæa, Clazomenæ, Chios, Samos §.

Thefe cities are mentioned by fome other ancient

* Herod. l. i. c. 142.
† Strab. l. xiv. p. 938.
‡ V. Paterc. l. i. c. 4.
‖ Paufan. l. vii. c. 2—4.
§ Suidas in v. Iwna.—Suidas feems to have taken his lift from Strabo, or Paufanias, with fome little variation.

writers;

THE PARIAN CHRONICLE. 155

writers; but not by any of them in the order, in which they are enumerated by Ælian *, and the author of the Chronicle.

It is observable, that six names may be transposed 720 different ways; and that twelve names admit of 479,001,600 different transpositions. Supposing then, that there is no particular reason for one arrangement rather than another, it will follow, that the chance of two authors, placing them in the same order, is, in the former case, as 1 to 720; and, in the latter, as 1 to 479,001,600.

It is therefore utterly improbable, that these names would have been placed in this order on the marble, if the author of the inscription had not transcribed them from the historian.

Epoc. 38. [Αφ ου Αμ- φικτυονες ενικησαν ελ]οντες Κυρ- ραν, και ο αγων ο γυμνικος ετεθη χρηματιτης απο των λαφυρων, ετη ΗΗ[Η]ΔΔΠΙΙ, αρ- χοντος Αθηνησι Σιμω[ν]ος. Α quo Amphictyones vice- runt, captâ Cyrrhâ, et cer- tamen gymnicum editum fuit pecuniarium ex spo- liis, anni CCCXXVII, ar- chonte Athenis Simone.

Τον Πυθικον αγωνα διεθηκεν Ευρυλοχος ὁ Θεσσαλος, συν τοις Αμφικτυοσι, τους Χιρραίους καταπολεμησας . . . επι αρ- χοντος Αθηνησι Σιμωνος, και νι- κησας εθετο χρηματικον αγωνα. Pythicum certamen insti- tuit Eurylochus Thessalus, unâ cum Amphictyonibus, cum Cirrhæos debellasset... archonte Athenis Simone, victoriâque partâ chrema- titem agonem decrevit. Pind. Schol. arg. 4. in Pyth. p. 163. edit. Oxon. 1697.

Epoc. 39. Αφ ου [ο στε- Φ]ανιτης αγων παλιν ετεθη, ετη

Επι μεν Αθηνησιν αρχοντος Δαμασιου, ὑστερον και στρατη...

† Ælian wrote about the year aft. Chr. 225. Saxii Onom.

ΗΗΗΔΓΔΙΙΙ.

ΗΗΗΔ[Δ]ΙΙ, αρχοντος Ἀ-θηνησι Δαμασιου του δευτερου. A quo coronarium certamen iterùm editum fuit, anni CCCXXII, archonte Athenis Damafiâ fecundo.

εθεντο. Archonte Athenis quidem Damafiâ, iterum coronarium ftatuerunt. Pind. Schol. arg. 2. in Pyth.

Epoc. 52. Αφ ου Ξερξης την σχεδιαν εζευξεν εν Ελλησποντω, και τον Αθω διωρυξε. A quo Xerxes navigiorum pontem junxit in Hellefponte, & Athonem perfodit.

Ξερξης διωρυξε και τον Αθω, εζευξε και τον Ἑλλησποντον. Xerxes perfodit et Athon, & Hellefpontum ponte junxit. Suidas v. Ξερξης. Vid. Ifoc. Paneg. p. 127, edit. Cantab. 1686.

Epoc. 53. Και το πυρ ερυη[σε εν Σικ]ελια, περι την Αιτνιαν *. Et ignis defluxit in Sicilia circa Ætnam.

Ερρυη δε περι αυτο το εαρ τουτο ὁ ῥυαξ του πυρος εκ της Αιτνης. Per idem ver ignis rivus ex Ætnâ effluxit †. Thucyd. l. iii. fub fin.

The eruption of mount Ætna, which Thucydides mentions in this paffage, happened in the archonfhip of Euthydemus, bef. Chr. 426. In the next fentence, he fpeaks of another eruption, πεντηκοσῳ ετει, fifty years before; that is, when Phædon was archon, in the year 476, or, according to the opinion of Corfini, when Dromoclides was archon, in 475. This is the eruption, mentioned by the author of the Chronicle; but he places it three or four years too early, in the archonfhip of Xanthippus, bef. Chr. 479.

* Αιτνιαν. Αιτνα for Αιτνη, Dor. but the ι in Αιτνιαν is a miftake, either of the author, or the ftone-cutter.

† This paffage is only produced as an imitation, or fomething like an imitation, of a writer, preceding the CXXIX Olympiad.

Epoc.

THE PARIAN CHRONICLE. 157

Epoc. 58. Αφ ου εν Αι-γος ποταμοις ο λιθος επεσε. A quo in Ægos flumen lapis cecidit.	Λιθος εκ του ουρανου επεσεν εν ποταμοις Αιγος. Lapis in Ægis fluvio de cœlo ruit. Euſeb. Chron. p. 168. 131.

It is worthy of obſervation, how the ancients differ with reſpect to the place, from which this ſtone is ſuppoſed to have fallen. Ariſtotle ſays, it was ſnatched up by a whirlwind, and fell εκ του αερος, out of the air *. Pliny and Diogenes Laertius aſſert, that it fell εκ του ηλιου, from the ſun †. Silenus, Plutarch, Philoſtratus, Euſebius, Ammianus Marcellinus, and Tzetzes ‡, tell us, that it fell εκ του ουρανου, from the ſky. Our author contents himſelf with ſaying, that it fell into the river Ægos. Does not this deviation from the opinion, and the language of the ancients, ſeem to encourage a ſuſpicion, that the writer of the Chronicle lived in later times, when men had learned to explode ſuch an abſurdity, as that of a ſtone, as big as a mill-ſtone, falling

---

* Ariſt. Meteor. l. i. c. 7.
† Plin. l. ii. c. 58.—Pliny ſays, it was, magnitudine vehis, a cart-load.—Diog. Laert. l. ii. § 10.
‡ Silenus apud Diog. Laert. l. ii. § 11. In this paſſage Scaliger reads διμυλον λιθον, a ſtone as large as two mill-ſtones. Scal. Animad. in Euſeb. Chron. p. 102. Kühnius thus reprobates the word διμυλον: "μυλου λιθος idem eſt quod μυλιτης, molaris ; διμυλος λιθος verò æque abſurdum eſt, ac ſi dicerem τριμυλος." Kühnii Obſerv. in loc.
Plut. in v. Lyſand. p. 439.—Plutarch calls it, παμμεγεθης λιθος, a very large ſtone.
Philoſt. in v. Apollon. l. i. c. 2.—This writer ſays, λιθοι, ſtones.
Euſeb. loc. cit.
Am. Marcell. l. xxii. p. 212. 236.—Marcellinus ſays, lapides, ſtones.
Tzet. Chil. vi.—Tzetzes likewiſe ſays, λιθοι, ſtones.

out

out of the air, from the sun, from the sky, or from heaven?

If, upon considering these parallel passages, it should appear, that they really exhibit a similarity of sentiment and expression, which could not result from chance, it will be necessary to enquire, from what source this coincidence arises.

It is not probable, that the historians, geographers, and miscellaneous writers of antiquity, living in different ages, and in distant countries, would, in cases of no particular importance, incidentally introduced, use the words of an inscription in the island of Paros. And if, in some instances, they might have borrowed the words of such an inscription, it is not probable, that they would have deviated from the general custom of their contemporaries, by suppressing the name of the author, whose expressions they adopted, and on whose authority they depended.

2. It is not probable, that the inscription has been copied by several writers, particularly by writers, who lived many centuries after its date; because, upon this supposition, it must have been generally known and consulted; which is so far from being the case, that there is not an author now remaining, who appears to have either seen or heard of such an inscription.

3. It is not probable, that the inscription was collected from preceding writers, as early as the cxxix Olympiad; and that others have drawn their information from the same original sources, and therefore employed the same expressions; first, because it is generally acknowledged*, that the Greeks, at that time, had no idea of any regular, chronological system, like the Parian Chronicle; and secondly, because we can hardly

---

* See chap. v. vi.

suppose,

suppose, that Greek writers of eminent abilities have servilely copied the words of their predecessors, on ordinary occasions, where they have not appealed to their authority. Professed compilers must be excepted.

I am very sensible, how difficult it is, in many cases, to trace resemblances, and fix upon unquestionable imitations, in different authors; but if there be any such imitations in the passages I have cited, and any validity in the subsequent observations, we may conclude, that the facts and dates, contained in the Parian Chronicle, have been collected, by some modern writer, from the historical records of antiquity.

CHAP. XIII.

VII. PARACHRONISMS appear in some of the epochas, which we can scarcely suppose a Greek chronologer, in the cxxix Olympiad, would be liable to commit.

The following articles, among many others, which might be mentioned, seem to fall under this imputation.

In the 31st Epocha, Pheidon the Argive, supposed to have been the eleventh from Hercules, is said to have made weights and measures, 895 years before the Christian æra.

There seems to be a considerable prochronism in this article. Eusebius and Syncellus place Pheidon in the year 800 *. Pausanias tells us, that Pheidon was a formidable tyrant, and interposed in a contest between the Eleans and the Pisæans, about the direction of the Olympic games, in the eighth Olympiad †, bef. Chr. 748. Strabo says, Pheidon himself assumed the power of superintending the games; but that he was soon afterwards deposed by the Eleans and Spartans. He makes him the tenth from Temenus ‡, who was unquestionably the fourth from Hercules.

Pheidon

---

* Euseb. Chron. p. 112. Ibid. Græc. 148. Syncell. p. 198.
† Pausan. l. vi. c. 22.
‖ Δεκατος μεν οντα απο Τημενου, decimum à Temeno. Strab. l. viii. p. 539 edit. 1707.—In the *Latin* translation of this passage, Pheidon is called, decimus ab HERCULE; for which, I think, there is

no

THE PARIAN CHRONICLE. 161

Pheidon was brother to Caranus, who founded the kingdom of Macedon. Chronologers are not agreed concerning the beginning of this prince's reign; but the moſt probable opinion ſeems to be that of archbiſhop Uſher, who places it about the year 794.

Paterculus brings Caranus, and conſequently Pheidon, two generations lower than Strabo has done; for he ſays, he was the SIXTEENTH from Hercules *.

Sir Iſaac Newton ſuppoſes Pheidon to have lived in the year 584; which is 311 years later, than the marble has placed him.

EPOC. 46. According to this epocha, the aſſaſſination of Hipparchus, and the expulſion of his brother Hippias, or that of the Piſiſtratidæ, happened in the ſame year. But it is univerſally agreed, that Hippias remained at Athens above three years after the death of his brother.

" The Athenians," ſays Herodotus, " during the ſpace of FOUR years, were no leſs oppreſſed by tyranny than before †." Plato makes this an interval of THREE years ‡. Thucydides, with hiſtorical accuracy, ſays, " Hippias continued in poſſeſſion of the tyranny at Athens THREE years; and in the FOURTH was depoſed

no authority, but that of Xylander, who reads 'Ηρακλεους, inſtead of Τημενου. Vid. Palmerii Exercit. p. 308.

Temenus was one of the three brothers, who conducted the celebrated expedition, called the Return of the Heraclidæ, bef. Chr. 1104. If Pheidon was ten generations, or 300 years, later, he muſt be ſuppoſed to have lived about the year 804.

* Sextus decimus ab Hercule. Paterc. l. i. c. 6.
† Επ' ετεα τεσσερα, per annos quatuor. Herod. l. v. § 55.
‡ Quo defuncto, τρια ετη, tres annos ſub fratre illius Hippiâ, tyrannide preſſi Athenienſes fuerunt. Plat. in Hipparcho, vol. v. p. 263. edit. Bipont. 1784.

Y   by

by the Lacedæmonians and the Alcmæonidæ, twenty years before the battle at Marathon *.

EPOC. 50. The author of the Chronicle afferts, that Darius, the fon of Hyftafpes, died in the archonfhip of ARISTIDES, the year after the battle at Marathon.

Ctefias indeed relates, that "Darius returned into Perfia, and died there, after an illnefs of thirty days †. But every one knows, how much the credit of Ctefias has been fufpected ‡; befides, the death of Darius is mentioned, in a mere EPITOME of his hiftory by Photius,

---

* Εν τῳ τεταρτῳ, quarto anno. Thucyd. l. vi. § 59.—Hipparchus was affaffinated, Olymp. LXVI. 3. bef. Chr. 514. Hippias was banifhed, Olymp. LXVII. 2. bef. Chr. 510. Hippiæ fuga in exeunte anno fecundo Olymp. LXVII conftitui debet. Corfin. Valefii Excerpt. Peirefc. p. 42.

† Δαρειος δε επανελθων εις Περσας, και θυσας, και ἡμερας νοσησας λ′, τελευτα, Darius autem ad Perfas reverfus eft, ubi celebratis facrificiis, quum triginta dies morbo laboraffet, mortuus eft. Ctefiæ Fragm. apud Phot. Bibl. cod. 72. Herod. Op. p. 816. edit. 1763.

‡ Μυθων απιθανων και παραφορων εμβεβληκεν εις τα βιβλια παντοδαπων πυλαιων, fabularum abfurdarum et infulfarum in libros fuos variam colluviem infarfit. Plut. in v. Artax. p. 1012.

Κτησιας ουκ αξιοπιςος, Ctefias non fide dignus. Arift. Hift. Animal. l. viii. c. 28.

In this paffage Ariftotle alludes to the INDICA of Ctefias. But might not Ctefias as well forge his Affyrian hiftory, as create the world of monfters he talks of in India? And might we not as juftly fufpect him of falfhood, when he pretends, that he compiled his hiftory from original records, as when he gravely affirms, that he was an eye-witnefs of what no perfon of fenfe can believe? Vid. Ctefiæ Indica apud Photium, cod. 73.

Herodotus, fay the authors of the Univerfal Hiftory, may be juftly ftyled the father of hiftory, and agrees better with the facred writings than any other profane hiftorian; whereas it will be difficult to find a more romantic and fabulous author than Ctefias, in the whole circle of antiquity, vol. xx. p. 84. edit. 1747. See alfo vol. iv. p. 265.

THE PARIAN CHRONICLE. 163

in such vague and general terms, as do not, by any means, ascertain the time of that event.

Herodotus says expressly, "In the FOURTH year after the battle at Marathon, when Darius had assembled the best of his forces, in order to invade Greece, the Egyptians, who had been subdued by Cambyses, revolted from the Persians *." And a little afterwards, he adds, "Darius died the year after the revolt of Egypt † :" that is, inclusively, the FIFTH year after the battle at Marathon, or the year bef. Chr. 486. Other authors corroborate the testimony of Herodotus ‡.

Diodorus Siculus informs us, that Xerxes, the son and successor of Darius, was assassinated in the fourth year of the LXXVIII Olympiad, bef. Chr. 465 years. This prince reigned 21 years ‖ : consequently his father must have died in the year 486.

Sir

---

* Τεταρτω ετει, quarto anno Ægyptii defecerunt. Herod. l. vii. § 1.

† Τω υςερω ετει, proximo anno ab Ægyptiorum defectione. Ibid. § 4.

‡ Several writers speak of the great preparations, which Darius had made for renewing the war. These must have taken up a considerable time.

Δαρειος, προ της τελευτης, παρασκευας πεποιημενος μεγαλων δυναμεων, Darius ante mortem magnarum copiarum apparatum fecerat. Diod. Sic. l. xi. p. 2.

Darius cùm bellum restauraret in ipso apparatu decedit. Just. l. ii. c. 10.

Darius ante QUADRIENNIUM quàm decederet, apud Marathonum pugnavit. Sulp. Sev. l. ii. c. 13.

Darius, cùm instauraret bellum, in ipso apparatu concidit, Olympiade septuagesimâ quartâ. Oros. l. ii. c. 8.—According to Orosius, Darius died bef. Chr. 484, six years after the battle of Marathon.

‖ Βασιλευσας των Περσων ετη πλειω των εικοσι, postquam ultra XX annos Persarum regno præfuisset. Diod. Sic. l. xi. p. 53.

Sir Isaac Newton observes, that "Darius began his reign in the spring, anno J. Per. 4193, bef. Chr. 521, and reigned THIRTY-SIX years, by the unanimous consent of all chronologers *."——" The reign of this prince," he says, "is determined by two eclipses of the moon, observed at Babylon, and recorded by Ptolemy; so that it cannot be disputed. The former was in the twentieth year of Darius, *an.* J. P. 4212, Nov. 19, at 11^h 45′ at night; the latter in the twenty-first year of the same prince, *an.* J. P. 4223, Apr. 25, at 11^h 30′ at night. Xerxes began his reign in the spring, *an.* J. P. 4229, bef. Chr. 485; for Darius died in the FIFTH year after the battle at Marathon, as Herodotus, l. vii. and Plutarch mention; and that battle was *an.* J. P. 4224, ten years before the battle at Salamis †."

Xerxes having determined to revenge the disgrace, received by his father at Marathon, spent four years in preparing for the invasion of Greece. In the FIFTH ‡ year he began his march, and passed the winter at Sardes. In the succeeding spring ‖, bef. Chr. 480, he crossed the Hellespont, and brought his forces into Eu-

---

Ξερξης ετη κα, Xerxes ann. XXI. Maneth. apud Euseb. Chron. p. 17. & apud Syncell. p. 75, 76. Vid. p. 208.

* Βασιλευσαντα τα παντα ετεα εξ τε και τριηκοντα, sex et triginta annis regni expletis. Herod. l. vii. § 4.

Δαρειος ετη λς΄, Darius ann. XXXVI. Maneth. apud Euseb. Chron. Græc. p. 17. African. apud Syncell. p. 75. Vid. Syncell. p. 78. 208.

Ctesias pretends, that Darius obtained the kingdom of Persia at twelve years of age, and reigned twenty-one years. Ctesiæ Fragm. loc. cit.—But when the former of these numbers is so manifestly erroneous, what dependence can we place upon the latter?

† Newt. Observ. on Daniel. c. 10. p. 141.

‡ Πεμπτῳ δε ετεϊ ανομενῳ, quinto autem anno ineunte. Herod. l. vii. § 20.

‖ Αμα τῳ εαρι, ineunte vere. Herod. l. viii. § 37.

rope.

rope. He engaged Leonidas at Thermopylæ, about the beginning of the month Hecatombæon*, and arrived at Athens, about the end of the same month. On the twentieth of Boëdromion, the Greeks obtained the celebrated victory at Salamis.

According to this account, which is clearly stated by Herodotus, Xerxes employed FIVE years in his military preparations for the invasion of Greece. Justin and Orosius † agree with Herodotus in this particular. Eusebius likewise places the battle of Salamis in the FIFTH year of Xerxes ‡. Diodorus mentions a preparation of three years ‖; and if we add the time which Xerxes spent in subduing the Egyptians, his account will coincide with that of Herodotus.

In opposition to all these testimonies, the author of the Chronicle affirms, that Xerxes succeeded to the throne of Persia NINE years before the battle of Salamis.

EPOC. 51. The author places the birth of Euripides 486 years before the Christian æra.

Diogenes Laertius places it in the first year of the LXXV Olympiad, when Calliades was archon, bef. Chr. 480; and Thomas Magister, in the same Olympiad. Plutarch, Hesychius, Suidas, and others, likewise affirm,

---

* Vide Corsini Fast. Attic. tom. iii. p. 165. Herodotus says, "The barbarians spent a month in passing the Hellespont, and bringing their forces into Europe; and in three months more entered Attica, when Calliades was archon of the Athenians." Lib. viii. § 51.

† Xerxes bellum à patre cœptum adversus Græciam per quinquennium instruxit. Just. l. ii. c. 10. Per quinquennium instruxit. Oros. l. ii. c. 9.

‡ Euseb. Chron. p. 130.

‖ Τριετη χρονον παρεσκευασαμενος. Diod. Sic. l. xi. p. 2.

that Euripides was born the very day, on which the Greeks defeated the Persians at Salamis *.

On the authority of these writers we may reasonably conclude, that there is a parachronism of five or six years, in this epocha.

Epoc. 54. In this epocha it is asserted, that Gelo became tyrant of Syracuse, two years AFTER the battle at Thermopylæ; whereas we are assured by the most eminent historians, that he had obtained the government of that city several years BEFORE Xerxes invaded Greece.

Diodorus informs us, that Gelo reigned SEVEN years, and DIED within two years after the battle abovementioned; that is, he became tyrant of Syracuse, in the year bef. Chr. 484, and died in 478 †. Aristotle likewise ascribes seven years to the tyranny of Gelo ‡. Pausanias relates, that Gelo was tyrant of Syracuse in the second year of the LXXII Olympiad, TEN years before the transit of Xerxes ‖. Though this writer seems to have mistaken Syracuse for Gela §, his testimony is totally repugnant to that of the Chronicle; for in another place, he positively asserts, that Gelo was tyrant of Syracuse, when Xerxes came into Europe ¶.

Diodorus, Ephorus, Herodotus, unanimously affirm, that the Greeks sent ambassadors to Gelo, as KING of

---

* Diog. Laert. in v. Socrat. l. ii. § 45.
Ετι Καλλιου [lege Καλλιαδου] αρχοντος, κατα την πεμπτην και εβδομηκοσ- την Ολυμπιαδα. Th. Magist. in v. Eurip.
Plut. in Sympos. l. viii. c. 1. Hesychius Milesius de Viris claris, in v. Ευριπιδης. Suidas, &c.
† Diod. Sic. l. xi. p. 30.
‡ Arist. Repub. l. v. c. 12.
‖ Pausan. l. vi. c. 9.
§ Vid. Dionys. Halic. l. vii. § 1.
¶ Pausan. l. viii. c. 42.

SYRACUSE,

SYRACUSE, to folicit his affiftance againft the Perfians, when Xerxes was preparing for his intended expedition *.

It may be prefumed, that Diodorus, a native of Sicily, was well acquainted with the records of his own country; and Herodotus, with the public tranfactions of his own time. It is certainly in the higheft degree improbable, that Diodorus, Ephorus, and Herodotus, fhould be deceived, in a circumftance, which was rendered particularly remarkable by a formal embaffy from the united ftates of Greece: for furely there muft have been public records, and other authentic memorials, of this late and important tranfaction.

We may therefore conclude, that the author of the Chronicle has miftaken the time of Gelo's acceffion, for that of his deceafe, and placed the former under the archonfhip of Timofthenes, bef. Chr. 478. where he fhould have placed the latter. By this parachronifm he has poftponed the fucceffion of Hiero to the year 472, which is fix years later, than Diodorus and other hiftorians have placed him †.

EPOC. 65. Here we are told, that the younger Cyrus ανεβ... when Callias was archon; i. e. in the third year of the XCIII Olympiad, bef. Chr. 406.

I can hardly fuppofe, that this paffage refers to the vifit, which Cyrus made his father in his laft illnefs; or to his attempt to affaffinate his brother at his coronation. It is fcarcely probable, that the author of the Chronicle would record either of thefe unimportant circumftances, and fay nothing of that memorable expe-

---

* Diod. Sic. l. xi. § 1. Ephor. apud Schol. Pind. Pyth. i. p. 175. Ω Βασιλευ Συρηκουσιων, κ. τ. λ, Herod. l. vii. § 161.—Corfini places this embaffy in the fecond year BEFORE the battle at Thermopylæ.
† Diod. Sic. l. xi. p. 30.

dition,

dition, in which this young prince marched at the head of thirteen thoufand Greeks, and a hundred thoufand barbarians, to difpute the crown of Perfia with Artaxerxes.

If thefe remaining letters ανεβ... relate to this expedition, ufually ftyled the Anabafis, here is a prochronifm of FIVE years; for it commenced in the archonfhip of Exænetus or Xenænetus*, in the fourth year of the XCLIV Olympiad, bef. Chr. 401, above five years after the date, fpecified in the Chronicle.

The LXVII epocha mentions only the RETURN of the ten thoufand Greeks.

Upon a prefumption, that the dates of thefe, or, at leaft, fome of thefe events are careleſsly and erroneouſly ſtated in the Chronicle, we may afk, Would a writer of reputation and learning, in one of the moft poliſhed and enlightened æras of ancient Greece, commit fuch miftakes, in oppoſition to the poſitive atteſtations of the moſt accurate hiſtorians, in events of PUBLIC NOTORIETY? Would a private citizen, or a magiſtrate of Paros, order a crude and inaccurate feries of epochas to be engraved, at a great expence, and tranfmitted to poſterity on a marble monument?—It is hardly probable.

* Ξενοφων ανεβεβηκε συν Κυρω επι αρχοντος Ξεναινετου, Xenophon afcendit cum Cyro fub archonte Xenæneto. Diog. Laert. l. ii. § 55.—Diodorus places the Anabafis under the fame archon. l. xiv. p. 249. The learned author of a Differtation, fubjoined to Spelman's tranſlation of Xenophon's Anabafis, is of opinion, that the year of the expedition was the third year of the XCIV Olympiad, bef. Chr. 402.

CHAP.

CHAP. XIV.

VIII. THE difcovery of the Chronicle is related in a very obfcure and unfatisfactory manner, with fome fufpicious circumftances, and without any of thofe clear and unequivocal evidences, which always difcriminate truth from falfhood.

It is remarkable, that the place, where it was found, is not afcertained.

The generality of writers, who have had occafion to mention it, have fuppofed, that it was found in the ifland of Paros.

Thus Du Pin : " We have no monument, from which we can, with more certainty, fix the Attic æra, or the beginning of the reign of Cecrops, than the Chronicle, found in the ifle of Paros *."

Du Frefnoy obferves, that " the Parian Chronicle takes its name from the ifland of Paros, in the Archipelago, where it was found †."

Dr. Rawlinfon, in a note to his tranflation of Du Frefnoy's Méthode pour étudier l'Hiftoire, affirms, " that thefe marbles were found in the ifland of Paros, one of the Cyclades ‡."

---

* Du Pin, Univ. Hift. Libr. tom. ii. l. i. p. 271.
† Elle tire fon nom de l'ifle de Paros, l'une de celles de l'Archipel, où cette Chronique fut *trouvée*, au commencement du XVIIe fiècle. Du Frefnoy, Tabl. Chron. tom. 1. p. clxvii. edit. 1744.
‡ New Method of ftudying Hiftory, vol. i. c. 2. § 3. p. 36.

Abbé Banier asserts, "that these marbles were dug up in the island of Paros *."

Others tell us, that they were not found at Paros, but in Asia Minor, at Smyrna.

Palmerius, who wrote a comment upon them, affirms, that "they were found at Smyrna, a celebrated city of Ionia †."

Petavius says expressly, "they were DUG OUT of the ground at Smyrna ‡.

If we consult the editors of the Marmora Arundelliana, we shall find no satisfaction in this particular.

Selden, in commenting on the words εμ Παρῳ, in the second line, only says, " We may reasonably CONJECTURE, that the author was a Parian ||;" but he does not once mention the place, where the Chronicle is supposed to have been found.

Prideaux is perfectly silent on this point.

Maittaire speaks of this fragment, as if he had not known where it was discovered. "Præterea," says he,

---

* CES MARBRES furent *déterrées* dans l'isle de Paros, & vendus au Comte d'Arondel. Banier, Mythol. tom. vi. p. 62. edit. Par. 1740.—This writer, and many others, suppose the Chronicle to have been written on a series of several pieces of marble. At present, there is only a shattered fragment remaining; but it is most probable, that the whole inscription was originally engraved on one tablet. Selden, who saw the greatest part of it, speaks of it in the singular number: epocharum marmor, chronologicum marmor, &c. edit. Ansl. p. iii. vid. supra, p. 53. *n*.

† Ea marmorum fragmenta inventa sunt Smyrnæ, quæ civitas erat inter Ionicas insignis. Palmer. Exercit. ad Chron. Marm. Arundel. p. 682.

‡ Antiquus ille chronologus, qui ex Arundellianis marmoribus, apud Smyrnam EFFOSSIS, nuper editus est. Petav. Rat. Temp. par. ii. l. ii. c. 9.

|| Autorem hinc Parium fuisse, æquum est ut conjectemus. Seld. Marm. Arundel. p. 72.

" hoc

THE PARIAN CHRONICLE. 171
" hoc marmor Smyrnæ magis, quàm in ULLA ALIA Afiæ parte, inventum fuiffe, NON LIQUET *."

Dr. Chandler BELIEVES it was found at Paros, and afterwards removed to Smyrna. "Marmor Chronicon, in infulâ Paro, UT FAS SIT CREDERE, repertum, dein ad Smyrnam tranflatum †."

This is the laft account we have of the Parian infcription.

On thefe evidences we may obferve, that neither Du Pin, Du Frefnoy, Banier, Palmerius, nor Petavius, appear to have received any certain information, relative to the place, where the Chronicle was difcovered; at leaft, they are not confiftent in their accounts; and yet, as we fhall fee hereafter, it was purchafed at Smyrna by one of their countrymen.

Selden's ÆQUUM EST UT CONJECTEMUS, Maittaire's NON LIQUET, and Chandler's UT FAS SIT CREDERE, leave us totally in the dark.

In the infcription itfelf we have no data, by which we can any ways difcover the place, where the marble was erected.

Palmerius conceives, that the author or the ftonecutter was an Ionian. Ἕως, he fays, is the Ionian dialect for ἕως, εμ Παρῳ for εν Παρῳ, and εγ Λυκωρειας for εκ Λυκωρειας ‡.

But Maittaire obferves, that ἕως is the poetic dialect, frequently ufed by Homer ‖; that εμ and εγ are mere archaïfms, very common in ancient infcriptions §; and that,

* Maitt. Marm. Arund. p. 571.
† Chand. Marm. Oxon. p. x.
‡ Palmer. Exercit. ad Chron. p. 682.
‖ Γἴως is ufed for ἕως, II. iii. 291. xi. 342. 488. xii. 141, & alibi paffim.
§ Hunc chronographum fuiffe Ionem, ut credam, minimè inducar, quod εμ Παρῳ pro εν Παρῳ, et εγ Λυκωρειας pro εκ Λυκωρειας, fcrip-

that, from such expressions as these we cannot infer, that the Chronicle was composed at Smyrna.

If this monument was erected in that city, for what purpose does the writer mention Astyanax, the archon of Paros, and not one circumstance relative to Smyrna? If it was erected at Paros, why does he not mention more archons of that city than one? Or how shall we account for his profound silence, with respect to all the events and revolutions, which must have happened in that island, and have been infinitely more interesting to the natives, than the transactions of any foreign country?

Sir Thomas Roe, who was ambassador at Constantinople, and whose letters, from the year 1621 to 1628, inclusive, are published under the title of NEGOTIATIONS, corresponded with lord Arundel on the subject of ancient manuscripts, coins, statues, and inscriptions; and, at the same time, recommended and assisted Mr. Petty, whom the earl had sent into Asia for the purpose of collecting antiquities; yet in his letters to his lordship, relative to the discoveries made by Mr. Petty, he does not once mention the Parian Chronicle.

In a letter to lord Arundel, dated, Constantinople, Jan. 20—30, 1624, Sir Thomas acknowledges the receipt of three letters from his lordship, in recommendation of Mr. Petty, sent by the earl in search of antiquities. He informs him, that he doubts he will find little worthy of his pains in those rude parts, "where barbarism has trodden out all worthy reliques of antiquity;" that he may find some few medals or coins; but that books have been so often visited, that Duck-lane is better furnished than the Greek church; that Mr. Marsham, by his assistance, had ransacked the country

scrit; quippe hæc magis ad archaïsmum, quàm ad Ionismum spectant.... Nisi fallor, ιι pro ε, et ου pro ο, poëtarum magis propria sunt, quamvis hæc usurpent frequentissimè etiam Iones. Maitt. Marm. Arund. p. 571. 615. 638.

for

for ſtatues, columns, and antique works; that he had lately fallen into a way of meeting with ſome rare ſtatues from Alexandria, by means of the patriarch, particularly of a negro of black marble, a piece not to be matched; that the ſaid patriarch has given him for his majeſty, with expreſs promiſe to deliver it, "an autographal Bible entire, written by the hand of Tecla, the protomartyr of the Greekes, who lived in the time of St. Paul; and he doth averr that to bee true and authenticall, of his owne writing, and the greateſt antiquitye of the Greeke church *."

* Negot. let. 241. p. 334.——This was the famous Alexandrian MS.
In a letter to the archbiſhop of Canterbury, dated Feb. 17—27, 1626, Sir Thomas ſpeaks of it in the following terms: " The patriarch alſo, this new yeare's tyde, ſent mee the old Bible, formerly preſented to his late majeſtie; which hee hath now dedicated to the kyng, and will ſend with that an epiſtle, as I thincke he hath ſignifyed to your grace, at leaſt I will preſume to mention it to his majeſtie. What eſtimation it may be of, is above my ſkill; but he valewes that as the greateſt antiquitye of the Greek church. The lettre is very fayre, a character that I have neuer ſeene. It is entyre, except the beginning of St. Matheiw. He doth teſtefye under his hand, that it was written by the virgin Tecla, daughter of a famous Greeke called Αβγιεριενος (ſtella matutina) who founded the moneſtarye in Egypt vpon Pharoas tower, a deuout and learned mayd, who was perſecuted in Aſya, and to whom Gregorye Nazianzen hath written many epiſteles. At the end wherof, vnder the ſame hand, are the epiſteles of Clement. She dyed not long after the councell of Nice. The booke is very great, and hath antiquitye enough at ſight. I doubt not his majeſtie will eſteeme it for the hand by whom it is preſented." let. 448. p. 618.
Who, in the name of wonder, was this famous Greek, called ΑΒΓΙΕΡΙΕΝΟΣ?
The patriarch wanted to magnify the importance of his preſent when he talked in this manner!—The council of Nice was held i 1 325. Gregory Nazianzen flouriſhed about the year 370. But lord Arundel was told, that the devout and learned writer lived in the time of St. Paul!—One ſtory is as credible as the other.

In

In the next letter to lord Arundel, dated Oct. 20—30, 1625, he says, "Mr. Petty hath vifited Pergamo, Samos, Ephefus, and fome other places, where hee hath made your lordſhip greate prouifions, though hee lately wrote to mee, hee had found nothing of worth *."

In a fubfequent letter to the earl, dated, Mar. 28, 1626, O. S. he says: "My laft letters brought your lordſhip the advice of Mr. Pettye's fhipwracke, and loffes vpon the coaft of Afya, returning from Samos... Although hee will not boaft to mee, yett I am informed, hee hath gotten many things rare and ancient. There was neuer man fo fitted to an employment, that encounters all accidents with fo vnwearied patience; eates with Greekes on their worft dayes; lies with fifhermen on plancks, at the beft; is all things to all men, that hee may obteyne his ends, which are your lordſhip's fervice. Hee is gone to Athens, whither alfo I have fent †."

This is the laft letter, in the Collection, from Sir Thomas Roe to lord Arundel.

In a letter to the duke of Buckingham, dated, Conftantinople, Nov. 5—15, 1626, he says: "Mr. Petty hath raked together 200 pieces, all broken, or few entyre; what they will prove I cannot judge. Hee had this advantage, that hee went himfelfe into all the iflands, and tooke all hee faw; and is now gone to Athens, where I haue had an agent nine monethes ‡."

In another letter to the duke of Buckingham, dated, Apr. 15, 1628, Sir Thomas gives his grace but a very indifferent idea of Mr. Petty's collections.

"I could haue LADEN SHIPPS with fuch ftones as Mr. Petty diggs; but GOOD THINGS undefaced are

* Negot. let. 315. p. 444.
† Negot. let. 41 p. 570.
‡ Negot. let. 359. p. 495.

THE PARIAN CHRONICLE. 175

rare, or rather NOT to be FOUND. Our search hath made many poore men INDUSTRIOUS to rippe up old ruines *.".

These are most probably the real sentiments of Sir Thomas Roe, with respect to Mr. Petty's discoveries, which he would scarcely have expressed with so much freedom to lord Arundel.

Mr. Petty's name is mentioned in several other letters; but there is not, in any of them, the least intimation of the Parian Chronicle; which is a remarkable circumstance. For, supposing it to be authentic, it was a most valuable monument of ancient learning; and must surely have occasioned much conversation at Smyrna, and other places in that country; more especially as we shall find, that it had been EXPOSED TO SALE, before it fell into the hands of Mr. Petty.

Gassendus, in his Life of M. de Peiresc †, gives us the following account of its first discovery.

" Per idem tempus accepit [Peirescius] aureum eruditi Seldeni librum, de Arundellianis Marmoribus, sive saxis Græcè incisis, quæ perilluftris ille comes transferri ex Asiâ in Angliam, hortósque suos, curaverat. Ac memorare quidem par est, marmora illa fuisse primùm operâ Peireskii detecta, erutaque, persolutis aureis quinquaginta, per Samsonem quendam, ipsius negotia Smyrnæ procurantem; & convehenda cum jam essent, nescio quâ venditorum arte, Samsonem conjectum in carcerem fuisse, marmoraque ipsa interea distracta. Sed et illud addendum est, maximoperè lætatum Peireskium, cùm accepit, præclaras illas antiquitatis reliquias in

* Negot. let. 611. p. 808.
† Nicolas Claude Fabri de Peiresc, counsellor in the parliament of Provence, was an eminent patron of arts and learning, and corresponded with almost all the literati of his time. He died at Aix in 1637, in the fifty-seventh year of his age.

tanti herois incidiffe manus ; ac tantò magis, quantò agnovit, Seldenem, veterem amicum, eas feliciter illuftráffe.

" Scilicet, cui unicus fcopus utilitas publica fuit, nihil putavit intereffe, feu fua effet gloria, feu alterius, dummodò quod effet è reipublicæ literariæ bono prodiret in lucem. Exiftimavit autem, thefaurum incomparabilem contineri in illis, præfertim rerum Græcarum epochis, quæ non modò hiftoricum, fed fabulofum etiam tempus fummè illuftrant, conciliántque ; dum memorabilia omnia, ab annis ufque octingentis ante Olympiadas, ad ufque quingentos quinquaginta poft earum initium, defcribunt *."

" About this time [fometime in the year 1629] Peirefc received the learned Selden's valuable commentary on the Arundel Marbles, or certain ftones, with Greek infcriptions engraved upon them, which had been conveyed out of Afia into England, by the direction of the illuftrious earl of Arundel, and placed in his gardens. Thefe marbles, I muft obferve, were firft difcovered, and dug out of the ground, in confequence of the application and order of Peirefc, who paid fifty pieces of gold † for that purpofe, by the hands of one Samfon, his agent at Smyrna. But when they were ready to be fent on board, by fome artifice of the venders, Samfon was thrown into prifon, and the marbles, in the mean time, left in a ftate of confufion. I muft likewife add, that Peirefc was extremely pleafed, when he was informed, that thefe celebrated reliques of antiquity had fallen into the hands of fuch an eminent perfonage, as lord Arundel ; and more particularly, when he found, that they had been happily illuftrated by his old friend Selden.

* Gaffend. de Vitâ Peirefcii, lib. iv. an. 1629.

† It is perhaps not eafy to afcertain the value of the *aurei quinquaginta*.

" As

" As a citizen of the world, whose only view was the benefit of mankind, Peiresc thought it immaterial, whether he himself, or another, received the glory, provided any thing could be brought to light, which might contribute to the advantage of the republic of letters. He was of opinion, that an incomparable treasure is contained in these Grecian epochas, which not only give a clear and consistent account of the dates of some important transactions, in the historic times, but of others also, in the fabulous and heroic ages; while they describe every memorable occurrence for 800 years before the Olympiads, and for 550 * after their commencement."

Several circumstances in this narrative are worthy of observation.

1. There is something very singular and unusual in the conduct of Peiresc, on the loss of this inscription, after he had purchased it for a considerable sum. His agent, it seems, was committed to prison, and the marbles were *distracta*, broken, separated, and thrown about in confusion.

It would have been natural for an ordinary virtuoso, who had received information of such a CURIOSITY, to have exerted all his activity and interest, in order to procure it. But Peiresc, a rich and indefatigable collector †, a philosopher, and an eminent patron of learning,

---

* The calculation of Gassendus in this place is erroneous. The epocha of Cecrops is bef. Chr. 1582. The Olympiads commenced an. 776, 806 years afterwards. The last remaining epocha on the marbles is 354; the date of the inscription 264. If we bring down our reckoning to the latter, the number of years after the Olympiads is 512; if to the former, it is only 422, instead of 550, as Gassendus has computed.

† M. Goguet, having occasion to mention M. de Peiresc, says, " Nothing escaped him, that could any way contribute to the advancement

ing, does not, as far as we can perceive, make the least effort to recover this inscription ; notwithstanding it was apparently of much greater value, than any other marble monument in the universe. On the contrary, he loses the money he had advanced, chearfully resigns his claim, and is glad to find the marbles were preserved in a foreign country.

His composure, on this occasion, would lead us to imagine, that he entertained some SECRET suspicion, relative to the authenticity of the inscription.

2. Peiresc, we are told, paid for these marbles *aureos quinquaginta*, "fifty pieces of gold." What lord Arundel paid for them we are not informed. Prideaux tells us, they were redeemed by Mr. Petty, majori pretio[*], "at a greater price;" and Dr. Chandler says, pretio LONGE majori [†], "for a far greater sum."

Supposing then, that Mr. Petty paid only thrice as much, as Peiresc had paid before, the owners or the venders received 200 pieces for the marbles. This, I apprehend, was an extraordinary acquisition, amply sufficient for the gratification of the author and the stonecutter, especially at Smyrna, in the earlier part of the last century. It was certainly as powerful a motive, in conjunction with others, which we do not know, as those which actuated either Annius of Viterbo, or any of his brethren, in the fabrication of inscriptions.

3. The sum, which was paid for these marbles, was much greater, than what a writer at Paros, 264 years before the birth of Christ, could possibly expect; and affords, as far as profit alone is concerned, a sufficient

---

vancement of human knowledge; and he spared no pains for that purpose. Goguet's Orig. of Laws, vol. iii. Dissert. 1. p. 251. Fabric. Bibl. Lat. l. iv. c. 5. § 7. p. 397.

[*] Prid. Marm. Oxon. pref. p. ix.
[†] Chand. Marm. Oxon. p. ii.

answer to the question, What advantage could any man propose, by the fabrication of the inscription, adequate to the trouble and expence, attending the execution of this project?

4. It is certain, that Peiresc was never in Asia; that he trusted to the integrity of his agent at Smyrna; and consequently was very liable to be imposed on in this negotiation. On the one side or the other, there was evidently some craft or imposition. Who Samson was, we are not informed: probably he was a JEW. He was however thrown into prison. This gives us no favourable opinion of his integrity. Gassendus indeed says, he was confined, *venditorum arte*, " by the iniquitous contrivance of the venders." If Samson was guilty of no fraud, the people, who sold the marbles, seem to have been capable of executing any scheme, which might gratify their avarice. For after they had received a considerable sum from Peiresc, they imprisoned his agent, and sold them a second time to Mr. Petty.

Such were the first OSTENSIBLE POSSESSORS of these marbles! and so dark and unsatisfactory is the account, which is transmitted to us of their discovery! They had been totally unknown, or unnoticed for almost nineteen hundred years, and, at last, they are dug out of the ground—no body can tell us WHEN or WHERE!

It will probably be objected, that the mutilated state of the marbles, when they were first brought to England, and examined by Selden, is a proof of their authenticity, as it cannot be supposed, that any man, in his senses, would deface his own inscription.

In answer to this objection we may observe, that the Chronicle may be a modern compilation, and yet not have come immediately from the hands of the original fabricator.

fabricator. It might have been ACCIDENTALLY defaced, before it was purchased for M. Peirefc.

We are informed, that after Samfon was imprifoned, the marbles were broken, feparated, and thrown about promifcuoufly at Smyrna. This will fufficiently account for their mutilation.

But, fecondly, fome occafional lacunæ might have been artfully contrived, to conceal falfe affertions and chronological errors; and, at the fame time, to give the marbles a venerable air of antiquity, which was not fufficiently confpicuous in the Greek characters. This artifice has been frequently practifed. We fhall fee a remarkable inftance of it in the XVI chapter, where this account is given of one H. Cajadus : " Lapides, datâ operâ detruncatos, ut aliqua ineffent ANTIQUITATIS VESTIGIA, obrui præcepit."

It is well known, that a true antiquary values a fragment, as much as a perfect piece; and his gufto is perhaps more ftimulated by the idea of what is loft, than gratified by the part, which is preferved.

The ftory of the Sibyl, who appeared to Tarquin, the laft king of Rome, is not inapplicable on this occafion.

A woman in ftrange attire came to Tarquin, and offered to fell him a collection of prophecies in nine volumes, for three hundred pieces of gold *. Upon his refufing to buy them on thefe extraordinary terms, the woman threw three of them into the fire, and afked the fame price for the remaining fix. Tarquin, looking upon her as a mad woman, treated her with contempt. Upon which fhe burnt three volumes more, and ftill

---

* We are told by Varro, and by Lactantius, who relates the ftory after him, and likewife by Servius, that the woman demanded three hundred philippi. This anticipation is a little abfurd : fuch a coin did not exift, till the time of king Philip, the father of Alexander the Great.

perfifted

perfifted in demanding as much for thefe three, as fhe had done for the whole collection.

The old woman formed a proper notion of human nature. Tarquin's CURIOSITY was immediately excited; and the fragments were purchafed at the price fhe demanded [*].

[*] A. Gell. l. i. 19. Dion. Halic. l. iv. c. 8. p. 259. Plin. l. xiii. 13. Serv. Æn. vi. 72. Varro and Lactantius report the ftory of Tarquinius Prifcus. Fragm. p. 35. Lact. l. i. c. 6.

CHAP. XV.

IX. THE world has been often imposed upon by spurious books and inscriptions.

Bishop Stillingfleet, having occasion to question the authenticity of a book, entitled, Scotorum Antiquitates, ascribed by Hector Boethius to one Veremundus, a Spaniard *, makes the following remarks, which are applicable to the present subject.

" It is well known, that it was no unusual thing in that age [about the beginning of the sixteenth century] to publish books under the names of ancient authors ... For, about that time, men began to be inquisitive into matters of antiquity; and therefore some, who had more learning, and better inventions than others, set themselves to work, to gratify the curiosity of those, who longed to see something of the antiquities of their own country. And such things were so eagerly and implicitly received by less judicious persons, that it proved no easy matter to convince them of the imposture †."

The celebrated Dr. Bentley makes the following observations to the same effect.

" To forge and counterfeit books, and father them upon great names, has been a practice almost as old as letters. But it was then most of all in fashion, when

---

* Veremundus is said to have lived about the year 1090. Fabric. Bibl. Med. & Inf. Lat. Hector Boethius flourished in 1526. Gesner. Or, in 1510. König. Bibl.

† Stillingfleet, Orig. Brit. pref. p. 50.

THE PARIAN CHRONICLE.

the kings of Pergamus and Alexandria *, rivaling one another in the magnificence and copioufnefs of their libraries, gave great rates for any treatifes, that carried the names of celebrated authors; which was an invitation to the fcribes and copiers of thofe times, to enhance the price of their wares, by afcribing them to men of fame and reputation; and to fupprefs the true names, that would have yielded lefs money. And now and then even an author, who wrote for bread, and made a traffic of his labours, would purpofely conceal himfelf, and perfonate fome old writer of eminent note; giving the title and credit of his works to the dead, that he himfelf might the better live by them. But what was then done chiefly for lucre, was afterwards done out of glory and affectation, as an exercife of ftyle, and an oftentation of wit. In this the tribe of the fophifts are principally concerned; in whofe fchools it was the ordinary tafk to compofe Ηθοποιιας †, to make fpeeches, and write letters in the name and character of fome hero, or great commander, or philofopher : Τινας αν ειποι λογους, "What would Achilles, Medea, or Alexander, fay in fuch or fuch circumftances?" Thus Ovid, we fee, who was bred up in that way, wrote love-letters in the names of Penelope, and the reft. It is true, they came abroad under his own name; becaufe they were written in Latin and in verfe, and fo had no colour or pretence to be the originals of the Grecian ladies. But fome of the Greek fophifts had the fuccefs

* Galen. in Hippoc. de Natura Hominis, com. ii. p. 17. edit. Bafil.

† Allocutio, quae a Graecis ηθοποιια dicitur, eft imitatio fermonis ad mores et fuppofitas perfonas accommodata: ut, quibus verbis uti potuiffet Andromache, Hectore mortuo. Prifcian. See the Ethopœiæ of Severus the fophift, at the end of the Rhetores Selecti, publifhed by Gale.

4   and

and satisfaction to see their essays, in that kind, pass with some readers for the genuine works of those, they endeavoured to express. This, no doubt, was great content and joy to them; being as full a testimony of their skill in imitation, as the birds gave to the painter, when they pecked at his grapes. One of them * indeed has dealt ingenuously, and confessed, that he feigned the answers to Brutus, only as a trial of skill; but most of them took the other way, and concealing their own names, put off their copies for originals; preferring that silent pride and fraudulent pleasure, though it was to die with them, before an honest commendation from posterity for being good imitators. And to speak freely, the greatest part of mankind are so easily imposed on in this way, that there is too great an invitation to put the trick upon them †."

If we were to take a general view of the republic of letters, we should be astonished at the number of suppositious books, which have been imposed upon the world by knaves and cheats.

Jamblicus, on the testimony of Seleucus, informs us, that Hermes Trismegistus was the author of 20,000 books; and, on the authority of Manetho, 36,525 ‡.

---

* Mithridates.—The publication, to which Dr. Bentley alludes, consists of 35 epistles, supposed to have been written by M. Brutus; and the same number of answers, with a preface, by Mithridates, to king Mithridates his cousin.—Epistolæ, quas nobis reliquit nescio quis, Bruti nomine, nomine Phalaridis, nomine Senecæ et Pauli, quid aliud censeri possunt, quàm DECLAMATIUNCULÆ? Erasm. Ep. l. i. 1. Fabric. Bibl. Græc. l. ii. c. 10. vol. i. p. 414.

† Bent. Dissert. upon Phal. p. 6. edit. 1777.

‡ Jamb. de Myst. sect. viii. c. 1.—Julius Firmicus also ascribes 20,000 volumes to Hermes. Mercurius Ægyptius conscripserat viginti millia voluminum de variis substantiis & principiis, & potestatum ordinibus cœlestium. Mathes. l. ii.

THE PARIAN CHRONICLE. 185

There are many volumes now extant under his name; but not one of them is genuine. Two of the most confiderable, the Pœmander, and the dialogue entitled Afclepius, are metaphyfical rhapfodies, containing a medley of Chriftian, Platonic, and Egyptian doctrines, without either tafte or confiftency; and appear to have been written fince the commencement of Chriftianity*.

Twenty or thirty thoufand books, produced by one author! The very idea fhocks all human credibility; and, if ever fuch a number really exifted, under the name of Hermes, we may fairly conclude, that the greateft part of them were forgeries †.

The two books of Egyptian hieroglyphics, which are afcribed to Horus Apollo, or Horapollo, and faid to have been tranflated out of the Egyptian language into Greek by one Philippus, are the fpurious production of fome Greek fophift.

An epic poem, called the Argonautics, eighty-fix

---

* Cafaubon calls the Pœmander, femichriftiani merum figmentum, and gives fufficient reafons for his opinion. Exercit. in Baron. Annal. num. 18. p. 55. Stillingfl. Orig. Sacræ, b. ii. c. 2. Afclepius is in the fame ftyle, and feems to be a production of the fame brain.

† Patricius affigns fome very probable reafons for the afcription of all thefe books to Hermes.—Quòd fuerit, fays he, in more antiquiffimorum hominum, ut fi cui libro authoritatem accedere cuperent, vel Dei alicujus, ut Ægyptii Mercurii, vel hominis alicujus infignis, nomine ornarent, reverentiâ fcilicet quâdam; vel etiam quòd vendibiliorem eo nomine fperarent fore; vel quòd fœtui proprio, alieni nominis quàm fui infignibus, gratiam majorem confequi fperarent ac immortalitatem; vel poftremò, quòd reverâ author libri ignoraretur, viderentúrque in eo contenta dogmata non nifi magni viri effe; aut etiam negligentiâ quadam, ac nullâ librorum expenfione, alicujus eos viri celebris nomine infigniverunt. Patric. Difcuff. Peripat. tom. i. l. 3. p. 29. Vid Galen. de Simpl. Medic. Facul. l. vi.

B b   hymns

hymns, and other pieces, pass under the name of Orpheus, the celebrated Thracian, who lived at the time of the Argonautic expedition *. But they are evidently supposititious. As the ancients have told us, that Orpheus could make wild beasts, trees, rocks, and rivers listen to his music, it is no wonder, that certain poets in later ages assumed his character, and sent their productions into the world under his auspices. His name was an incomparable passport and recommendation to the writings of obscure bards. Aristotle asserted, that no such poet as Orpheus ever existed: "Orpheum poetam docet Aristoteles nunquam fuisse †." Cicero seems to agree with Aristotle; and Vossius, Huetius, and others, maintain the same opinion ‡.

But, without calling his existence in question, we may be fully assured, that none of his works are now remaining.

---

* Suidas says, a little extravagantly, that Orpheus lived "eleven generations before the Trojan war." But who shall pretend to ascertain the age of a poet, who is said to have been the son of Apollo and Calliope, and to have gone down to the regions of Pluto to fetch his wife? Saxius places him 1255 years bef. Christ.

† Cic. de Nat. Deor. l. i. § 107.

‡ Puto enim, triumviros illos posseos, Orphea, Musæum, Linum, non fuisse; sed esse nomina ab antiquâ Phœnicum linguâ, quâ usi Cadmus et aliquamdiu posteri. Voss. de Art. Poet. c. 13. p. 78. Huet. Dem. Evang. prop. iv. c. 8. § 19. p. 184. edit. 1680.——Vid. Suid. in v. Ορφευς, "where," says Dr. Bentley, "there is an account of half a score of such counterfeit writers." Dissert. on Phal. p. 10. Ælian. Var. Hist. l. viii. c. 6. Diog. Laert. in procem. § 5. Pliny places Orpheus in the list of magicians. Nat. Hist. l. xxx. c. 1.

Some writers pretend, that the Argonautics, the hymns, and other poetical pieces, which are extant under the name of Orpheus, are the works of Onomacritus, who lived about 520 years before the Christian æra.——This notion may be as groundless, as the other.

Musæus

Musæus is said to have been the son, or the disciple of Orpheus *. The poem of Hero and Leander, which is published under his name, is probably the work of some Greek poet in the fifth or sixth century †. It is observed, that he has borrowed very largely from the Dionysiaca of Nonnus ‡. We often meet with the name of Musæus; but never find the least intimation of this poem, in any ancient writer. Tzetzes, I believe, is the first, who expressly mentions it ‖. It was first printed in 1486.

We have a history, De Excidio Trojæ, of the Destruction of Troy, under the name of Dares Phrygius. In an epistle prefixed, it is pretended, that this Dares was present at the siege; that his manuscript was discovered at Athens many years afterwards, by C. Nepos, and translated by him into Latin.

---

* Diod. Sic. l. iv. p. 232. Suidas.

† Musæum hunc recentiorem circumcirca tempora Coluthi, Tryphiodori, Joannis Gazæi, Nonni, Christodori, Leonis Magistri, multis scilicet post Christum natum annis, floruisse certissimum est, præter orationis structuram, ipso operis titulo, ubi se grammaticum appellat, Μουσαιου του γραμματικου τα καθ' Ἡρω και Λεανδρον; et istiusmodi inscriptionem in pluribus me legisse memini manuscriptis codicibus. Allat. de Patriâ Homeri, c. 4. p. 75.

An quæso, nisi monitus criticorum vaticiniis, Musæo, Orpheo, Lino, Phocylidi, et aliis INNUMERIS, tum Pelasgis, tum Romanis, poemata spuria multa, et illegitima, assignata fuisse, hodiéque assignari INSULSE, ut veteri Phocylidi quæ supersunt, Musæo de Herone et Leandro poema, scire quis unquam potuisset? Maussaci Dissert. Crit. de Harpocratione, p. 399. edit. 1683.

If we may depend on the authority of Josephus and Sextus Empiricus, there were no writings remaining, in their days, among the Greeks, of higher antiquity, than the poems of Homer. See notes to chap. ix. p. 127.

‡ Paræus in Musæum.

‖ Tzet. Chil. ii. hist. 38. v. 435.—Tzetzes flourished about the year 1176.

But the inelegant, not to say, the despicable style, in which it is written, as well as many other circumstances, clearly demonstrate the falsity of these pretences.

There is another production of the same character, in six books, De Bello Trojano, of the Trojan War, bearing the name of Dictys Cretensis. In the preface, and an epistle, which accompanies this work, it is asserted, that the author attended Idomeneus to the siege of Troy, and wrote the history of that expedition in the Greek language, but in Phœnician characters; that his work was buried with him at his own request, in a coffer made of pewter or tin; that, in consequence of an earthquake, the coffer was discovered, in the reign of Nero; and some time afterwards translated into Latin, by one Q. Septimius Romanus.

This legendary tale, and some others, which I shall have occasion to mention, are evidently formed upon the old story of king Numa *, who is said to have ordered, that his books should be safely enclosed in a stone chest, and buried by his side. After they had lain in the ground 490 years †, they were, it seems, accidentally discovered, and appeared as fresh, as if they had been newly written ‡! Some people imagined, they were kept in this EXCELLENT PRESERVATION by a miracle ‖. Others probably, a little more sagacious than the rest, upon observing the Egyptian papyrus, of which

---

* Varro Fragm. p. 51.   Liv. l. xl. c. 29.   Plin. l. xiii. c. 13. Plut. v. Numæ, p. 74.   Val. Max. l. i. c. i. § 12.   Lactan. l. i. c. 22.   Aur. Vict. c. 3.

† Numa died, bef. Chr. 671; and his books were found in the year 181.   Corsin.   Plin. loc. cit.

‡ Non integros modò, sed recentissimâ specie.   Liv. loc. cit.

‖ Majore miraculo, quòd tot infossi duraverint annis.   Plin. loc. cit.

they were made, the freshness of the writing, and the contents, looked upon them as forgeries. It is however agreed on all hands, that Q. Petilius, the prætor, by a decree of the senate, caused them to be publicly burnt; which certainly would not have been suffered, if there had been any reason to believe, they were the genuine remains of the religious Numa [*].

A small volume, containing 148 epistles, has been repeatedly published under the name and character of Phalaris, tyrant of Agrigentum. In the year 1695, the Hon. Mr. Boyle printed a new edition of these Epistles, which occasioned a memorable controversy between him and Dr. Bentley. The latter, in a Dissertation [†], well known to the learned, considers the chronology, the language, the contents, and the first appearance of these epistles; and incontestably proves, that they are the spurious productions of some sophist, who lived in a much later age, than the real Phalaris. To this Dissertation, the learned author has subjoined some critical remarks on the Epistles of Themistocles [‡], Socrates, and Euripides; and on Æsop's Fables, shewing, that they are likewise suppositious.

[*] Inclyta justitia religióque Numæ Pompilii erant. Liv. l. 1. c. 18.

[†] Bentley's Dissertation was printed at the end of the second edition of Mr. Wotton's Reflections on ancient and modern Learning, in 1697. The Examination of Bentley's Dissertation, by the Hon. Mr. Boyle, appeared about nine months afterwards; and a second edition of it, before the end of the year 1698. This drew from Dr. Bentley another edition of his Dissertation, in 1699, with a preface, and very large additions, in answer to the examiner.

[‡] The very judicious and accurate Corsini deduces a new argument against the authenticity of the epistles, ascribed to Themistocles, from a mistake, which the author has made in the thirteenth epistle, concerning the Corinthian month Panemus. Fast. Attic. Dissert. iii. § 22.

Some

Some of the dialogues, which are publiſhed among the works of Plato, were written by other authors. Eraſmus thinks, this is ſo very evident, that he, who does not perceive it, muſt have no diſcernment *.

Diogenes Laertius obſerves, that the dialogues, entitled, Eryxias, Acephalus or Siſyphus, Axiochus, and Demodocus, are undoubtedly ſpurious †. The Definitions, the Dialogue on Virtue, and that on Juſtice, are generally placed in the ſame claſs ‡. The Epinomis has been aſcribed to Philippus Opuntius, one of Plato's diſciples ‖; the ſecond Alcibiades to Xenophon §, and Phædon to Panætius ¶.

* Sunt aliquot inter Platonicos dialogos, quos nemo non ſentit ſuppoſititios eſſe, niſi qui nihil omninò ſentit animo. Eraſmi Epiſt. ad tom. iv. Hieron. Op. p. 5.

† Diog. Laert. l. iii. c. 62.

Eryxias is aſcribed to Æſchines, the Socratic philoſopher. Suidas in v. Αισχινης.

Siſyphus or Acephalus, to Æſchines. Diog. Laert. l. ii. § 60. iii. § 62. Suid. loc. cit.

Axiochus to Æſchines. Diog. Laert. Harpoc. in v. Αξιοχος. Suidas loc. cit. et in v. Αξιοχος.

Demodocus : ει δη του Πλατωνος το συγγραμμα, ſi modò eſt opus Platonis. Clem. Alex. Strom. l. i. p. 315.

‡ The 'Οροι, or Definitions, are ſuppoſed to have been written by Speuſippus. Diog. Laert. l. iv. § 5. Lambecii Comment. de Biblioth. Cæſar. l. vii. p. 137.

The Dialogue on Virtue is placed by Suidas among the works of Æſchines.

‖ Diog. Laert. l. iii. § 37.

§ Athen. l. xi. p. 506.

¶ Menagii Obſerv. in Diog. Laert. l. iii. § 62. Vid. Fabric. Bibl. Græc. vol. ii. p. 9. Placcii Theatrum Pſeudonymorum. p. 511. Patric. Diſcuſſ. Peripat. tom. i. l. 3.

⁎ In what relates to the want of authenticity, in ſome of Plato's Dialogues, and the works of others, I give the ſentiments of learned writers, without any deſign to adopt or maintain their opinions, when they are not confirmed by unqueſtionable evidence.

Laertius

THE PARIAN CHRONICLE.

Laertius reckons up "near 400 books," which, he says, were undoubtedly written by Ariſtotle *. Patricius has collected the titles of 747, which have been aſcribed to that philoſopher †. But many of theſe pieces, as he has ſufficiently proved, are ſuppoſititious. Galen and Ammonius give us an anecdote, which accounts for this inundation of ſpurious publications, under the name of Ariſtotle.

"When the Attali and the Ptolemies," ſays Galen, "were rivaling one another in forming and enriching their reſpective libraries, the knavery of forging books and titles began [to be a common practice.] For, in order to get money, many artful ſchemers prefixed the names of celebrated authors to their manuſcripts, and, under ſuch fictitious characters, ſold them to thoſe princes ‡."

Ammonius relates the ſame ſtory. "It is reported," ſays he, "that Ptolemy Philadelphus, being deſirous of collecting the works of Ariſtotle, as indeed he was of collecting all ſorts of books, gave rewards to thoſe, who brought him any treatiſe of that philoſopher. Some therefore, with a deſign to make an advantage of his liberality, affixed the name of Ariſtotle to the compoſitions of other authors ‖."

On

---

* Ἀ τον ἀριθμόν ἐγγὺς ἥκει τετρακοσίων, quæ ad quadringentorum numerum ferè perveniunt. Diog. Laert. l. v. § 34.

† Si hi, ex variis authoribus, atque ipſo Ariſtotele, collecti, libri triginta ſeptem, reliquis à Laertio enumeratis, atque iis, qui extant, addantur, ſeptingentorum quadraginta ſeptem numerum adimplebunt. Patric. Diſcuſſ. Peripat. l. ii. p. 18.——The ſame books were probably mentioned by different authors, under different titles. This circumſtance ſeems to have deceived many writers, who have enumerated the works of the ancients.

‡ Galen. in Hippoc. de Nat. Hom. com. ii. p. 17.

‖ Πτολεμαῖον τον Φιλάδελφον παιδ σπουδαζειν ὡς περι τα Ἀριςοτελους συγγραμματα,

On this account, it is almoſt impoſſible for us to know, which are the genuine productions of Ariſtotle.

The treatiſe on Elocution, uſually aſcribed to Demetrius Phalereus, though not unworthy of his character, is moſt probably the work of ſome other Demetrius, or ſome rhetorician of a later age, who has aſſumed his name *.

A hundred and thirty comedies were circulated at Rome, under the name of Plautus; but we are aſſured,

---

συγγξαμματα, ὡς και περι τα λοιπα, και χρηματα διδοναι τοις προσφερουσιν αυτω βιβλους του φιλοσοφου· ὁθεν τινες χρηματισασθαι βουλομενοι, επιγραφοντες συγγραμματα τω του φιλοσοφου ονοματι, προσηγον. Aiunt Ptolemæum Philadelphum incenſum ſtudio fuiſſe circa Ariſtotelis libros, ſicuti et circa alios, et munera dediſſe iis, qui ſibi adferrent libros philoſophi. Quare quidam ditari inde volentes, inſcripſerunt libros nomine philoſophi, eique detulerunt. Ammon. Com. in Ariſt. Categ. p. 10.

* The ſcholiaſt on the Nubes of Ariſtophanes, quoting a paſſage in the treatiſe on Elocution, ſays, ὡς ἐφη Διονυσιος ὁ Ἁλικαρνασσευς εν τω περι Ἑρμηνειας: For this and other reaſons, Valeſius aſcribes the treatiſe on Elocution to Dionyſius Halicarnaſſeus. Valeſii Excerpta, p. 65. Menagii Obſerv. in Diog. Laert. l. v. § 81. Hed. de Bibl. Text. l. i. c. 9. p. 55.

Voſſius, Gale, &c. aſcribe it to ſome other Demetrius. Auctor videtur alius Demetrius, rhetor Alexandrinus. Voſſ. Inſtit. Orat. l. vi. c. 2.——Tandem in ſententiam Voſſianam tranſivi. Gale præf. ad Rhet. Select.——Propendet animus ut credam, Demetrium Alexandrinum aureoli hujus libelli auctorem eſſe. Hudſon. præf. ad Dionyſ. Halic.——Demetrii alicujus rhetoris libellus. Fabric. Bibl. Græc. l. iv. c. 31. § 1. vol. iv. p. 424.——Demetrius was a very common name. Diogenes Laertius mentions twenty, and Fabricius above a hundred Demetrii. Bibl. Græc. vol. x. p. 390.

The editor of Daniel ſecundum LXX. contends, that the treatiſe on Elocution is really the work of the celebrated Demetrius Phalereus. Diſſert. iv. § 15.

that

that Varro, an excellent judge in this case, included only twenty-one in the list of that author's works*.

Among the various pieces, which have been falsely ascribed to Cicero, the CONSOLATIO is the most remarkable. This tract made its first appearance in the year 1583, and is generally supposed to have been the work of Sigonius. " The essay de Consolatione," says Dr. Bentley, " as coming from a skilful hand, may perhaps pass for Cicero's with some, as long as Cicero himself shall last †." There is however an obvious and striking circumstance attending it, which alone seems to destroy all its pretensions to authenticity; and that is, the passages quoted by Lactantius ‡ from Cicero's real work, do not exist in the present Consolatio.

In the second century, we find the practice of forging books so very common, and so eagerly pursued, that it was impossible to guard against literary impositions ‖. We have a memorable instance of those fraudulent schemes in the case of Galen. That eminent physician having been the author of many volumes, not only on medical subjects, but on philosophy, grammar, and rhetoric §, left his reputation should be injured by spurious publications, gave the world a particular account of his

---

* A. Gell. l. iii. c. 3.
† Bentley, Dissert. on Phal. p. 8.—See the opinions of several writers on this subject collected by Placcius, in his Theatrum Pseudonymorum, num. 646. p. 179—181.
‡ Lactan. l. iii. c. 14. 18. Vid. Lipsii Opera, tom. i. edit. Moreti, p. 411. Clerici Art. Crit. tom. ii. p. 333.
‖ Nemini non notum, quàm fertile et fœcundum scriptorum fictitiorum fuerit sæculum secundum à Christo nato. Nihil magis tunc temporis in usu fuit, quàm libros emittere sub nominibus antiquiorum. Quod infinitis exemplis luculentò constat. Hodius, de Bibl. Text. Orig. l. i. c. 9. p. 53.
§ Suidas in v. Γαληνος.

writings *. Yet, notwithstanding this precaution, above forty books were fathered upon him, which are not included in his catalogue †.

In this manner a multitude of spurious productions have been published under the names of Homer, Æsop, Euripides, Hippocrates, Aristophanes, Lysias ‡, Demosthenes, Plutarch, Lucian, Virgil, Ovid, Seneca, Quintilian, and almost every other eminent author of Greece and Rome ||.'

The forgeries of Annius Viterbiensis are well known. In the year 1497, this impudent monk published a volume, containing, as he pretended, the Antiquities of Berosus in five books; one book of Manetho's Supplement to Berosus; one book of Xenophon's Æquivoca; two books of Fabius Pictor on the Golden Age, and the Origin of Rome; one book of Myrsilus Lesbius on the Pelasgic War; one book of Cato's Origines; one book of an Itinerary by Antoninus Pius; one book of C. Sempronius, on the Division of Italy; a chronological tract by Archilochus; one book of Metasthenes § on the Assyrian and Persian Annals; an

---

* Περι των ιδιων βιβλιων, Of his own books.

† Galeno, quanquam de libris suis librum edidisset, quo testatum relinqueret, quinam à se conscripti libri essent, sunt tamen reperti homines audaculi, qui illi, præter à se nominatos ascripserunt libros plusquam quadraginta. Patric. Discuss. Peripat. tom. i. l. 3. p. 29.

‡ Harpocration, in his excellent Lexicon on the Ten Orators of Greece, when he mentions any oration of Lysias, or of others, the authenticity of which is not sufficiently ascertained, usually subjoins the words, ει γνησιος, "if it be genuine." And this useful caution he repeats, on many occasions, in the course of his references. v. p. 11. 13. 16. 17. 22, 23. & alibi passim.

|| Vid. Erasmi Epist. ad tom. iv. Hieron. Op. p. 5. Placcii Theatrum Pseudonymorum.

§ Ita eum inepte vocat, qui est Megasthenes. Voss. de Hist. Lat. l. iii. c. 8. p. 609.

Epitome

Epitome of History by Philo in one book; a tract of Marius Aretius on the Situation of Sicily; and a Dialogue, containing a description of Spain, by the same author *.

These fragments were illustrated by the comments of Annius himself; and for some years passed for the genuine works of the authors, whose names they bear. They are now universally exploded, as the fictions of the editor.

The learned Dr. Prideaux, having occasion to mention the forgeries of Annius, the British History of Geoffrey of Monmouth †, and other productions of the same stamp, subjoins this reflection: " All these are no other than the fictions of the first editors. They framed them to perpetuate their names by the publication; and they have truly done so, for they are still remembered for it; but no otherwise, than under the style of INFAMOUS IMPOSTORS ‡."

It is remarkable, that no province of literature has been so grievously infested with cheats and forgers,

---

* Berosi, sacerdotis Chaldaici antiquitatum libri quinque, &c. Romæ, 1497. folio. This collection was afterwards printed at Venice, Paris, Basil, Antwerp, and other places.

† Geoffrey of Monmouth lived in the time of Henry the First and Stephen, and was bishop of St. Asaph in 1152. In his British History he affirms, that Brutus, the great-grandson of Æneas, and after him above seventy glorious monarchs, reigned in this island, during a period of 1053 years, before the invasion of Julius Cæsar. He continues his narrative to the death of Cadwallader, in the year 689.

This history contains the story of king Lear and his daughters; an account of the wonderful exploits of Uther Pendragon, and king Arthur; the prophecies of Merlin, and many similar curiosities. See above, chap. iii.

‡ Prid. Connect. vol. ii. p. 804.

as that of Jewish and ecclesiastical antiquity*. Here we read of the BOOKS of Abel, Seth, Enoch, Shem, Abraham, and Og the giant; the TESTAMENTS of Adam, Noah, Abraham, Job, Moses, Solomon, and the twelve patriarchs; the LITURGIES of Matthew, Mark, John, James, Peter, the Virgin Mary, and Jesus Christ; the ACTS of Andrew, John, Mark, Matthias, Paul, Peter, Philip, Thomas, Pilate, Caiaphas, and Thecla; the EPISTLES of Luke to Galen, Peter to James, John to a man who had the dropsy, Paul to the Laodiceans, and the Virgin Mary to Ignatius; the GOSPELS of James, Andrew, Thomas, Philip, Bartholomew, Matthias, Barnabas, Thaddæus, Peter, Paul, Nicodemus, Judas Iscariot, and Eve; the REVELATIONS of Peter, Stephen, Paul, Thomas, Solomon, Moses, Job, Elias, Abraham, Noah, Adam; the MAGICAL WRITINGS of Solomon, Joseph, Abraham, Ham, and Noah †.

To this list we may add the following extract from a decree of pope Gelasius I. made in the year 494, De Libris apocryphis, &c.

Itinerarium nomine Petri apostoli, quod appellatur S. Clementis, libri viii. apocryphum.

Actus nomine Andreæ apostoli, apoc.

Actus nomine Philippi apostoli, apoc.

Actus nomine Petri apostoli, apoc.

---

* Illud me vehementer movet, quòd videam primis ecclesiæ temporibus quamplurimos extitisse, qui facinus palmarium judicabant, cœlestem veritatem figmentis suis ire adjutum; quo faciliùs videlicet nova doctrina à gentium sapientibus admitteretur. Officiosa hæc mendacia vocabant, bono fine excogitata. Quo ex forte dubio procul sunt orti LIBRI SEXCENTI, quos illa ætas & proxima viderunt. Casaub. in Baron. Annales Exercit. 1. num. 18. p. 54.

† Fabric. Codex Pseudepigraphus Vet. Test. Cod. Apoc. Nov. Test. passim.

Actus

Actus nomine Thomæ apoftoli, apoc.
Evangelium nomine Thaddæi, apoc.
Evangelium nomine Thomæ apoftoli, quo utuntur Manichæi, apoc.
Evangelium nomine Barnabæ, apoc.
Evangelium nomine Bartholomæi apoftoli, apoc.
Evangelium nomine Andreæ apoftoli, apoc.
Evangelia, quæ falfavit Lucianus, apoc.
Evangelia, quæ falfavit Hefychius, apoc.
Liber de Infantiâ Salvatoris, apoc.
Liber de Nativitate Salvatoris, et de S. Mariâ, et de obftetrice Salvatoris, apoc.
Liber, qui appellatur Paftoris, apoc.
Libri omnes, quos fecit Lenticius, difcipulus diaboli, apoc.
Liber, qui appellatur de filiabus Adæ, vel Genefis, apoc.
Liber, qui appellatur Actus Theclæ & Pauli apoftoli, apoc.
Revelatio, quæ appellatur Thomæ apoftoli, apoc.
Revelatio, quæ appellatur Pauli apoftoli, apoc.
Revelatio, quæ appellatur Stephani, apoc.
Liber, qui appellatur Tranfitus S. Mariæ, apoc.
Liber, qui appellatur Pœnitentia Adæ, apoc.
Liber, qui appellatur Diogenes, nomine gigantis, qui poft diluvium cum dracone pugnaffe perhibetur, apoc.
Liber, qui appellatur Teftamentum Job, apoc.
Liber, qui appellatur Sortes apoftolorum, apoc.
Liber, qui appellatur Laus apoftolorum, apoc.
Liber Canonum apoftolorum, apoc.
Epiftola Jefu ad Abgarum regem, apocrypha, &c. *

* Fabric. Cod. Apoc. p. 65. 135. Varrerii Cenfura, p. 14. &c.

The decree, from which this catalogue is taken, is supposed by Dr. Cave *, and some other ecclesiastical writers, to be supposititious. But the learned Casaubon speaks of it in much more favourable terms. For having mentioned the gospel according to the Egyptians, the prophecy of Ham, the apocalypse of Moses, and other notorious forgeries, he calls it, " insigniter salutare decretum," a very salutary decree, in which, he says, many books of this despicable sort are specified and condemned †.

However, whether it is genuine or not, it will serve to shew us, what numbers of absurd and scandalous publications were imposed upon the world, in the first ages of Christianity, under the respectable names of apostles and evangelists. Hanc legem, says Varrerius on a quotation from the same decree, hic duximus subjiciendam, ut melius intelligatur, quantùm præpostera hominum ingenia fallacibus hujusmodi et fucosis artibus delectentur ‡."—Supposing the decree itself is a forgery, it is but an addition to the impositions already mentioned.

If we descend to the primitive fathers, we shall find a multitude of spurious productions under their names. Cave ‖ enumerates thirty pieces of that kind, which have been ascribed to Cyprian ; thirty, which have been attributed to Athanasius ; thirty, which have appeared under the name of Jerom ; sixty, which have been published as the works of Austin ; seventy, which have been fathered on Chrysostom ; and so on, in proportion to the reputation of each respective writer.

The number of forgeries, false records, and counter-

* Cave, Hist. Liter. sub an. 492.
† Casaub. in Baron. Annal. Exercit. i. p. 22. 54.
‡ De Beroso Censura, p. 14.
‖ Cave, Hist. Liter.

feit

feit antiquities, imposed upon the world by the advocates of the church of Rome *, in support of their religion, or, more properly speaking, their SYSTEM of SUPERSTITION, exceeds almost all imagination, and affords a deplorable instance of the depravity of mankind, and the facility, with which knaves and bigots have suppressed every suggestion of conscience, reason, and religion, while they were engaged in the pursuit of what is absurdly, if not ironically, called a PIOUS FRAUD !

If we confine our observations to the present century, and to our own country in particular, we shall meet with several notorious instances of literary craft and imposition.

The late Psalmanazar wrote a fictitious history of Formosa †, and invented a new language, which, he pretended, was the language of that island. The imposition was supported for some time; and the author was caressed as a prodigy of abstinence, piety, and learning. But in the latter part of his life, his conscience began to upbraid him; and, in a posthumous publication, he acknowledged, that the account, which he had given of Formosa, and of his travels and conversion from paganism to Christianity, was an infamous fiction ‡.

In

* See a book, entitled, Roman Forgeries, published in 1673.
† An historical and geographical Description of Formosa, 8vo. 1704.—A second edition of this work was published in 1705, with a preface, containing, " an answer to every thing, that had been objected against the author and his book."
Psalmanazar died in 1763, about the eighty-sixth year of his age.
‡ Memoirs of ****, commonly known by the name of George Psalmanazar, a reputed native of Formosa, written by himself, in order to be published after his death, &c. 8vo. 1764.
In his will he says : " The principal manuscript I thought myself in duty bound to leave behind, is a faithful narrative of my education,

In the year 1747, the literati were furprifed at the appearance of an Eſſay on Milton's Uſe and Imitation of the Moderns, in his Paradiſe Loſt, by William Lauder *; the tendency of which was to ſhew, that Milton was a plagiary. In purſuance of this deſign, he charged Milton with having borrowed many parts of his plan, many paſſages, ſentiments, and images, from the Sarcotis of Maſenius, the Adamus Exul of Grotius, the Triumphus Pacis of Staphorſtius, the Comœdia Apocalyptica of John Fox, the Locuſtæ of Phineas Fletcher, the Bellum Angelicum of Taubman †, and other ſimilar productions.

Some

---

education, and the ſallies of my wretched youthful years, and the various ways, by which I was, in ſome meaſure, unavoidably led into the baſe and ſhameful impoſture, of paſſing upon the world for a native of Formoſa, and a convert to Chriſtianity, and backing it with a fictitious account of that iſland, and of my own travels, converſion, &c. all or moſt of it hatched in my own brain, without regard to truth and honeſty." p. 5, 6.

* Lauder commenced his attack upon Milton in the Gentleman's Magazine for January 1747; and continued his animadverſions, at different times, in that publication. An imaginary ſucceſs prompted him to reprint his extracts and obſervations, with conſiderable additions, in a ſeparate volume, 8vo. which appeared in December 1749.

† Jacobus Maſenius was profeſſor of rhetoric and poetry, in the Jeſuits college at Cologn. His Sarcotis conſiſts of five books, and was printed about the year 1654. An elegant edition of this poem, and of ſome other pieces, by Maſenius and Grenan, was publiſhed at Paris in 1771, with ſome obſervations on Lauder's controverſy.

Grotius is ſaid to have written his tragedy, entitled, Adamus Exul, when he was only eighteen years of age. It was printed at Leyden in 1601; but was not inſerted in the collection of his poems.

Caſpar Staphorſtius was a Dutch poet and divine. His Triumphus Pacis was a congratulatory poem, on the concluſion of the

Some of the examples, which he produced, in support of this accusation, bore such a striking resemblance to passages in the Paradise Lost, that many of his readers were inclined to applaud his sagacity, and the propriety of his remarks.

But while the enemies of Milton were shouting, *Io triumphe!* and insulting the memory of the injured poet, an acute and learned writer rose up in his defence, and effectually exposed this master-piece of fraud and imposition, by demonstrating, that Lauder had inserted several passages of Hog's translation * of Paradise Lost, and other lines of his own composition, into the extracts, which he had produced from Masenius, Staphorstius, and others; and then urged those very lines as a proof, that Milton had copied them †.

As this charge was unanswerable, Lauder thought proper to throw himself on the candor of the public,

---

peace between the states of Holland, and the commonwealth of England, in 1655.

John Fox, the martyrologist, published his Comœdia Apocalyptica, or Christus Triumphans, in 1551.

Phineas Fletcher was Fellow of King's College, Cambridge. His poem against the Jesuits, entitled, Locustæ, vel Pietas Jesuitica, was printed in 1627.

Taubman, the author of Bellum Angelicum, printed about the year 1604, was the celebrated commentator on Plautus and Virgil.

* Paraphrasis poetica in tria Johannis Miltoni, V. C. poemata, viz. Paradisum Amissum, Paradisum Recuperatum, et Samsonem Agonisten. Autore Gulielmo Hogæo. Londini, 1690.

† Milton vindicated from the charge of plagiarism, brought against him by Mr. Lauder; and Lauder himself convicted of several FORGERIES and gross IMPOSITIONS on the public. By John Douglas, M. A. [now bishop of Carlisle.] 8vo. 1751.

A second edition of this pamphlet was published in 1756.

by subscribing a penitential acknowledgment, dictated by a learned friend, of all his interpolations in the writers he had quoted *.

In the year 1762, an enterprizing writer published an epic poem in six books, entitled Fingal, and other pieces, of a singular character, under the name of Ossian, which were said to have been translated from the Galic or Erse. The truth of this assertion has been frequently controverted. It is however strenuously maintained by these, who are advocates for the literary glory of Caledonia. But the very existence of Ossian, if ever there was such a poet, is, like the history of Orpheus, enveloped in fable and romance; and though we may allow the pretended translator to have collected some traditionary stories, some ancient fragments, and some strolling ballads, we may reasonably suspect, that the greatest part of these poems have been composed by the editor, as he has never condescended to favour the world with the works of Ossian in their original language, though such a publication has been frequently requested †; and would have not only silenced all ob-

---

* This confession was entitled, A Letter to the Rev. Mr. Douglas, occasioned by his vindication of Milton, &c. By Wm. Lauder, A. M. 4to. 1751. It was dictated by the late Dr. Johnson, who, at first, had conceived a favourable opinion of Lauder's abilities and integrity. Lauder however in the year 1754, retracted his confession, defended his essay, and made a new attack upon Milton, in a pamphlet, entitled, " King Charles I. vindicated from the charge of plagiarism, brought against him by Milton ; and Milton himself convicted of forgery, and a gross imposition on the public. —Lauder died in Barbadoes, about the year 1771.

† Dr. Johnson required, that the original should be deposited in either the king's or the marischal college at Aberdeen, and submitted to public inspection; but this was never done. Hawkins's Life of Johnson, p. 488.

THE PARIAN CHRONICLE.

jections, but have been esteemed a valuable curiosity in the republic of letters *.

About the beginning of the year 1777, the attention of the public was excited by a volume of Poems, which were said to have been written at Bristol by Thomas Rowley, a secular priest of that city, and others, in the fifteenth century †. These pieces were read with surprise and admiration, and occasioned a variety of conjectures, relative to their authenticity. It was asserted, that the original manuscripts had been found in an old chest in Redcliff church, at Bristol, by one Chatterton the sexton; that Chatterton gave them to his nephew, the master of a writing-school in Pile-street ‡; and that, after the death of the latter, they fell into the hands of his son, Thomas Chatterton, who sent some of them to the editors of the magazines, and disposed of others.

Some learned writers have maintained, that they are the genuine productions of Rowley ‖; others have supposed, that they were not written by Rowley, but forged by Chatterton §, who probably derived the first idea of

such

* It is said, that Ossian was the son of Fingal, a king of Scotland, celebrated for his prowess; that he lived in the beginning of the fourth century; and that these poems are superior to those of all other Caledonian bards, both in genius and antiquity.

† In the reigns of Henry VI. and Edward IV.

‡ Account of Chatterton by Dean Milles.

‖ Their authenticity is asserted in several publications, particularly the following:—" Poems, supposed to have been written at Bristol, by Thomas Rowley, &c. with a Commentary. By Jeremiah Milles, Dean of Exeter, 4to. 1782."

" Observations upon the Poems of Thomas Rowley, in which the authenticity of those poems is ascertained. By Jacob Bryant, Esq. 8vo. 1782."

§ Thomas Chatterton, the hero of this controversy, was born Nov. 20, 1752, and educated at a charity-school in Bristol. At the age of fourteen, he was articled clerk to an attorney in that city.

such a project from some old parchments, which might have been found, as he afserted, in a chest in Redcliff church.

This opinion seems to be much more probable than the other, for the following reasons.

1. It is hardly to be imagined, that all the poems, ascribed to Rowley, could have lain in a chest, unobserved and unexamined, for the space of 300 years; and that there should not, during this long interval, have been one, among all the learned vicars of Redcliff church, who had the curiosity to examine, and the sagacity to discover, the contents of this wonderful repository.

2. The phraseology, the splendid descriptions, the poetical images, the harmony of the versification, very unusual with writers of the fifteenth century, the manifest imitation of later poets, some apparent anachronisms, and OTHER CIRCUMSTANCES, are strong presumptive evidences, that they are not the compositions of Rowley.

Chatterton's abilities for a work of this nature can hardly be doubted, if we attend either to his comments on the poems attributed to Rowley, or to many similar pieces, which, we are assured, are his genuine and acknowledged productions *.

But,

city. In April 1770, he came to London, in hopes of advancing his fortune by his pen; but he was so miserably disappointed, that about four months afterwards, in a fit of despair, he put an end to his life, at the age of seventeen years and nine months.

* See Remarks on Chatterton's Miscellanies by the Author of this Dissertation, in the Critical Review for August 1778, where it is shewn, that there have been many EARLY GENIUSES, equal or superior to Chatterton, in the republic of letters.

On this occasion, the present Dissertator, though he owns these insignificant remarks, would wish to intimate, that his concern in the

THE PARIAN CHRONICLE.

But, not to dwell any longer on fuppofititious BOOKS, let us proceed to fictitious INSCRIPTIONS.

the fame Review extended only from Auguſt 1764 to September 1785 incluſive ; and that he is not, at prefent, accountable for any criticiſms, which appear in that publication.

CHAP. XVI.

ABOUT the year 1435, Cyriacus Anconitanus, furnamed the Antiquary, collected inscriptions, and other remains of antiquity, in different parts of Europe, Asia, and Africa *. He pretended to have found a multitude of inscriptions in Spain, as well as in other countries, which Ambrosius Morales, and other Spanish historians, quoted upon his authority. But the learned and judicious Antonius Augustinus, archbishop of Tarragon, assures us, that many of these inscriptions were fictitious; and that, in his time, none of them were to be seen in Spain †.

In

---

* Cyriacus's inscriptions, in three volumes, folio, entitled, Antiquarum Rerum Commentaria, were never entirely published. Some of them only were communicated by himself to his friends; about 200 were printed by C. Moronus in 1660, and others have appeared in different collections.

A small volume in 12mo. entitled, Kyriaci Anconitani Itinerarium, was published by Laurentius Mehus, at Florence, in 1742, containing eight Letters by Kyriacus, and a preface by the editor, in vindication of the author's literary character. But this publication contains no inscriptions, nor any very important information.

† Cyriaci Anconitani inscriptiones plurimas in Annalibus Hispaniæ Ambrosius Morales temerè descripsit. B. Mirari equidem soleo in tot tantisque antiquis inscriptionibus, quas ille attulit, nullas hodiè in Hispaniâ legi. A. Illud incommodi est, videri Joannem Annium & Cyriacum, similísque farinæ homines, Hispanos irridere voluisse, confictis Hispanorum rebus gestis sub Noâ, Tubale; serie item contextâ regum falsorum, quasi nostris regnassent temporibus; fictis adhæc lapidibus, de bello cum Viriatho, & Sertorio; civili quoque Cæsaris ac Pompeii, &c. Augustini Antiquitatum Dialogi. xi. p. 161.

Augustinus's

THE PARIAN CHRONICLE. 207

In 1534, Petrus Apianus and Bartholomæus Amantius publiſhed a large collection of antiquities at Ingolſtadt, in which they inſerted a conſiderable number of thoſe, which had been either collected or invented by Kyriacus *. The learned writer I have juſt now cited affirms, that many of theſe inſcriptions are forged by different authors †.

About the year 1520, Alexander Geraldinus pretended to have found in various parts of Ethiopia, on both ſides of the equinoxial line, many Roman inſcriptions and antiquities ‡, more valuable (if genuine)

Auguſtinus's Dialogues were publiſhed in the Spaniſh language in 1587, and tranſlated into Latin by And. Schottus, 1617. The author died in 1582, aged 71 years. Voſſ. de Hiſt. Lat. l. iii. c. 10. p. 809.

Reineſius ſpeaks favourably of Cyriacus. Inſcript. Antiq. præf. p. ii.

* This collection bears the following title: Inſcriptiones ſacroſanctæ vetuſtatis, non illæ quidem Romanæ, ſed totius ferè orbis, ſummo ſtudio ac maximis impenſis terrâ marique conquiſitæ, feliciter incipiunt. Magnifico viro, domino Raymundo Fuggero, &c. Petrus Apianus Mathematicus, & Bartholomæus Amantius Poeta. D. E. D. Ingolſtadii, anno MDXXXIV.

Primi, qui excerpta ex Kyriaci ſchedis typis excuderunt, fuere Petrus Apianus & Bartholomæus Amantius. Kyriaci Itin. præf. p. 59.

† In antiquitatibus orbis totius, à Petro Apiano & Bartholomæo Amantio foras datis, fictæ multæ ſunt à diverſis auctoribus inſcriptiones. Aug. Dial. xi. p. 162. Menagiana, tom. iv. p. 263.—One of the firſt in this collection is the fooliſh prophecy of II. Cajadus, which will be mentioned hereafter.

‡ Alexandri Geraldini Itinerarium ad regiones ſub æquinoxiali plagâ conſtitutas. [anno 1520; complectens antiquitates & ritus populorum Æthiopiæ, Africæ, Atlantici oceani, & Indicarum regionum. Acceſſerunt auctoris opuſcula alia, edente Onuphrio Geraldino, ejus abnepote.] 8vo. Romæ, 1631.—Geraldinus was made biſhop of St. Domingo, the capital of Hiſpaniola, in 1516, and died in 1525.

than

than all the inscriptions and antiquities, which the rest of the world could produce. But it is observable, that no traveller, besides himself, ever saw these curiosities; and, as M. de la Mothe le Vayer remarks, " it is the greatest impertinence to raise imaginary pillars, and bear testimony to the conquests and dominion of the Romans, in places, where apparently no Roman ever set his foot, and in direct opposition to their own historians *." Geraldinus appears to have been as great a traveller, and—as great a romancer, as Leo Africanus: par nobile fratrum !

In 1636, Curtius Inghiramius published a volume of Tuscan Antiquities †, containing a multitude of Latin inscriptions, relative to the origin of Volaterra, Sena, Rome, &c. which, he says, he found under-ground at Scornellum, near Volaterra. The inscriptions, he tells us, were written by one Prosperus Fesulanus, who lived in the time of Cicero ‡, and deposited by him in that place, with an epistle to the finder, in which he prophetically describes the said Inghiramius ; lays many strict injunctions on him not to communicate the originals to any one ; and denounces the most horrible calamities on such as should presume to steal, to touch them, to depreciate the credit of the finder, or rob him of the glory, to which he was entitled for the discovery of these inestimable treasures ‖.

It

---

* De la Mothe le Vayer, des anciens Historiens Grecs & Latins.
† This work is entitled, Ethruscarum Antiquitatum Fragmenta, quibus urbis Romæ, aliarumque gentium primordia, mores, & res gestæ indicantur, à Curtio Inghiramio reperta Scornelli prope Vulterram. Francofurti, anno salutis MDCXXXVII. Ethrusco vero cIɔ cIɔ cIɔ cIɔ ccccxcv. Folio. A former edition was printed at Florence in 1636.
‡ Bef. Chr. 60.
‖ Alius, si forte invenerit, eas scripturas tangere non audeat; alioquin

It is easy to see the author's views in throwing out these denunciations. Though they were perfectly absurd and ridiculous, they were plainly intended to check the impertinent curiosity, the animadversions, and the ridicule of his opposers.

The whole performance however bears the most obvious marks of fraud and imposition *. The characters do not in the least correspond with the mode of writing in the time of Cicero; the Latinity is mean and barbarous; the customs, which are occasionally mentioned, were unknown in ancient Rome; and the stories, which are told of the patriarch Noah, are alone sufficient to expose the grossness of the cheat.

To these remarks we may add, that the artist very simply and inadvertently wrote his inscriptions on paper, which was known to have been made about the time of the pretended discovery †.

Some have ascribed this performance to Postellus ‡; some, to Paganinus Gaudentius; others affirm, that the author was Thomas Phædrus or Fœdrus, who was keeper of the Vatican library, about the year 1490. It is most probable, that Inghiramius himself was the real fabricator of all these ridiculous inscriptions ‖.

alioquin superûm infernorumque deorum iram expertus peribit infelix... Si quis has scripturas quovis modo sibi arripuerit, famæ et corporis jacturam faciet... Si quis nomen tuum augere his scripturis, vel tuum deprimere fuerit ausus, rerum suarum, vitæ, & honoris, maximum damnum passus omnibus ludibrio erit. Verum nec hæredes tui nec tu, inventas scripturas aliis dare audeatis, nam malum instat, sed transcriptas poteris dare cui volueris, &c. p. 3, 4.

* Vid. Leon. Allatii Animadversiones in Antiquitatum Etruscarum Fragmenta, ab Inghiramio edita, 4to. Paris, 1640.
† Ibid. p. 91.
‡ Voss. de Hist. Lat. l. i. c. 9. p. 41.
‖ Fabric. Bibl. Lat. l. iv. c. 13. § 2. p. 601. Vid. Saxii Onomast. vol. iv. p. 442. Placcii Theat. Pseudon. p. 523.

But

But the most enterprizing and eminent practitioner in the art of making fictitious inscriptions, was Annius of Viterbo, whom I have already mentioned. Antonius Augustinus gives us the following account of the process, which Annius observed in his forgeries.

" Mihi Latinus Latinius * Viterbiensis, vir doctus, bonæque fidei, de Joanne Annio, Viterbiensi monacho, narrare jucundè solebat. Lapidi insculpendas curâsse literas, quem vineæ infodi jusserat, non procul à Viterbio. Cúmque fodienda esset vinea, ad lapidem usque ut fodiendo pervenirent jussit; narrans in libris se reperisse, templum ibi orbis terrarum antiquissimum latere. Terrâ jam effossâ, primus, qui lapidem invenit, vinitor accurrit; paulatim detegi sarcophagum imperat. Hic stupens, lapidis antiquitatem, & literas à se confictas, admiratur; ac describens, ad urbis senatores lætus confugit, & civitatis honori fore persuadet, in amplissimo publicè spectari loco. Viterbii enim urbis originem contineri, quæ bis mille annis Romanâ esset urbe à Romulo conditâ longè antiquior, utpote ab Iside & Osiride conditæ. Fabulas hic suas, quibus abundabat, venditavit, factúmque ut ille jusserat. Fertur manuscripta inscriptio ficta, typis etiam evulgata, hoc initio, Ego sum Isis †."

" Latinus Latinius, a native of Viterbo, a man of learning and veracity, used to relate, with some humour, the following anecdote of John Annius, a dominican friar of that city.

" Annius got an inscription engraved on a stone, which he buried in a vineyard near Viterbo. When

* Latinus Latinius was born at Viterbo about the year 1513. He published notes on Tertullian, and a work, entitled, Bibliotheca sacra et profana, sive observationes, correctiones, conjecturæ, & variæ lectiones.

† August. Dial. xi. p. 160.

THE PARIAN CHRONICLE.

the labourers were employed in digging the ground, he directed them to proceed, till they came to the spot, where the stone was depofited; telling them he had found in his books, that the ruins of the moſt ancient temple in the world lay under-ground in that place. After the earth was removed, the ſtone actually appeared; upon which the vine-dreſſer, who firſt diſcovered this wonderful curioſity, ran to Annius, and acquainted him with what he had found. The farcophagus was ordered to be removed with all poſſible care. Annius, in the mean time, ſeemed to be aſtoniſhed at the antiquity of the ſtone, and extremely delighted with the inſcription. In the height of his pretended exultation, he flew to the magiſtrates of Viterbo, expatiated on the nature and importance of the diſcovery, and perſuaded them, that this venerable monument of antiquity would be an everlaſting honour to the city, if they would remove it to a conſpicuous place, where it might be publicly exhibited. He obſerved, that it related to the origin of Viterbo; and that Rome, founded 2000 years ſince by Romulus, was far inferior in point of antiquity to Viterbo, which was built by Iſis and Oſiris. With theſe romantic ſtories, which he readily invented, he amuſed the public; and his orders were inſtantly obeyed. An inſcription was circulated in manuſcript, and afterwards printed, beginning with theſe words, EGO SUM ISIS, I am Ifis."

A project of the ſame kind was managed, with ſome ſucceſs, by one Hermicus Cajadus, or Hermio Gajado, a Portugueſe poet, about the year 1505 *. When his countrymen had made a conqueſt of ſeveral places in Africa, and the Eaſt Indies, he compoſed ſome Latin verſes, in the ſtyle of a Sibylline prophecy, foretelling theſe conqueſts; and having engraved them on three marble columns, he MUTILATED THE STONES, and

* Cajadus died of intoxication in 1508. Ladvocat.

DEFACED some of the inscriptions, in order to give them an appearance of antiquity. He then buried them in the ground; and, at a proper opportunity, contrived a scheme for the discovery, which was artfully managed, and attended with great exultation. The inscription, which was undefaced, was read, admired, touched and kissed, with the profoundest veneration; and afterwards published as a divine prophecy *.

The Duilian inscription has been reckoned a most

---

* Is Latinis carminibus commentus fuerat Sibyllinam vaticinationem, in columnis marmoreis incisam, quæ per ambages significabat, Indos sub imperium & ditionem Lusitanorum esse venturos, eosque lapides data opera DETRUNCATOS, ut aliqua inessent ANTIQUITATIS vestigia, obrui præcepit. . . . Ubi vero defossa marmora aliquod vitium fecisse, ex humore terreno, judicavit, ad certam diem, simulata delectationis causa, invitat amicos in villam suam, quæ proxima erat loco, ubi obrutum latebat vaticinium. Cum igitur accubuissent omnes, ecce villicus nunciat Hermico, mercenarias ejus operas, dum in fundo fossionibus incumberent, incidisse in lapides, in quibus inscriptæ essent literæ, indices magni cujusdam thesauri, eodem loco defossi; sic enim rustici opinabantur. Nec mora, omnes simul, alacritate ingenti, relictis epulis, accurrunt, defossas intuentur columnas, confestimque extrahi jubent; in quibus incisa hujusmodi erant carmina Sibyllina:

Sibyllæ vaticinium, occidiis decretum.
Volventur saxa literis, & ordine rectis,
Cum videas occidens orientis opes.
Ganges Indus Tagus erit, mirabile visu,
Merces commutabit suas uterque sibi.
Soli æterno, ac lunæ decretum.

Tum vero omnes, pro se quisque legere, admirari, versus illos fatidicos venerari, manu tangere, exosculari . . . . Ita Sibyllina fabula vires acquirit eundo, ac tandem per totum terrarum orbem divulgata, fides ei ubique et auctoritas adjungitur, hodiéque typis excusa circumfertur in fronte codicis, cui titulus est, " Inscriptiones antiquæ." Varrerii Censura in quendam Auctorem, qui sub falsa Inscriptione Berosi Chaldæi circumfertur, p. 15. edit. 1598. Fabric. Bibl. Lat. l. iv. c. 13. vol. ii. p. 607.

curious

THE PARIAN CHRONICLE. 213

curious and valuable relic of antiquity [*], yet Selden seems to question its authenticity; for having occasion to mention its age, in speaking of the Parian Chronicle, he intimates his suspicions in these words, si nimirùm genuina est [†].

Reinesius asserts, that Fulvius Ursinus has published many fictitious inscriptions [‡].

Fleetwood, in his Inscriptionum Antiquarum Sylloge, informs his readers, that though he was, as much as possible, on his guard against false and fictititious inscriptions, he often found, that he had inadvertently inserted, " plurimas apertè spurias," many that are evi-

---

[*] C. Duilius commanded the Roman fleet in the first Carthaginian war, and gained a complete victory. To perpetuate the memory of this triumph, a pillar of white marble was erected to his honour at Rome. This pillar is called Columna rostrata, from the rostra, or beaks of ships, with which it was adorned. On the basis of the column was an inscription, recording the exploits of Duilius, and the value of the booty, which was taken in the Carthaginian ships. The remains of this pillar were accidentally dug up, in the year 1560, in the place, which was formerly the Forum Romanum: and, by the order of Cardinal Alexander Farnese, was removed to the capitol.

The inscription, which is in old Latin, is supposed to have been written 260 years before the Christian æra, and is reckoned the most ancient Latin monument now remaining.

Justus Lipsius endeavoured to supply the deficiencies in the inscription. Pet. Ciacconius did the same, and explained the sense in a learned commentary, entitled, Pet. Ciacconii in Columnæ Rostratæ C. Duilii inscriptionem, à se conjecturâ suppletam, Commentarius. Lug. Bat. 1597. Græv. Thesaur. tom. iv. p. 1807. Univ. Hist. vol. xvii. p. 224. 506. xii. p. 171. edit. 1740.

[†] Seld. Marm. Arund. in edit. Ansâ, p. 3.

[‡] De Ursino dixeram, cautè me arripere solere, quas ab ipso profectas scirem, inscriptiones; & paratus sum, si quis postulet, FICTITIAS cum PLURIMIS extrusisse probare. Remesii ad Rupertum Epist. 50. p. 456. Epist. 43. p. 418. Epist. 51. p. 487. 490. Fabric. Bibl. Lat. l. iv. c. 5.

dently

dently spurious *. And Stillingfleet affirms, that there are many counterfeits in Gruter's collection †.

As a farther confirmation of what I have here observed, I shall subjoin the remarks of a learned writer, who in this instance, has advanced none of his usual paradoxes.

" Falsarum inscriptionum architectos proximum nostro sæculum INNUMEROS tulit; egregios artifices, qui, quas ipsi magnâ, ut sibi quidem videbantur, arte concinnassent, has aut in marmoribus, aut in tabulis æneis, plumbeisve, aut lateritiis fistulis, aut in antiquis denique numismatis, lectas à se fuisse mentirentur. Sed et aliquot ante ætatibus fraus eadem in usu fuit. Plena sunt pergamena manu exarata fictis in otio inscriptionibus, epitaphiis, elogiis; quæ cum inde eruuntur à viris etiam alioqui magnis ac probis, sed minus justo suspiciosis, ab eorumdem suffragio pondus illa accipiunt; ac deinde mirificè inquinant perturbantque prophanam historiam, utinam verò non etiam ecclesiasticam.

" Superiore porrò sæculo, insigniores harum inscriptionum fabricatores fuere Jovianus Pontanus, Pomponius Lætus, Joannes Camers, Cyriacus Aconitanus, aliique ‡. Hos enim in primis nominatim designat Antonius Augustinus, Dialogo xi. p. 161. E Cyriaci verò officinâ plurimas in Annales Hispaniæ transfudit Ambrosius Morales ||, et exinde Gruterus in Thesaurum suum; è tot autem inscriptionibus nullum hodie in

---

* Epist. dedic. p. 10.

† " Not only authors, but other monuments of antiquity, were then counterfeited, as appears by many in Gruter's Collection of Inscriptions." Stillingf. Orig. Brit. pref. p. 1.

‡ Jovianus Pontanus fl. circa 1460. Saxii Onomast. Pomponius Lætus, circa 1484. Ibid. Joannes Camers, circa 1510. Ibid.

|| Ambrosius Moralis, sive de Morales, circa 1574.

Hispaniâ

THE PARIAN CHRONICLE. 215

Hispaniâ legi, testis est idem Antonius Augustinus, vir summæ eruditionis, limatique judicii, qui de Joanne Annio, Italisque aliis præterea conqueritur, quòd suæ, nempe Hispaniæ, genti epigrammata et marmora obtruserint, nec visa illis, nec ab Hispanis reperta; atque ea demum ille cum Amadisii Gallici et Orlandi Furiosi nugis commentisque confert. Inscriptionum hujusmodi immensam supellectilem, quadraginta amplius digestam voluminibus, olim collegit Pyrrhus Ligorius; quæ Romæ extare dicitur in bibliothecâ Barberinnâ et Farnesianâ. Quâ in vastâ mole atque congerie, Spanhemius, vir eruditus, confitetur, p. 141. "plura esse aut dubiæ fidei, aut confessæ novitatis." Nec tantam ille crevisse segetem putat, nisi ex plurimorum fraude, qui Ligorio viro bono fucum fecerint. Farraginem eam esse subdit, quæ possit incautis imponere, avidis ad quamcumque ciborum novitatem, viris etiam alioquin eruditis, sed, ut dixi, minime suspiciosis. Neque enim HEBETES ac STULTI sunt, qui dant operam, ut hâc arte fallant. Sic Muretus olim Scaligero ipsi imposuit, quem induxit ut crederet, Attii et Trabeæ *, veterum, ut aiunt, poetarum carmina quædam esse; quæ idem Muretus, à se conficta, sub eorum nominibus Scaligero submiserat. E veteribus etiam schedis Josephi Scaligeri describitur à Grutero posita, ut quidem ait, Nicomediæ inscriptio: quis hanc, amabo, ad Scaligerum Nicomediâ attulit?

"Atqui non Gruterum modò, sed et eos, qui volumini ejus amplificando suam veluti symbolam contulerunt, fefellerunt ii, qui vel ex marmoribus ea se descripsisse elogia testati sunt; vel eruta ex membranis fallacibus insculpere lapidibus, superiore præsertim sæculo, ad aliquam patriæ suæ laudem, incautè sategerunt; vel QUI

---

* See an account of this imposition in Fabric. Bibl. Lat. l. iv. c. 1. p. 198. edit. 1728.

DENIQUE

DENIQUE INSIGNI FRAUDE INSCULPSERE IPSI, AC
TELLURI SUFFODERUNT, QUÆ DEINDE VEL IPSI-
MET, VEL POSTERI, EFFOSSA INGENTI AURO VEN-
DERENT. Vix enim repertum crutúmve talem fuiſſe
lapidem reperias, ante annum MDX. Poſt hunc annum
innumera ſunt, eo quem diximus aſtu, reperta. Itaque
in illo Theſauro Gruteriano INFINITI CARBONES LA-
TENT. Neque ex ſexaginta ferè inſcriptionibus, quæ
Conſtantiniani hujus ſæculi eſſe æſtimantur, vel una
quidem ſincera eſt, ſi inſcriptionem Arcûs Conſtantiniani exceperis *."

Similar obſervations occur in almoſt every author,
who has written upon the ſubject.

* Harduini Opera Selecta, p. 501.

CHAP. XVII.

THE examples, which I have produced in the foregoing chapter, will, I think, be sufficient to shew, what frauds have been committed, in the fabrication of inscriptions; and with what CAUTION we should credit such memorials.

In a question of importance, like the present, a writer, who is in pursuit of truth, will examine every circumstance with impartiality and freedom; and if he sees so many difficulties on every side, that he can form no SATISFACTORY conclusion, he will suspend his opinion, and be content to remain in the number of those, " who neither believe nor disbelieve every thing:" Ουτε πασι πιςευοντες, ουτε πασιν απιςουντες *.

This precaution is the more necessary, in the present instance, as suppositious books and inscriptions have been so numerous, and are, in reality, a disgrace to the republic of letters. Without any breach of charity we may assert, that he, who obtrudes any thing upon the world, under the name of antiquity, which has no title to that venerable character, deserves to be branded, as the worst of impostors; or, to use the language of Plautus, sent to live,

> Apud fustitudinas, ferricrepinas insulas,
> Ubi vivos homines mortui incursant boves †.

Whoever

---

* Arist. Rhet. l. ii. c. 14.

† Plaut. Asin. act. i. sc. 1. 20.—Fustitudinas and ferricrepinas are words coined by Plautus. Mortui boves is a humorous phrase

Whoever was the author of the Parian Chronicle, he stands in a higher clafs, than many of the modern forgers I have mentioned. His performance is written in a clear and claffical ftyle. It bears the marks of real learning, and a competent knowledge of Grecian hiftory; fo that in whatever light it is viewed, it is no contemptible production.

It is however worthy of obfervation, that the illuftrious Sir Ifaac Newton paid NO REGARD to its authority, in his Chronology of ancient Kingdoms.

The fixteenth century, and the former part of the feventeenth, prior to the difcovery of the marbles, produced a multitude of grammarians, critics, commentators, and writers of every denomination, deeply verfed in Grecian literature, and amply qualified for the compilation of fuch a fhort fyftem of chronology, as that of the Arundelian marbles.

Above all, the fcience of chronology was particularly ftudied and inveftigated about that time. " Nunc fervet chronologia," fays Scaliger in the year 1605; " omnes hoc ferrum excalfaciunt *." And Cafaubon treats thofe perfons with contempt, who were unacquainted with the improvements, which had been made in that department of learning, after the revival of letters. " Scientia temporum," fays he, " quantopere fuerit poft renatas literas exculta, quàm admiranda acceperit incrementa, ASINUS eft qui ignorat inter literatos; malignus, & beneficiorum DEI erga hoc feculum ingratus æftimator, qui diffimulat. Stupenda enim funt,

---

phrafe for ftrappadoes or whips, made of leather. A late tranflator renders thefe lines,

" In Club-ifland, and in that of Rattle-chain,
Where the dead oxen gore the living men."

* Scal. Epift. inter Opufcula, p. 521.

quæ

quæ viri fummi in noftrâ præfertim Galliâ & Germaniâ præftiterunt *."

Innumerable fyftems of chronology had been publifhed before the year 1625; from which it was eafy to extract a feries of memorable events, and give the compilation a Grecian drefs.

The avidity, with which all relics of antiquity were then collected, and the price, at which they were purchafed, were fufficient inducements to any one, whofe avarice, or whofe neceffity, was ftronger than his integrity, to engrave his lucubrations on marble, and tranfmit them to Smyrna, as a commodious emporium for fuch rarities †.

Whether

---

* Cafaub. in Baron. Annal. exercit. 1. num. 99. p. 111.— Cafaubon's preliminary difcourfe is dated 1614. He died July 1, 1614, aged 55.

† In thofe days, there were numbers of learned Greeks, ready to engage in any fraudulent fcheme, which was calculated to procure them any emolument. I fhall take the liberty to mention one of this clafs.

Critopulus Metrophanes was fent into England and Germany, by Cyril Lucar, patriarch of Alexandria, to gain information concerning the ftate and doctrine of the proteftant churches in Europe.

Archbifhop Abbot, in a letter to Sir Thomas Roe, then ambaffador at Conftantinople, recommends this gentleman in the following terms.

——" I recommend unto you this bearer Critophilus Metrophanes, a Greeke, borne in Byrræa, and fent unto mee five or fix yeeres fince by Cyrill, then patriarke of Alexandria ; and now of Conftantinople. Hee hath remained all his time in Oxford, where I have taken care, that hee hath bene well and fufficiently maintained, and thereby hath attained unto fome reafonable knowledge of the Englifh tongue, not neglecting his ftudies otherwife. Hee is a learned man, and hath lived in that univerfity with good report, whereof he is able to fhew letters teftimoniall to the good contentment,

A DISSERTATION ON

Whether this was the cafe with the Parian Chronicle or not; whether it is an authentic monument of antiquity,

ment, as I hope, of that reverend man, from whom he was fent [*].

. . . . Lambeth, Nov. 20, 1622.

In a fecond letter to Sir Thomas, the archbifhop gives a very different character of this learned Greek, as follows.

. . . . The Grecian Critopylus Metrophanes hath taken his journey very lately, into France or Holland, pretending from thence to go by land to Conftantinople. I bred him full five yeeres in Oxford, with good allowance for diett, cloaths, bookes, chamber, and other neceffaries; fo that his expence, fince his comeing into England, doth amount almoft to three hundred pounds. Whiles hee was in that univerfity, hee carried himfelfe well; and at Michaelmas laft I fent for him to Lambeth, taking care that in a very good fhippe, hee might bee conveyed with accommodation of all things by the way. But by the ill counfell of fome body, hee defired to go to the court at Newmarket, that hee might fee the king before his departure. His majefty ufed him well; but there hee was putt into a conceite, that hee might gett fome thinge to buy him bookes to cary home to the patriarke. The meanes that hee gaped after were fuch as you can hardly beleeve; at firft, that hee fhould have a knight to bee made for his fake; and then, after that, a baronet, wherein a proiector fhould have fhared with him: after that, the kinge was to be moved to give the advowfon of a benefice, which a falfe fimoniacal perfon did promife to buy of him. I caufed my chaplaines to diffwade him from thefe thinges, and interpofed mine owne cenfure in it, as thinking thefe courfes to bee vnwife, vnfitt, and vnworthy. But, to fatisfy his defire, I bought him new out of the fhoppe many of the beft Greeke authors, and among them Chryfoftome's eight tomes. I furnifhed him alfo with other bookes of worth, in Latin and in Englifh, fo that I may boldly fay, it was a prefent fitt for mee to fend to the patriarke of Conftantinople. In the meane time, fince Michaelmas laft, I lodged him in my owne houfe, I fett him at my owne table, I cloathed him, and provided all conveniences for him; and would once againe

[*] Roe's Negot. let. 63. p. 102.

have

quity, or a modern compilation; whether its authority is indisputable, or, as I am inclined to think, APOCRYPHAL, have sent him away in a good shippe, that hee might safely have returned: but he fell into the company of certain Greeks, with whom wee have been much troubled for collections and otherwise; and although I knew them to bee counterfeits and vagabonds (as sundry times you have written unto me) yet I could not keepe my man within dores, but hee must bee abrode with them, to the expence of his time and mony. In breefe, writing a kind of epistle unto mee, that he would rather loose his bookes, suffer imprisonment, and loss of his life, then go home in any shippe; but that he would see the parts of christendome, and better his experience that way. I found that hee ment to turne roague and beggar, and more I cannot tell what; and thereupon I gave him ten pounds in his purse, and leaving him to Sir Paul Pindares care, at my remooving to Croydon, about a fortnights since, I dismist him. I had heard before of the basenes and slavishnes of that nation; but I could never haue beleeved, that any creature in humane shape, having learning, and such education as he hath had heere, could, after so many yeeres, have bene so farre from ingenuity, or any gratefull respect. But he must take his fortune, and I will learne by him to intreate so well no more of his fashion. Onley I have thus at large acquainted you with the vnworthy carriage of this fellow, which, though it bee indecent in him, yet for the patriarks sake I grudge it not vnto him... I remayne, &c. *

Croyden, Aug. 12, 1623.

Sir Thomas answers:

.... I have lett the good patriarch know the devious course taken by Metrophanes, of your bounty, and care for him, and all the circumstances of his departure. Att first hee seemed somwhat astonished; butt his affection towards him prevailed to make his excuse .... Hee hath given order to write into Holland, France, and diuers other parts, to recall this straye sheepe, to whom hee beares an entire loue; and if hee come hither, intends to make him a kind of coadiutor in judging of causes, and to conferr vpon him all the dignity hee can † ....

Constant. June 24, 1623.

* Roe's Negot. let. 3. p. 171. † Ibid. let. 142. p. 214.

PHAL, I shall now leave to the determination of the judicious and impartial reader.

Though

In a third letter, the archbishop says:

———I hold it fitt to give the patriarcke this account of Metrophanes; that in July last I gave him viaticum to carry him to Constantinople by land; and for a long time after, I heard of him, but saw him not; only in February or March last, hee came unto mee, and told mee, that hee was resolved then speedily to go home by sea, and would know what service I would command him. I told him, that for seven or eight moneths, hee had not knowne mee, and now I would not know him; he might go where hee list, and might do what hee pleased. I thought then hee had gone away; but now, two daies past, being in my coach at London, I saw him go by me; but what hee intendeth, or what hee hath done with the bookes which I gave him for the patriarche, I can yeeld no account [*].

Lambeth, June 20, 1724.

Sir Thomas answers:

... I have acquainted the patriarch with your graces first and last letters concerning Metrophanes; who can heare nothing against him, that affection doth not enterprett to the better. Hee expects him daily, and your worthy present of bookes. I feare they will be pawned in the way. Of wandering Greeks there is SO GREAT A STORE, that I am forced daily to deny my passports [†]....

Constantinople, Dec. 9—19, 1624.

In a fourth letter, the archbishop gives this farther account of the good patriarch's "straye sheepe."

.... I knowe not what to saye to the patriarke touching Metrophanes. His roguish countreymen did vndoe him: hee had bene fairely caried to Constantinople by sea, and I gave him viaticum to that purpose; but hee is gone with pretence to travaile throughe Germany by lande, in whiche course I cannot see how hee should carye the bookes alonge with him. I do muche feare, that hee hath

---

[*] Roe's Negot. let. 173. p. 253.   [†] Ibid. let. 229. p. 320.

fared

Though its authenticity, I believe, has hitherto been unqueſtioned; nay, though it has been held in the higheſt eſtimation by men of diſtinguiſhed learning, I flatter

fared ſo well in theſe parts, that hee will hardly reduce himſelfe to the ſtrict life of the Coloires in the Greek church *....
Lambeth, Mar 30, 1625.

Sir Thomas, in his anſwer to the archbiſhop, ſays,

.... " Of his Metrophanes, hee [the patriarch] hath at laſt heard from Nurenburgh, who writes him a ſtrange diſcourſe, that Gondomar did ſeeke to debauch him, and ſend him to Rome; but failing, attempted his life, which made him forſake England; with many other friuolous aduentures. I wiſhed the patriarch to beleeve little: but hee willingly heares nothing againſt him, vpon whom hee hath ſett his affection. The truth is, they are futiliſſima natio. Long ſlavery hath made them, for the moſt part, lyars, baſe, and treacherous †."
[No date.]

Metrophanes ſpent ſome time at Tubingen, Helmeſtadt, Altdorff, and other places in Germany. Upon his return home he obtained preferment in the Greek church at Conſtantinople, and afterwards became patriarch of Alexandria !

He wrote a confeſſion of faith for the Greek church, entitled, Ὁμολογια της ανατολικης Εκκλησιας, which was republiſhed, with a Latin verſion by Joannes Horncius, at Helmeſtadt, in 1661. The original, ſays Königius, is compoſed, " ſtilo puro et elegante." Königii Bibl. p. 537. Conringius, in a preface to the Ὁμολογια, ſpeaks of his abilities in theſe terms : Potuit ſanè, quod rogatus erat, optimè omnium præſtare ; quandoquidem valebat ingenio, judicio, et doctrinâ non proletariâ.

The deſign of this note is, not to charge Metrophanes with any forgery ; but to ſhew, that there were men of learning among the Greeks, and unprincipled adventurers, who might be prompted to impoſe upon the world, by views of lucre, by vanity, or even by REVENGE. And this may ſerve as a caution to thoſe, who may hereafter be induced to purchaſe antiquities in the Eaſt.

* Roe's Negot. let. 262. p. 373.   † Ibid. let. 347. p. 488.

myſelf

myself there can be no impropriety in this disquisition. On the most important subject, that can possibly engage the attention of the human mind, we are directed to avoid an implicit credulity, and " to prove all things" by an impartial examination.

If the objections, which I have here alleged against the authenticity of this celebrated Chronicle, should be answered with liberality and candor, I shall readily join with the author in admitting its authority; for truth, and truth only, is the object of this enquiry *.

If, on the contrary, this essay should be treated with asperity; if I should be accused of depreciating a venerable monument of ancient learning; if any dictatorial critic should exclaim in the language of Horace,

————fragili quærens illidere dentem,
Offendet solido !   Sat. l. ii. 1. 77.

or, in the plenitude of his benevolence, should advise me to

————remember Milo's end,
Wedg'd in the timber, which he strove to rend,

I shall comfort myself by reflecting, that sarcasms and contumely are no arguments; that the antiquities of Berosus and Manetho, as they are exhibited by Annius of Viterbo, have been warmly defended; and that the most violent exclamations have been raised against those, who have called in question the most notorious forgeries, the letters of Abgarus †, Lentulus ‡, Pilate,

* Ego quid sentiam simpliciter indicavi, libenter παλινῳδήσων, et in diversam iturus sententiam, si quis docuerit rectiora. Porrò, si quis, cum id non possit, tamen odiosius obstrepit, ne studio rapi, quàm judicio mavult, ne cum hoc quidem unquam tria verba commutaverim. Erasmi præf. ad tom. iv. Hieron. p. 4.
† Fabric. Cod. Apoc. vol. i. p. 317.
‡ In some copies the epistle bears this title : Lentulus Hierosolymitanorum

THE PARIAN CHRONICLE.

late *, Seneca to St. Paul †, and, above all, that collection of ancient rubbish, the Oracles of the Sibyls ‡.

lymitanorum præfes, S. P. D. Romano S. Vid. Fabric. Cod. Apoc. vol. i. p. 302.
* Ibid. p. 298.
† Eight letters from Seneca to St. Paul, and fix from the Apoftle to Seneca. Ibid. vol. ii. p. 892. Sixt. Sinenf. Bibl. l. ii.
‡ A collection of Sibylline Oracles, in eight books, was published by Xyftus Betuleius, in 1545, 8vo. by Joh. Opfopæus, in 1589, 8vo. by Servatius Gallæus, in 1688, 4to.—The learned H. Dodwell calls this collection a counterfeit by fome Chriftian author; and obferves, that it was not reduced into the form, in which we now have it, before the end of the fecond century. Dodwell, Letter of Advice, &c. p. 114. Blondel on the Sibyls. Banier, Mythol. l. iv. ch. 2. Clerici Art. Crit. tom. ii. p. 345.

Suppofing there were really fuch prieftefles, as are ufually called Sibyls, it is amazing, that men of fenfe and learning fhould contend for the divine infpiration of FANATICAL OLD WOMEN! Perfius fpeaks like a more rational philofopher, when he fays.

———VETERES AVIAS tibi de pulmone revello.
Sat. v. 92.

F I N I S.

INDEX.

A.

ABBOT, archbishop, his letters to Sir Thomas Roe, 219—222.
—— his account of Metrophanes, ibid.
Accius imagines, that Hesiod lived before Homer, 124, 125.
Acusilaus, his genealogical tables, 75.
Ægius Spoletinus, an error in his translation of Apollodorus, 153.
Ægos-potamos, a stone said to fall in or near that river, 38.
—————— observations on that story, 157.
—————— Conon defeated there, 79.
Æschylus, present at the battle of Marathon, 36.
Ætna, eruptions of that mountain, 156.
Africanus, his opinion of Grecian chronology, 100.
Alexander, the time of his birth, 41.
—————— a spurious history of, 91.
Alexandrian library, 69.
—————— MS. 55, 173.
Alphonsus, his encomium on Q. Curtius, 146.
Alyattes reigns in Lydia, 32.
Ammoneans, who they were, 65.
Ammonius, his account of literary forgeries, 192.
Amphictyon, 24.
Amphictyones assemble at Thermopylæ, 24.
—————— take Cirrha, 32.
Anabasis, the meaning of that word, 39.

INDEX.

Annius of Viterbo, the books he forged, 194.
——— his inscriptions, 210, 211.
Antiquities, collected with avidity, 219.
Apianus, Pet. his inscriptions, 207.
Apollodorus, some account of his writings, 96.
——————— a passage in his Bibliotheca corrupted, 150.
——————— a passage improperly translated, 151.
——————— his account of Deucalion, ibid.
Apollonius Tyaneus, 65.
Archaïsms in the Chronicle, 56—58.
Archias, conducted a colony to Syracuse, 31.
Archilochus, his character, 80.
Aristeas, his history of the LXX. a contemptible fiction, 44, 128.
——— written by some Hellenistic-Jew, 138.
Aristides, when he was archon, 130.
Aristobulus, when he lived, 137.
Aristotle, an account of his library, 147.
——— his numerous commentators, ibid.
——— many pieces falsely ascribed to him, 191.
——— the number of his books, ibid.
Arundel, Thomas earl of, his genealogy, 45.
——— letters to him, 172.
Arundel-house, 47.
Astyanax, archon at Paros, 23.
Athenæus, on the number of the Athenians, 140.
Athenians, when they began their year, 116.
Athens taken by Lysander, 79.
——————— by Sylla, 147.
Attic months, 116, 117.
——— year, ibid.
Attica, its twelve cities, 29.
——— the number of its inhabitants, 140.
Augustinus, Ant. his remarks on spurious inscriptions, 206.
Autochthon, 23.

B. BABY-

B.

BABYLONIAN empire, its antiquity, 85.
——— Babylonians, their aftronomical obfervations, 65, 66.
——————— why they wrote on tiles, 66.
Banier, his account of Minos, 28.
——— afferts, that the Chronicle was dug up in the ifle of Paros, 170.
Bentley, his tranflation of the 55th epocha, 37.
——— his remark on the modern pronunciation of μ, 58.
——— his account of literary forgeries, 182.
——— his Differtation on Phalaris, 189.
——— his opinion of the Confolatio, afcribed to Cicero, 193.
Βιβλιοταφος, a literary undertaker, or a COLLECTOR of books, 147.
Boëthius, Hector, when he wrote, 182.
Books and volumes, mentioned by Mofes, &c. 67.
Boyle, Hon. Mr. his controverfy with Bentley, 189.
Brutus, Marcus, epiftles afcribed to him, 184.

C.

CADMUS goes into Greece, 25.
——— Cajadus, H. his forged infcriptions, 211, 212.
Callifthenes wrote a hiftory of Greece, 91.
——————— a fictitious hiftory under his name, 91, 92.
Capellus, on the date of the deftruction of Troy, 117.
Cafaubon, his opinion of literary forgers, 196.
Cave on fuppofititious books, 198.
Cecrops I. reigns at Athens, 24.
Cenforinus, a conjectural emendation of a paffage in his treatife de D. N. 113, 115.

Cures

INDEX.

Ceres comes to Attica, 26.
Chandler, Dr. publishes his Marmora, 51.
——— his edition of the Chronicle commended, ibid.
——— ascribes the Chronicle to Demetrius Phalereus, 129.
Chatterton, an account of him, 203.
Chronology, not observed by the ancient Greeks, 83.
——— when it began to assume a new form, 98.
——— when particularly studied, 218.
——— many systems published, 219.
Cicero, not the author of the Consolatio, 193.
Cirrha, the inhabitants besiege Delphi, 32.
Clemens Alexandrinus, his chronological citations, 109.
Comedies, carried in carts, 33.
Comet, mentioned in the Chronicle, 40.
Conon gains a victory, 79.
Corinth, the burning of that city, 97.
Corn, first sown in the Rharian plain, 27.
Corsini, on the Attic months, 116.
——— the destruction of Troy, 117.
——— the epistles ascribed to Themistocles, 189.
Cranaus reigns at Athens, 24, 150.
Creon, first annual archon, 31.
Crœsus, 34, 102.
Ctesias, his account of Cyrus, 89.
——— his character, 162, 164.
Curtius, Q. not mentioned by the ancients, 144—148.
——— epistles under his name, 148.
Cybele, her image appeared, 26.
Cyclades, possessed by the Carians, &c. 78, 79.
Cynossema, the battle at that place, 86.
Cyriacus Anconitanus, his inscriptions, 206.
Cyril Lucar, his extravagant account of the Alexandrian MS. 173.
——— his partiality for Metrophanes, 222.
Cyrus takes Sardes, 34.

INDEX.

Cyrus, various accounts of his birth, &c. 88—90.
———— the younger, his anabasis, 39, 167, 168.

D.

DAMIS the Assyrian, his memoirs, 65.
Danaus sails from Egypt, 25.
———— goes into Greece, 25.
Daniel secundum LXX, published at Rome, 128.
Dares Phrygius, the history ascribed to him, 187.
Darius began his reign, 35, 164.
———— his preparations for invading Greece, 163.
———— the time of his death, 162, 163.
Decalogue, written upon stones, 75.
Delphi, the temple of, plundered, 41.
Demetrii, many of that name, 135, 192.
Demetrius Judæus, 134.
———— Phalereus, not the author of the Chronicle, 128—141.
———— numbered the inhabitants of Attica, 140.
———— governor of Athens, 140.
———— retires into Egypt, 135, 139.
———— probably not the author of the treatise on Elocution, 192.
———— killed by the bite of an asp, 136.
Deucalion, the deluge in his time, 24.
———— circumstances relating to him, 151.
Dictys Cretensis, the history ascribed to him, 188.
Διδασκειν δραμα, the meaning of that phrase, 34, 35.
Διμυλος λιθος, a remark on that expression, 157.
Diodorus Siculus, his opinion of the Grecian chronology, 104.
———— his date of the Trojan war, 114.
Dionysius Argivus, his date of the Trojan war, 113.
———— Halicarnasseus, his date of the Trojan war, 114.
———— the tyrant, dies, 40.
———— his son succeeds him, ibid.

Diotimus,

INDEX.

Diotimus, archon at Athens, 41.
Diphtheræ, used for writing, 67.
Docere fabulam, the import and origin of this phrase, 34, 35.
Dodwell, his opinion of those, who pretended to copy inscriptions, 64.
Douglas, Mr. his vindication of Milton, 201.
Du Fresnoy says, the Chronicle was found in Paros, 169.
Du Pin reports, that the Chronicle was found in Paros, ibid.

E.

Eϱ, instead of εκ and εν, 56.
Egypt, its history full of incredible fictions, 85.
Eleusis or Eleusin, 27.
——— the Eleusinian mysteries, 27.
Ephorus, an account of his writings, 91.
——— makes Homer and Hesiod contemporaries, 125.
Erasmus, his opinion of the epistles of Phalaris, &c. 184.
——————— of some of the dialogues ascribed to Plato, 190.
Eratosthenes, some account of him, 93.
——————— his chronology, 94.
——————— his date of the Trojan war, 113.
Erichtheus reigns at Athens, 26.
Erichthonius joins horses to a chariot, 25.
Ethopœiæ, what they were, 183.
Euhemerus, an account of him, 63.
Eumolpus celebrates the mysteries, 27.
Euripides, when born, 36, 165.
——— dies, 39.
Eusebius differs from the author of the Chronicle, 119.
Ezekiel represents Jerusalem on a tile, 66.

F.

FORGERIES, literary, some account of, 182—205.
——————— when the forging of books began to be in fashion, 183.
——————— under the name of Homer, Virgil, &c. 194.
——————— of Jewish and apostolical writers, 196.
——————— of the fathers, 198.
——————— of the Popish writers, 199.
——————— of Pſalmanazar, ibid.
——————— of Lauder, 200—202.
——————— of Ossian's works, 202.
——————— of Chatterton, 203, 204.
——————— of the inſcriptions of Cyriacus Anconitanus, 206.
——————— of Pet. Apianus, 207.
——————— of Barth. Amantius, ibid.
——————— of Alex. Geraldinus, ibid.
——————— of Curt. Inghiramius, 208, 209.
——————— of Annius Viterbienſis, 210, 211.
——————— of H. Cajadus, 180, 211, 212.
——————— of others, 213—216.

G.

GALE, Dr. an error in his edition of Apollodorus, 153.
Galen, his account of literary impoſtors, 191.
—— publiſhed an account of his writings, 193.
—— books falſely aſcribed to him, 194.
Gaſſendus, his Life of M. Peireſc, 175.
——————— an error in his computation, 177.
Gelaſius Cyzicenus, pretends to have found an ancient manuſcript, 65.
——————— pope, his decree, 196, 197.

INDEX.

Gelo, when he became tyrant of Syracuſe, 37, 166.
Γελοια, joci, applied to Æſop's Fables, 142.
Γενεα, the uſe of that word, 84.
Genealogies, on tables of braſs, 75.
Generations, according to Herodotus, 85.
Geoffrey of Monmouth, his Britiſh Hiſtory, 65.
——— romantic, 195.
Geraldinus, his inſcriptions, 207, 208.
Goths wrote on rocks, 65.
Grecian chronology, 83—99.
——— the ſentiments of Africanus on that ſubject, 100.
————————— of Juſtin Martyr, ibid.
————————— Plutarch, 100—102.
————————— Joſephus, 102.
————————— Varro, 103.
————————— Thucydides, 103.
————————— Diodorus Siculus, 104.
Greeks, their hiſtory, 83—107.
——— their firſt writers, 83.
——— Herodotus, 83, 86.
——— Thucydides, 86.
——— Hippias the Elean, 90.
——— Ephorus of Cuma, 91.
——— Calliſthenes, ibid.
——— Theopompus, 92.
——— Timæus Siculus, ibid.
——— Eratoſthenes, 93.
——— Apollodorus, 96.
——— Polybius, 97.
——— Philochorus, &c. 97.
Greek writers never refer to the Parian Chronicle, 107.
——————— often quote their predeceſſors, 110.
Greeks, modern, Sir Th. Roe's account of them, 223.
Grotius, his Adamus exul, 200.

INDEX

Gruter, his inscriptions, 214, 216.
Guilandinus, his account of the papyrus, 68.

H.

HALIRROTHIUS, 24, 150.
Hardouin, his opinion of many inscriptions, 214—216.
Harmodius and Aristogiton assassinate Hipparchus, 35.
Harpocration, his useful caution, 194.
Hellen, son of Deucalion, 24, 152.
Hellenes, an appellation of the Greeks, 24, 152.
Heraclidæ, their return, 91.
Hercules purified, 28.
——— fetches the belt of Hippolyta, 77.
Hermes Trismegistus, books ascribed to him, 184.
——————— forgeries under his name, 185.
——————— reasons assigned for these forgeries, ibid.
Hermippus, an accurate historian, 137.
Herodotus, his chronology, 83—86.
——— did not write the Life of Homer, 123.
——— agrees with the sacred writings, 162.
Hesiod flourished, 30.
——— his "Works and Days" written on lead, 66.
——— corrected by Acusilaus, 102.
——— his poems turned into prose, ibid.
——— supposed to have been older than Homer, 124.
——— his contemporary, 125.
——— later than Homer, ibid.
Hiero, 37, 167.
Hipparchus assassinated, 161.
Hippias deposed, 161, 162.
——— the Elean, 90.
Hody, Dr. his opinion concerning the LXX. 128.
Homer, a fragment of his, 27.

INDEX.

Homer, the age in which he lived, 31, 121—127.
────── the opinion of Apollodorus on that subject, 122.
────── of Archemachus, 123.
────── Aristarchus, ibid.
────── Crates Mallotes, 124.
────── Eratosthenes, 123.
────── Euphorbus, 121.
────── Euphorion, ibid.
────── Eusebius, 122.
────── Euthemenes, 123.
────── C. Hemina, ibid.
────── Herodotus, 121.
────── the author of a Life of Homer, 123.
────── Juvenal, 122.
────── C. Nepos, ibid.
────── V. Paterculus, ibid.
────── Philochorus, 123.
────── Pliny, 122.
────── Porphyry, 121.
────── Solinus, 122.
────── Sosibius, 121.
────── Theopompus, ibid.
────── the Parian Chronicle, 124.
────── supposed to have been contemporary with Hesiod, 125.
────── prior to Hesiod, 125.
────── the most ancient Greek writer, 127, 187.
Horace expected his works would be immortal, 61.
Horus Apollo, books ascribed to him, 185.
Howard, Thomas, his genealogy, 45.
────── Henry, duke of Norfolk, 47, 48.
Hyagnis invents flutes, 26.
Hypodicus teaches a chorus, 37.

J. JAMES,

INDEX.

I.

JAMES, Richard, an account of him, 46.
Icaria, a borough in Attica, 33.
Idæi Dactyli, 26.
Inscription, the Sigean, 54.
——————— the Nemean, ibid.
——————— the Delian, ibid.
——————— the Marmor Sandvicense, 55.
——————— the Farnesian pillars, ibid.
——————— the Marmor Cyzicenum, ibid.
——————— the Duilian, 213.
Inscriptions, mistakes in them, 60.
——————— liable to be defaced, ibid.
——————— on stones, bricks, &c. 65, 66.
——————— their introductory forms, 71, 73.
——————— collected with avidity, 219.
——————— their authority precarious, 206—217.
——————— many of them supposititious, ibid.
——————— those of Cyriacus Anconitanus, 206.
——————— of P. Apianus and B. Amantius, 207.
——————— of Alex. Geraldinus, 207.
——————— of Curt. Inghiramius, 208, 209.
——————— of J. Annius, 210, 211.
——————— of H. Cajadus, 211, 212.
——————— of F. Ursinus, 213.
——————— of Fleetwood, ibid.
——————— of Gruter, 214, 216.
——————— of Pontanus, 214.
——————— of Pomponius Lætus, ibid.
——————— of Pyrrhus Ligorius, 215.
Johnson, Dr. his favourable opinion of Lauder, 202.
——————— his request concerning Ossian, ibid.

INDEX.

Ionia, colonized, 30.
────. its twelve cities, 153—155.
Josephus, his fictions, 62, 63.
─────────── his opinion of Grecian chronology, 102, 103.
─────────────── of the Greek writers, 102.
─────────── the time of his birth, 103.
Isocrates supposes the Athenian constitution had subsisted 1000 years, 119.
Isthmian games, instituted, 29.
Ἱστορεω, the use of that word, 63.
Junius, Patricius, an account of, 46.
Justin Martyr, his opinion of the Grecian chronology, 100.

K.

KAT' ενιαυτον, its acceptation, 31.

L.

LATINIUS, Latinus, his account of Annius, 210.
Lauder, his forgeries, 200, 201.
Laws, engraved on wood, 76.
──── on stone, &c. ibid.
──── of the XII tables, ibid.
──── when engraved, ibid.
Leagues, engraved on marble, 75.
Leuctra, the battle at, 40.
Libraries, an account of many celebrated ones, 68.
─────── the Alexandrian, 69.
─────── the Pergamean, ibid.
Λογοποιος, fabularum scriptor, 143. Sed vid. Maii Observ. Sacr. l. iii. c. 9. p. 121. Fabric. Bibl. Græc. vol. i. p. 392.
Lot's wife, a ridiculous account of her statue, 63.

INDEX.

Lycæa, a festival instituted by Lycaon, 28.
Lycoria, a town on Parnassus, 23.
Lycurgus, when he lived, 101, 102.
Lysander defeats Conon, 79.

M.

M, No Greek word ends in μ, 57.
Maittaire publishes the Marmora, 49.
——— an account of this work, 49, 50.
Manetho pretends to copy the pillars of Thoth, 62.
Marathon, the battle of, when fought, 36, 78.
Marmor Sandvicense, 55.
Marsham, Sir John, his account of the Grecian chronology, 87.
Masenius, Jacobus, his Sarcotis, 200, 201.
Menestheus reigns at Athens, 29.
Metrophanes, Crit. some account of him, 220—223.
Miletus inhabited at the time of the Trojan war, 30.
——— Neleus builds a new city of that name, 30.
——— its government reëstablished, 78.
Miltiades besieges Paros, ibid.
Minerva Hippia, 35.
Minos, [I] reigns in Crete, 26.
——————— the Chronicle supposes two princes of that name, 28.
Minos, [II] BANIER's account of him, ibid.
——————— resides in Paros, 77.
——————— sacrifices to the Graces, ibid.
——————— his four sons by a Parian lady, ibid.
Mithridates, epistles ascribed to him, 184.
Musæus, poems ascribed to him, 187.

INDEX.

N.

NELEUS builds Miletus, &c. 30, 153.
—— the disciple of Aristotle, 147.
Nemean games instituted, 29.
Nitocris, when she lived, 85.
Nomos, the meaning of that term, 26.
Numa, his books, 188.

O.

OBJECTIONS :—that the Chronicle contains several archaisms, 56.
——— that it was usual to write on stones, 61.
——— the Chronicle might have been quoted under another name, 112.
——— might have been written by Demetrius Phalereus, 128 —141.
——— other writings have lain a long time in obscurity, 142 —148.
——— that the marble is mutilated, 179.
Olympiads, used by Polybius, 97.
——— by the Greek historians, 98.
Olympic catalogues, ibid.
——— games, when instituted, 101.
——— year comprehended part of two Julian years, 43.
Orestes, 30.
Orpheus publishes his poems, 27.
——— books ascribed to him, 186.
——— his evidence questioned, ibid.
Orthian song, 26.
Ossian's works, their authenticity suspected, 202.
Ovid congratulates himself on the immortality of his works, 60.

Π, the double form of that letter, 53.

Palmerius affirms, that the Chronicle was found at Smyrna, 170.
Panathenæa, when instituted, 25, 152, 153.
Panchæa, a fabulous region, 63.
Pandion reigns at Athens, 27.
Panemus, a Grecian month, 116, 189.
Panionia, instituted, 30.
Papyrus, when the use of it was introduced, 68.
Παραλιας, 25.
Parapegma, the meaning of that word, 104—106.
Parchment, when used for books, 67, 70.
Parian Chronicle, A GENERAL ACCOUNT of it, 43—51.
———————— when engraved, 43.
———————— brought to England, 45.
———————— copied by Selden, 46.
———————— a great part of it lost, 47.
———————— carefully preserved at Oxford, 50.
———————— its CHARACTERS have NO CERTAIN MARKS of antiquity, 53—58.
———————— not engraved for PRIVATE USE, 59—61.
———————— not engraved by PUBLIC AUTHORITY, 71—82.
———————— records the transactions of different countries, 82.
———————— PRIOR to any settled chronology, 83—107.
———————— its singular precision, 107—109.
———————— not MENTIONED by any ANCIENT WRITER, 108—111, 140.
———————— OBJECTIONS against the argument from the SILENCE of the ancients, 112—148.
———————— the author's date of the TROJAN WAR, 116.
———————— the age of HOMER, 124—126.

INDEX.

Parian Chronicle differs from the Chronicon of Eusebius, 119.
—————————— not composed by DEMETRIUS PHALEREUS, 129—141.
—————————— the beginning supplied, 132.
—————————— ostentatiously engraved on marble, 148.
—————————— seems to have been collected from OTHER WRITERS, 149—159.
—————————— PARACHRONISMS in some of the epochas, 160—168.
—————————— the history of the DISCOVERY, 169—180.
—————————— where found, uncertain, 169—171.
—————————— whether engraved on one tablet, or more, 170.
—————————— whether the author was an Ionian, or not, 171.
—————————— purchased by Mr. Peirese, 176.
—————————— its first possessors, ibid.
—————————— to be received with caution, why, 217.
—————————— not regarded by Sir Isaac Newton, 218.
—————————— not a despicable work, ibid.
—————————— its origin APOCRYPHAL, 221.
Parians send a colony into the Adriatic, 79.
Paros, the history of that island, 77—80.
—— governed by the sons of Minos, ibid.
—— its various names, 80.
—— its extent, ibid.
—— its first inhabitants, 77.
—— attacked by Miltiades, 78.
Peirese, M. de, an account of him, 175.
—————————— purchases the Chronicon, 176, 178.
—————————— his character by Goguet, 177.
—————————— never in Asia, 179.
Peloponnesian war, its beginning and end, 79, 87.
Pergamus, kings of, 70.
Persius explodes credulity and superstition, 225.
Petavius, on the time of the destruction of Troy, 118.

INDEX.

Petavius affirms, that the Chronicle was found at Smyrna, 170.
Petty, William, an account of, 45, 172—175.
Phædrus, when he wrote, 142.
——————— seems to be noticed by Martial, ibid.
——————— not mentioned by Seneca, 143.
——————— reasons assigned for this omission, 143, 144.
Phalaris, epistles ascribed to him, 184, 189.
Pheidon invents weights and measures, 31.
——————— when he lived, 160, 161.
Philadelphus, his splendid age, 44.
——————— married his sister, 128.
——————— his rigorous treatment of Demetrius Phalereus, 136.
——————— said to have bought all Aristotle's works, 147.
Philip, king of Macedon, 41.
Philippus, a coin mentioned by Varro, 180.
Philochorus, 98.
Pillar of salt, 63.
Pillars of Seth, Hermes, Acicarus, 61, 62.
——— of Osiris, Bacchus, 75.
——— erected by the Greeks and Romans, 75.
Piræus, when fortified, 32.
Pisistratus, 33.
Plataeæ, or Platæa, the battle of, 37.
Plato, dialogues falsely ascribed to him, 190.
Plautus, comedies falsely ascribed to him, 192.
——— his description of Club-island, 218.
Pleias poëtarum, 44.
Pliny, a mistake in his N. H. 65.
——— on the Babylonian calculations, ibid.
——— his account of the papyrus, &c. 66.
Plutarch, his opinion of Grecian chronology, 100—102.
Poëtarum pleias, 44.
Polybius, an account of his writings, 97—99.
Prideaux publishes the Marmora, 48.

Prideaux,

INDEX.

Prideaux, his death, 48.
——— his character of Aristeus, 44.
——— his opinion concerning the LXX. 128.
——— his remarks on the forgeries of Annius, 195.
Pſalmanazar, his forgeries, 199.
Ptolemean kings, 70.
Pythian games, celebrated, 33, 155.

R.

RAWLINSON aſſerts, that the Chronicle was found in Paros, 169.
Roe, Sir Thomas, his letters to archbiſhop Abbot, 45, 173, 221—223.
——— to lord Arundel, 172—174.
——— to the duke of Buckingham, 174, 175.
Rowley, poems aſcribed to him 203, 204.

S.

SALAMIS, the battle of, 36, 79.
Salmaſius, his explanation of the word parapegma, 105.
Samſon purchaſes the Chronicon, 176.
——— impriſoned, 179.
Sanchoniatho pretends to have copied ancient records, 62.
——————— the books of Taaut, 64.
Sappho ſails to Sicily, 32.
Selden publiſhes the Marmora, 46.
——— dies, 48.
——— his works publiſhed, 49.
Semiramis, when ſhe lived, 85.
Septuagint verſion, when made, 128.
Seſoſtris, his pillars, 62.
Seth, his pillars, 61, 62.

Seventy

INDEX.

Seventy interpreters, their cells, 138.
Sibyl sells her books to Tarquin, 180.
Sibylline oracles, fanatical impostures, 225.
Simonides invents the art of memory, 37.
────── dies, 39.
Simson, his construction of a passage in D. Laertius, 136.
Socrates, dies, 39, 131.
────── a dispute concerning his age, 130.
Solon, his interview with Crœsus, 102.
────── when he was archon, ibid.
Sophocles gains a victory in tragedy, 38.
────── dies, 39.
Sosibius, his date of the Trojan war, 113.
Spanheim, his character of Aristeas, 138.
Stesichorus goes into Greece, 36.
────── the second of that name, 40.
Stillingfleet, his account of literary frauds, 182, 214.
Syncellus, a passage in his chronography corrected, 125.

T.

TAAUT, called by the Greeks Hermes, 64.
Tatian, his chronological citations, 109.
Taubman, his Bellum Angelicum, 200, 201.
Telestes, 39.
Temenus, one of the Heraclidæ, 160, 161.
Terpander, 32.
Tertullian, a remarkable passage in his works, 63.
Teucer builds Salamis, 30.
Themistocles, not archon eponymus, 32.
────── epistles falsely ascribed to him, 189.
────── fortifies Piræus, 32.
────── lays the Parians under contributions, 79.
Theopompus, 92.

Theseus

INDEX.

Theseus unites the twelve cities of Attica, 29.
────── the time of his birth, 101.
Thespis exhibits tragedy, 34.
Thucydides, the authenticity of a passage in his works suspected, 31, 32.
────────── styles his history an everlasting possession, 61.
────────── his chronology, 86, 87.
────────── his division of the year, 86.
────────── his opinion of Grecian chronology, 103.
Timæus Siculus, his writings and character, 92, 93.
Treaties, engraved on pillars, 75.
Triptolemus, 27.
Troy, the siege of that city commenced, 29.
──── an error in the date of that event, ibid.
──── the epocha of the Trojan war, 113.
──── the opinion of the ancients on that subject, 113—118.
──────────── of Apollodorus, 114.
──────────── of Aretes, 115.
──────────── of P. Cato, 113.
──────────── of Censorinus, 114, 115.
──────────── of Dicæarchus, 115.
──────────── of Diodorus, 114.
──────────── of Dionysius Argivus, 113.
──────────── of Dionysius Halicarnasseus, 114.
──────────── of Duris Samius, 115.
──────────── of Eratosthenes, 113.
──────────── of Eusebius, 114.
──────────── of the Greek chronologists, ibid.
──────────── of the author of the Life of Homer, 115.
──────────── of Paterculus, ibid.
──────────── of Solinus, 114.
──────────── of Sosibius, 113.
──────────── of Tatian, 114.
──────────── of Timæus, ibid.
──────────── of the Parian Chronicle, 116.

INDEX.

Troy, the day of the month, on which the city was taken, 116, 117.
—— the opinion of the ancients on this subject, 116.
—— the sentiments of the moderns, 117.
Tyrant, the import of that word, 33.
Tyrtæus commands the Spartan army, 32.

V.

VARRERIUS on the decree of pope Gelasius, 198.
    Varro, on the papyrus, 68.
—— his division of time, 103.
—— his account of the Sibyl, 180.
Veremundus, when he wrote, 182.
Vespasian restores 3000 brazen plates, 76.
Vossius, on the word parapegma, 105.

W.

WILKINS publishes Selden's works, 49.
    Writing, on pillars, stones, bricks, &c. 65, 75.

X.

X signifies 600, 71.
, Xanthus, a poet of Sardes, 39.
Xenophon, when born, 87.
——— his Grecian history, ibid.
——— the Olympiads in his history an interpolation, 88.
——— his Cyropædia, 89, 90.
Xerxes reigns in Persia, 36.
—— makes a bridge over the Hellespont, 36, 156, 164.
—— his invasion of Greece, 164, 165.

Y.

YOUNG, Patrick, some account of him, 46.

ERRATA.

p. 4.	l. 11.	read,	κ]α-
9.	7.	—	Τεω.
15.	16.	—	Hellefponto.
18.	5.	—	Μικαν[ο]ς.
27.	18.	—	Phurnutus.
34.	20.	—	εδδαξεν.
37.	34.	—	An feni.
84.	9.	—	confift.
85.	20.	—	πεντηκοντα.
100.	1.	—	his.
109.	15.	—	are.
127.	4.	—	Sextus Empiricus.
129.	34.	—	literariam.
156.	12.	—	Hellefponto.
163.	21.	—	πυλαιαν.
176.	14.	—	Peirefc.
195.	33.	—	prophecies.
211.	20.	—	the origin of Viterbo, &c.

The Latin tranflation of this paffage, p. 210, is obfcure and equivocal. Notwithftanding the word *longè*, and the extravagance of the affertion, it is very probable, that Annius's rodomontade is to be underftood in this fenfe:

———" the origin of Viterbo, which was built by Ifis and Ofiris, two thoufand years before Rome was founded by Romulus."

I have not been able to meet with the original of the learned Spaniard, from which Schottus made his Latin tranflation.

www.ingramcontent.com/pod-product-compliance
Lightning Source LLC
Chambersburg PA
CBHW020755230426
43666CB00007B/710